101 Week Gift Projects from Wood

James A. Jacobson

Ken—

We hope these projects are highly enjoyable for you. The good thing about them is that they don't take too long. Have fun!

Love,

Nori + Tim

Sterling Publishing Co., Inc. New York

Dedication
For A.R.J.

ACKNOWLEDGMENTS

I wish to thank and acknowledge the following companies for providing photographs and granting permission to use them: Stanley Tools, Division of the Stanley Works, New Britain, Conn.; Makita U.S.A., Inc., La Mirada, Calif.; Porter-Cable Professional Power Tools, Jackson, Tenn.; Delta International Machinery Corp., Pittsburgh, Pa.; Forest City Tool, Hickory, N.C.; Dremel, Racine, Wisc.; Warren Tool Co., Inc., Rhinebeck, N.Y.; Woodcraft Supply Corp., Parkersburg, W. Va.; The Foredom Electric Co., Bethel, Conn.; Black & Decker, Hunt Valley, Md.

Acknowledgments and thanks are also extended to the following individuals for providing ideas, assistance, and projects: Jerry Lipchik and Becky Lipchik, Granite City, Ill.; Mike and Karen O'Meara, St. Paul, Minn.; Christin Weggemann, Eagan, Minn.; the late Leanne DeLaurenti, Pocahontas, Ill.; Jessica Weggemann, Eagan, Minn.; Mike Field, Caseyville, Ill.; Carol Banghart, Wilton, Conn.; Mallory Weggemann, Eagan, Minn.; Peter and Kathy Jacobson, Blacksburg, Va., and Namibia (Southwest Africa); Ann and Chris Weggemann, Eagan, Minn.

A very special thanks to Anita R. Jacobson, Collinsville, Ill., and Andy Matoesian, Granite City, Ill.

Library of Congress Cataloging-in-Publication Data

Jacobson, James A.
 101 weekend gift projects from wood / by James A. Jacobson.
  p. cm.
 Includes index.
 ISBN 0–8069–0322–8
 1. Woodwork. I. Title. II. Title: One hundred and one weekend gift projects from wood.
 TT180.J263 1993
 684′.08—dc20
                   93–8446
                   CIP

10 9 8 7 6 5 4
Published by Sterling Publishing Company, Inc.
387 Park Avenue South, New York, N.Y. 10016
© 1993 by James A. Jacobson
Distributed in Canada by Sterling Publishing
© Canadian Manda Group, P.O. Box 920, Station U
Toronto, Ontario, Canada M8Z 5P9
Distributed in Great Britain and Europe by Cassell PLC
Villiers House, 41/47 Strand, London WC2N 5JE, England
Distributed in Australia by Capricorn Link Ltd.
P.O. Box 665, Lane Cove, NSW 2066
Manufactured in the United States of America

Sterling ISBN 0-8069-0322-8

CONTENTS

INTRODUCTION

Having just finished making wooden gifts for three grandchildren's birthdays, I find myself facing the gift needs for the month of May. While some will be purchased, I will make most of these gifts from wood.

While you could develop the capacity to ignore special occasions and/or forego the giving of a gift, that wouldn't be much fun. It's more fun to get a few tools or use the ones you already have and start making gifts from wood. Most people enjoy receiving gifts that are handmade, especially when they're made by somebody they know and care about.

Gift-making may also appeal to those people looking for a way to manage stress or simply to become involved in a rewarding hobby. Making gifts from wood is an easy and productive way to get into woodworking. It is a type of activity that you can get involved in with a minimum of investment. Also, the money saved from buying gifts can help offset the costs of tools and supplies.

The availability of accessories that you can use to enhance your wooden gifts has greatly expanded in recent years. You may want to limit the accessories to items that you can make from wood. However, if you want to dress up your projects, there are a wide range of commercial items available for you to use. There are many mail-order suppliers, in addition to local craft stores, where you can purchase clock inserts, pens of every type, Shaker pegs, candle cups, lazy Susan hardware, spice jars, music movements, marbles, and anything else that can be used to enhance a gift project.

Local hardware, do-it-yourself, or discount stores offer a festival of supplies for the gift maker. Dowels, screws, Plexiglas®, mirror glass, glues, paints, and almost any other supply that you need can be found either at a local store or via mail order. Items that used to be available only to commercial manufacturers are now readily available to the consumer public. You will be amazed at the kinds of things that can be purchased that will make your wooden gifts more attractive and useful. Equally important, you will discover that these items are, as a rule, reasonably priced.

This is the second book on making gifts from wood that I have written. It is the result of my attempt to keep up with the ongoing demand for gifts that all of us face. Each of the gift projects presented is new. Material lists, a list of suggested tools to use, and specific instructions are provided with each gift project. You can follow these guidelines or, if you're so inclined, modify the gift to suit individual needs or tastes. This approach allows you to personalize your gifts. For example, you may decide to stain or paint your gift to suit the recipient's surroundings, or to coordinate the color of a desktop gift with the desk itself. Creativity is encouraged.

The gift projects are designed so that the beginning woodworker can successfully make them and enjoy the process. They are also designed to avoid insulting the skill and expertise of the more experienced woodworker. The availability of tools may present the only significant barrier to crafting a particular gift project. If that's the case, you may want to consider buying the needed tool. Think of the money you're saving by making your own gifts! However, if the pocketbook or purse simply won't allow it, try the shop at the local high school or junior college. In a pinch, borrow the tools needed.

Most of the projects are designed to be small and require a minimum of space for crafting. This prevents those apartment dwellers from being overwhelmed by the size of a project. Using small power or hand tools, a portable workbench, and a good shop vacuum, you should be able to manage quite well as a woodworker.

James A. Jacobson

TOOLS AND ACCESSORIES

One of the interesting things about making the projects in this book is that you have lots of options when it comes to what tool to use. Having been a woodworker for many years, I've accumulated many tools. Even though I have an array of tools, including most of the floor power tools, I actually use very few tools to make small projects. In part, this has to do with habit, but it also reflects how easy it is to make gift projects with only a few tools. Woodworking is one of those wonderful activities that allows you to "do your own thing," and this includes using the tools that will serve you best.

As you will discover, any number of gift projects can be made with tools found around most households. The projects do not require a major investment in tools or tool accessories. However, as you begin making gift projects you may find buying one or several tools a practical and enjoyable investment. While some woodworkers may prefer hand and small power tools, others may be inclined to use and invest in floor power tools.

You may have to purchase tool accessories to make a particular project, such as router bits, drill bits or a carbide burr. However, an effort has been made to minimize the number of tool accessories required for the projects. Also, the same accessories can be used for crafting many different projects. This will save money.

With some exceptions, the gift projects are within the reach of those woodworkers with limited or even no experience. While it may take the beginner a bit more time to do a project, the task is achievable and will result in a finely made gift. Your level of skill will also determine what tools you will want to use. As a beginner, you may want to initially work with hand tools and small hand-held power tools. The following overview of tools and accessories will help familiarize woodworkers of all skill levels with available tools that can be used to make gift projects.

Those who need to buy tools and accessories should learn about the different types available before purchasing any. Most communities have a variety of stores, from discount houses to main-street hardware stores that sell woodworking tools. In addition to local sources, there are many mail-order suppliers that carry everything a woodworker needs or wants. Buy some current woodworking magazines and review the ads. Write for catalogues and become familiar not only with the products but also their prices. Do your homework. As a rule, it pays to buy quality tools.

You should also talk to people who use tools on a regular basis, for example, school shop teachers, carpenters, people who make and sell craft items, and anyone else who is a source of information. When you do buy a tool, be certain to read the manual that comes with it. Familiarize yourself with the various parts of the tool, how it works, how to maintain it and, above all, how to use it safely.

Woodworking is a series of related functions or tasks. Tools, whether hand-powered or electric-powered, help you achieve these various tasks. The following presentation—geared for beginners—discusses these different tasks and the tools best suited to perform them. It also demonstrates how accessories permit tools to perform a greater variety of tasks or, in some instances, a specific task. For those experienced in woodworking, it is hoped that the material and photographs will reveal some new ideas and new tools.

Procedures

Safety must be given top priority in woodworking. It's the key priority to an enjoyable and productive woodworking experience. Always, for example, wear safety glasses or a safety mask. There are many different types of eye and face coverings available. Find one that fits properly and will provide protection.

As indicated earlier, never use any tool until you understand how it works and the kind of hazards that it presents when using it. Read the tool manual and become familiar with all aspects of the tool. You need to constantly be aware that most power tools involve sharp steel rotating at high speeds. They are unforgiving. Become familiar with the recommended safety practices that all tool manufacturers include in their manuals. Also, use common sense and learn from your experiences when working with wood.

Also purchase earplugs or other ear devices to protect your hearing from the high-pitched noises of power tools. Floor-model power tools are especially noisy, and you need to protect your hearing. Most tool suppliers carry ear protective devices that are designed for woodworking. Your local pharmacy may be another source of appropriate ear protection.

When using carving knives, grinders with carbide burrs, and other hand tools, wear leather gloves to help protect your hands and fingers. For those who plan to do a lot of carving, there are specially designed gloves that will protect your fingers and hands from a slip of a knife.

It is advisable to hang a danger sign next to tools that present any special risks. There are several such signs in my shop. These signs help stress the importance of safety. While it is not my intent to generate inappropriate fear, you need to be realistic about safety whenever working with tools. Think and practice safe woodworking. It's a lot more fun and much less painful.

One final thought on safety. Every home and apartment should have appropriately placed fire alarms and several quality fire extinguishers. The workshop is a potential fire hazard and must be treated accordingly. You need to be especially aware of the potential fire dangers in your shop when using the various finishing products. Read the labels and follow the directions for use. Practice effective fire prevention, but also be prepared for any emergency.

Measuring

While measuring is one of the least dramatic functions in the woodworking process, it remains one of the most important. The problem with measuring is that we take it for granted and become careless when doing it. As a result, many mistakes that occur when making projects are measuring mistakes. Take your time and double check the measurement before sawing or doing whatever task is required.

A metal tape measure at least 12 feet long will be very helpful when you are making projects. A tape this long will prove very important when you're at the local lumber dealer selecting your wood. It is also useful for purposes other than woodworking.

A metal straightedge such as a 12-inch ruler with rubber backing is also useful when crafting. Many tasks require a good straightedge. There are some metal yardsticks available that can also serve you well.

A try square can be very helpful when you need to make a straight line on a board for sawing (Illus. 1). The handle fits over one edge of a board, and the blade lies flat on its surface. Run a pencil along the edge of the blade and you will have a straight cutting line. A try square is especially helpful if you're cutting your boards with a handsaw, because it permits you to make a square cut. While the try square is by no means an indispensable device for making gift projects, it can be helpful if you plan on primarily using hand tools.

The combination square is a good alternative to the try square, especially if you want a tool that is more versatile (Illus. 2). An effective alternative to both the try and combination square is a small steel square. While most hardware stores, discount houses, and mail-order suppliers

Illus. 1. Try square (photo courtesy of Stanley Tools).

carry all three of these devices, don't rule out finding a used one at a flea market or yard sale.

In my own shop, I tend to use an old try square

Illus. 2. Combination square (photo courtesy of Stanley Tools).

whether I'm cutting a board by hand or with a radial arm or table saw. While I also have a combination square and large and small steel squares, using a try square has become a habit. Use whatever is available to you and whatever works the best.

There is an assortment of other devices that you will find useful when crafting gift projects. For example, a school compass is an inexpensive device that can be used to both measure and draw circles. Plastic templates with an array of circles of different diameters can also be useful. Plastic coffee can covers or similar items can also be used to make a circle pattern.

Sawing

Sawing can be accomplished with a variety of tools. If you prefer crafting your gift projects with hand tools, you may want to consider a handsaw (Illus. 3). Should you prefer this type of saw, be certain to purchase one designed for crosscuts. You may want to discuss your sawing needs with an experienced woodworker or an informed store employee. Another type of handsaw that will allow you to do intricate cuts is a coping saw (Illus. 4). If you want to cut holes or other shapes in

Illus. 3. Handsaw (photo courtesy of Stanley Tools).

Illus. 4. Coping saw (photo courtesy of Stanley Tools).

Illus. 5. Keyhole saw (photo courtesy of Stanley Tools).

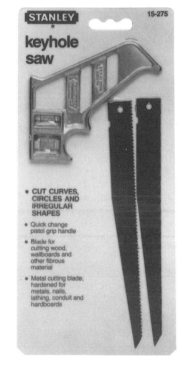

wood, you may want to use a keyhole or similar saw (Illus. 5). Use a hacksaw to cut metal and, in a pinch, a piece of wood (Illus. 6). Keep extra blades available for both the hacksaw and coping saw. The coping saw is especially prone to breaking blades, especially if you try to force a cut. If you're inclined to a more exotic type of handsaw, you may want to try the Japanese saws.

The mitre saw is another saw that you should consider, especially if you are interested in making picture or mirror frames (Illus. 7). While the saw can be purchased with a unit that sets the

Illus. 6. Hacksaw (photo courtesy of Stanley Tools).

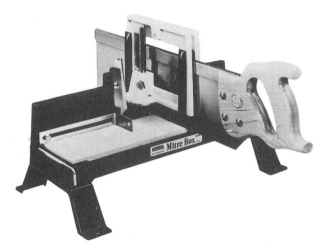

Illus. 7. Mitre box (photo courtesy of Stanley Tools).

cutting angle, you may want to buy a mitre saw and make your own box from wood. One of the gift projects requires mitre cuts.

If you prefer, sawing can be more easily accomplished using a hand power tool. An all-purpose tool that can accomplish most of your sawing needs is a sabre saw (Illus. 8). In addition

Illus. 8. Sabre saw (photo courtesy of Makita U.S.A., Inc.).

to making straight cuts, a sabre saw can make almost any other type of cut, especially decorative ones. For internal cuts, you need only drill a hole that will accommodate the sabre-saw blade. You will find that there is a sabre-saw blade designed for almost every sawing task. I tend to use blades that give a smooth, clean, finished cut.

Another saw that can be used to crosscut is the circular saw (Illus. 9). If you like doing repair jobs around the house in addition to making projects, this type of saw is very helpful. It's important to keep in mind that the circular saw is for straight cutting only. Incidentally, as with all power tools, read the manual for this saw carefully.

Illus. 9. Circular saw (photo courtesy of Porter-Cable Power Tools).

Many homeowners and woodworkers already own one of several floor-model power saws. The radial arm saw (Illus. 10) is a very popular and affordable power tool. Another floor-model saw found in many homes and shops is the table saw (Illus. 11). Both saws, given their size and power, require careful use. Be certain to read and follow all the instructions and safety precautions in the owners' manual.

Floor-model power tools are considerably more expensive than power hand tools, so before buying these larger tools make sure you are committed to woodworking. If you're planning on making gift projects in quantity to give or to sell,

Illus. 10. Radial arm saw (photo courtesy of Delta International Machinery Corp.).

these larger tools may be desirable. Also, it's important to remember that floor-model power tools require a considerable amount of room. Cars cannot be parked in my garage because it is full of tools. Don't rule out the use of your basement for a shop. Wherever you place and use your floor-model power tools, install a vent fan or some type of vacuum system.

The band saw, another floor-model power tool, is a very versatile piece of equipment (Illus. 12). If you use a wide blade, you can rip or crosscut boards. Narrow blades allow the user to make decorative cuts. I use the band saw to cut round gift projects. As with any of the other floor model power tools, there are many different types of band saw on the market, including bench models. You will find some excellent books available on how to use a band saw, a radial arm, and table saw.

For those gift makers interested in creating lots of projects that require mitre or straight cuts,

Illus. 12. Band saw (photo courtesy of Delta International Machinery Corp.).

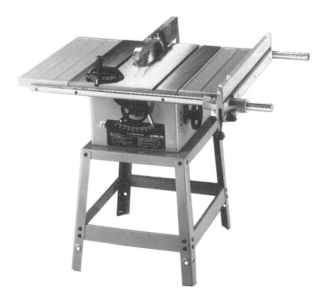

Illus. 11. Table saw (photo courtesy of Delta International Machinery Corp.).

the electric mitre saw may be worth considering (Illus. 13). If you're so inclined, however, you can make mitre cuts on both a radial arm saw and table saw. The priority in any mitre work is the accuracy of the cut, not what tool is used to accomplish it. Mitre joints have to fit tightly together. Be certain to familiarize yourself with the owners' manual, because the electric mitre saw is a potentially dangerous tool. As with any floor-model power saw, watch where you place your hands and fingers.

Illus. 14. Variable-speed scroll saw (photo courtesy of Delta International Machinery Corp.).

Illus. 13. Electric mitre saw (photo courtesy of Delta International Machinery Corp.).

The scroll saw (Illus. 14) is a popular and affordable floor-model tool. This saw allows you to make very detailed and decorative cuts in wood and other materials of varying thickness. It's a fun tool to use and is excellent for making gift projects from wood. While the floor-model scroll saw can do magical things to wood, you can still do much decorative cutting with a hand-held sabre saw. If you're considering woodworking as a hobby, you may want to purchase a floor-model scroll saw. Shop around, because there are many different brands and styles of scroll saws available.

Drilling

Many of the gift projects require that you have some capability for drilling holes. In woodworking, this function is more accurately called boring, but for our purposes, the term drilling is acceptable. As with sawing, there are different tools and accessories that can be used to drill. For example, if you like working wood with hand tools, you'll love the traditional bit and brace. My own preference is to use both hand and floor-model drills, for both convenience and accuracy. As a matter of fact, I use a small pneumatic drill and bit along with an air compressor for some drilling tasks.

If you need a tool to achieve your drilling tasks for making gift projects, consider an electric hand drill (Illus. 15). Electric hand drills can be found in most homes or apartments. Many have the cordless-type hand drill that has become popular in recent years. If you have to buy a drill, consider one that has a ⅜-inch chuck and adequate power. This type of unit will meet most of your drilling needs, even when a project is being

Illus. 15. Electric drill (photo courtesy of Makita U.S.A., Inc.).

crafted from one of the hardwoods. You should also consider buying a drill that has variable speeds and is reversible. They're both useful features to have on a drill.

For the ultimate drilling tool, you may want to consider buying a drill press (Illus. 16). This type of tool allows you to do more accurate drilling

Illus. 16. Drill press (photo courtesy of Delta International Machinery Corp.).

and also permits the use of a wide range of accessories. For serious woodworking, it's indispensable. Many manufacturers have both floor- and bench-model drill presses on the market. Some of the gift projects in the following pages can be crafted more easily if you have use of a drill press.

Bits or bores, as they're called in woodworking, are used with the drills. Twist drills of specific sizes will be needed for the gift projects (Illus. 17). For wood screws, you may want to use a set of combination drills and screw-sinks (Illus. 18). Another device that can be useful with wood screws is the standard countersink (Illus. 19). If you want to use an electric or cordless drill to set wood screws, buy a set of insert bits (Illus. 20).

Many different types of bits can be used to bore holes in hardwood and softwood. One of the least-expensive wood bits is what is generally

Illus. 17. Twist drill set (photo courtesy of Stanley Tools).

Illus. 18. Screw-sinks (photo courtesy of Stanley Tools).

Illus. 19. Countersink (photo courtesy of Stanley Tools).

is called a power-bore (Illus. 22). While more expensive than spade bits, wood bores are more accurate and easier to use. As with any bit, don't drop these on a concrete floor.

Illus. 22. Power-bore bits (photo courtesy of Stanley Tools).

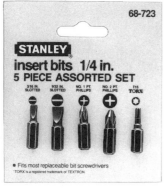

Illus. 20. Insert bits (photo courtesy of Stanley Tools).

The brad-point bit is clearly the best overall bit for boring into wood (Illus. 23). The design of the point allows both accuracy and quick penetration at the marked hole location. The bit also allows for easy and accurate hole boring in thick wood, whether it is hardwood or softwood. Brad-point bits, unlike spade and power-bore bits, are available in fractions of an inch.

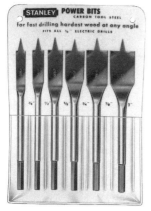

Illus. 21. Spade bits (photo courtesy of Stanley Tools).

Illus. 23. Brad-point bit (photo courtesy of Forest City Tool).

called a spade bit (Illus. 21). The spade bit is available in various diameters and can be used in both an electric drill and a drill press. These bits are generally available and, if you need to, can be easily sharpened.

Another wood bore that I often use in the shop

Forstner bits, used primarily by European woodworkers, have in recent years become very popular in the United States (Illus. 24). While quite expensive, they are very effective bits, especially if you want to bore a hole at an angle or into end grain. They also leave a clean, flat bottom in a drilled hole. Forstner bits are available in sizes from ¼ to 2 inches. By the way, you can use both brad-point and Forstner bits in most electric hand drills. The shanks on the larger diameter bits are reduced to be accommodated in a ⅜-inch drill chuck.

Illus. 25. Multi-spur bit (photo courtesy of Forest City Tool).

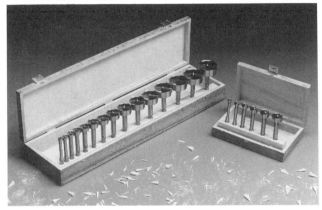

Illus. 24. Forstner bits (photo courtesy of Forest City Tool).

Several gift projects require a multi-spur bit (Illus. 25). In that multi-spur bits generally are manufactured with a ½-inch-diameter shank, a drill press is required for their use. They can also be used on a lathe. Multi-spur bits cut extremely fast, and you can drill relatively deep holes with them. Whenever using the bits, reduce the speed of your drill press. It's also important to clamp the piece being drilled when using these bits. The bit can grab the chunk of wood as you are holding it, spin it around, and cause serious injury to a finger or hand.

You may have to order your multi-spur bits from a mail-order supplier. On occasion, a local hardware store may have them in stock.

One accessory you may want to use in making gift projects is the circle cutter (Illus. 26). These cutters should be used on a drill press. They're very functional for cutting large holes, especially in softwood. You can adjust the cutting arm to vary the diameter of the holes being cut. While

Illus. 26. Circle cutter (photo courtesy of Stanley Tools).

larger holes for some projects can be cut with a sabre saw, the circle cutter is an effective alternative.

When using a circle cutter, be sure to reduce the speed of the drill press. The piece being worked on also has to be clamped. Again, be careful when drilling or using accessories on a drill press.

While you can buy a variety of wood plugs in different diameters, I tend to make my own. Use a plug cutter to cut plugs from scraps. Cutters work best on a drill press and are available in ¼-, ⅜-, and ½-inch diameters. I use the plugs as a decorative design on some gift projects. Plugs cut from a red hardwood like padauk add a nice decorative touch to a project made from hard maple or some other light wood. Plugs are also great for plugging a drilled hole of a recessed wood screw.

There are many other accessories that can be used with a drill press or an electric drill. The ones described in this section will assist you in making gift projects. As you shop the mail-order catalogues and discount and hardware stores, you will find additional clever and interesting devices that can make your woodworking easier and more fun.

Routing

Routing, more accurately called shaping, can be done with either a floor-model shaper or a router. The tool of choice for most small woodworking projects, including gift projects, is the router (Illus. 27). Many homeowners already own a router, because it is a useful and affordable hand power tool. The router can be effectively used by holding it in two hands. When mounted on a router table, the tool becomes more versatile (Illus. 28).

Illus. 27. Router (photo courtesy of Porter-Cable Power Tools).

When the router table is used, the router is attached under the table. The router bit, secured in the router collet, protrudes through a hole in the table. This configuration allows you to move the wood into the revolving bit. When the router is hand-held, the bit and tool are moved into the wood. As a rule, more effective routing can be accomplished with the tool secured to a table.

Illus. 28. Router table (photo courtesy of Porter-Cable Power Tools).

The router is a very noisy and intimidating device. Ear protection is mandatory with this tool. Most router bits, made of high-speed or carbide steel and very sharp, rotate at about 25,000 revolutions per minute. It's critical that you read the tool manual and become familiar with how the tool is to be used.

A router with ⅞, 1, or 1½ horsepower is adequate for making gift projects and most other routing tasks. There are more powerful ones on the market, including plunge routers, that you may want to consider. If you need to buy one, shop the mail-order suppliers and discount and hardware stores. There are many brands available with an array of different features.

The device that holds the router bit in place is called the collet. Routers usually come with a ¼-inch collet. Some also have a ½-inch collet. Router bits have shanks that are either ¼ or ½ inch in diameter. When buying router bits, be certain to purchase a bit whose shank will fit the collet of your tool.

There are a great variety of router bits available today. Given the popularity of routers, the bits manufactured today are of better quality and are less expensive. Several different bits will be needed to make gift projects. For example, a roundover bit will be very useful. A rabbeting bit will be needed when you are making mirror frames. If you want to rout a groove on a shelf to support decorative plates, you may want to have a roundnose bit. Become familiar with the bits that are available and what type of shapes they will cut in wood. For each gift project, information is provided as to what kind of bit should be used.

If you're so inclined, a small rotary tool with a routing attachment can be useful on small projects (Illus. 29). Small router bits for use in the rotary tool are also available. The rotary tool is quite useful when you are making small projects from wood.

Illus. 30. Wood lathe (photo courtesy of Delta International Machinery Corp.).

Illus. 29. Rotary tool with routing attachment (photo courtesy of Dremel).

Turning

Several gift projects require the use of a wood lathe (Illus. 30). Unlike many other large floor-model power tools, the wood lathe and turning tools can, in some instances, be used to make the entire project. In other instances, they can be used to make one part of a project. If you're looking for one single tool with which to get in-

volved in woodworking, consider the lathe. While it's rather expensive, especially with the various turning tools and accessories that are required, it remains one of the most enjoyable ways of working with wood.

Most of the gift projects that require turning can be done by the beginner. If you do not have a lathe, try using one at the local public school or junior college. The projects present you with the opportunity to do both spindle and faceplate turning.

Carving and Shaping

Most people who see someone carving or whittling want to try it. Once they have, they don't want to stop. Carving is a fun way to work with wood. It is very relaxing and can be done with a few tools, a minimum of space, and very little wood. Those who are inclined to whittling a gift project should consider a whittling kit (Illus. 31). Another option is to use a sharp jackknife. Details can also be carved on a project with any number of different carving tools (Illus. 32). There are many excellent mail-order suppliers of carving and whittling tools and accessories.

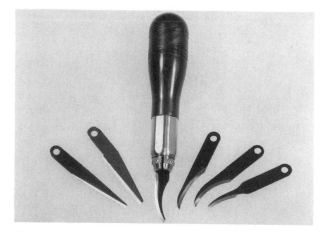

Illus. 31. Whittling kit (photo courtesy of Warren Tool Co., Inc.).

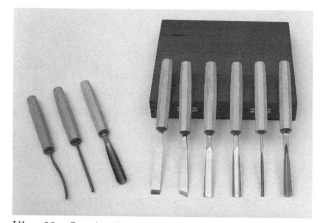

Illus. 32. Carving Tools (photo courtesy of Warren Tool Co., Inc.).

Illus. 33. Electric grinder (photo courtesy of Makita U.S.A., Inc.).

Illus. 34. Carbide burrs (photo courtesy of Woodcraft Supply Corp.).

Illus. 35. Rotary tool and accessories (photo courtesy of Dremel).

To minimize the work, instructions are given to rough-shape most projects on a band or scroll saw. This allows you to remove lots of wood quickly that otherwise would have to be removed by hand. If you prefer, after cutting the project to its rough shape, you can finish it by hand. My preference is to shape and finish projects using an electric grinder (Illus. 33). When you use a variety of large and small carbide burrs with the grinder, you can remove lots of wood quickly (Illus. 34). This is a potentially dangerous procedure, so read the tool manual and shape with care.

A smaller but equally useful carving tool is the rotary tool. There are a variety of accessories that are available for use with these tools (Illus. 35). While you cannot remove wood as quickly as with the electric grinder, rotary tools allow you to do detail and more controlled work.

Another effective and enjoyable tool to carve and shape with is the flexible shaft tool (Illus. 36). This tool affords you maximum control and is great fun to use. It is by no means a mandatory tool for making gift projects, but certainly one that could be useful.

Another tool that you can use for either shaping or finishing gift projects is the small electric

Illus. 36. Flexible shaft tool (photo courtesy of Foredom Electric Corp.).

finishing sander (Illus. 37). Some of these tools have a vacuum and bag system that keeps the sanding dust to a minimum. Using coarse-grit abrasive paper, you can remove lots of wood and also shape a project. One effective method of shaping and finishing is to use an electric grinder and carbide burrs to shape a project, and a small finishing sander, with a fine-grit abrasive, to give the project a final, smooth finish.

Illus. 37. Finishing sander (photo courtesy of Makita U.S.A., Inc.).

Sanding

The surface of all gift projects must be prepared for finishing. While you can use a block of wood and some abrasive paper to prepare a project's surface, you may want to consider some power sanding tools. A small belt disc sander can do much to reduce the effort involved in surface preparation (Illus. 38). You will definitely want to use one of the many small finishing sanders that are on the market.

Illus. 38. Belt/disc sander (photo courtesy of Delta International Machinery Corp.).

As you review the mail-order tool catalogues, you will discover a variety of power, sanding or finishing tools, in both hand and floor models. Select one that will make the surface preparation of wood easy. The final appearance of your gift project is pretty much determined by how well you sand or prepare the surface for finishing. As always, read the owners' manuals that accompany these sanding tools.

Each project has specifics on surface preparation that you will find helpful.

Other Tools and Accessories

While the foregoing presents the major tools that you will need or find useful in crafting gift projects from wood, there are many other items that can also be useful. For example, if you live in an apartment and do not have a place for crafting projects, you may want to consider a portable workbench (Illus. 39). These units fold up and can be tucked away when not in use.

There are a multitude of small tools that you will also find helpful in your crafting. Most of these items can be used for other purposes around the household. For example, a utility

17

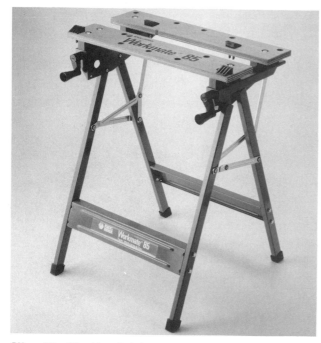

Illus. 39. Workbench (photo courtesy of Black & Decker).

Illus. 42. Nail Set (photo courtesy of Stanley Tools).

knife with replaceable blades (Illus. 40) has many uses when crafting and for jobs around the household. Another knife that is very useful is the hobby knife (Illus. 41). While knives with different blades are available, those with pointed blades are excellent for cutting veneer for gift project bookmarks.

Illus. 40. Utility knife (photo courtesy of Stanley Tools).

Illus. 41. Hobby knife (photo courtesy of Stanley Tools).

You will need a hammer to assemble projects or to smash the ones that don't turn out right. To drive finishing nails under the surface of the wood, you may want to have a nail set (Illus. 42). After the nails are set, you can patch the hole with a touch of wood putty. It gives the project a more finished look.

Clamps are always useful in a shop. The basic C-clamp is available in a variety of sizes. There are many different and very useful clamps available for woodworking. Shop around and purchase those that best serve your immediate and long-term needs. Clamps can be expensive, so check around for the best prices.

One final tool that is great fun to use is a wood-burning set (Illus. 43). As you will discover when making many of the gift projects, a design can be burned into the surface of the project. These devices are easy to use, even for beginners. You may want to consider buying one that uses points of different sizes. Many of the projects lend themselves to some kind of surface design.

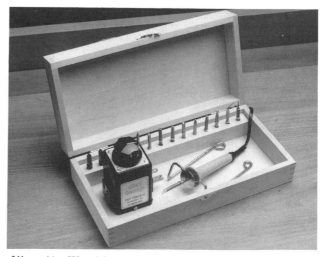

Illus. 43. Wood-burning set (photo courtesy of Woodcraft Supply Corp.).

WOOD, SUPPLIES, AND FINISHING PRODUCTS

Wood

While many of the gift projects can be made from pine, others are best crafted from one of the hardwoods. If you're so inclined, you may want to use one of the hardwoods for all of your gift projects. As you probably know, hardwoods come from trees that shed their leaves, which technically are known as *deciduous* trees. Oak, maple, cherry, and walnut are considered hardwoods. Softwoods come from trees that have needles, technically called *conifers*. Pine, spruce, cedar, fir, and other evergreen trees are all softwoods.

Hardwood and softwood differ in cost. You will find that hardwoods are more expensive than softwoods. Black walnut, for example, is significantly more expensive than white pine. You will be able to buy pine at most local lumber companies, but you will have to shop around to find a hardwood dealer. If you can't find a hardwood dealer locally, check the national woodworking magazines for mail-order suppliers of hardwood. These dealers will also be able to supply you with some of the imported woods that are plentiful and are not exported from the rain forests.

Beginning woodworkers should note that the hardwoods are more difficult to work with than the softwoods. In some instances, a floor-model power tool may be required. Experiment with the woods and your tools to learn what works best for you.

When shopping for wood, take along a tape measure and, when possible, select your own boards. You should have a good idea of how much lumber you need for a given set of projects before you start. When buying pine, ask for No. 3 Common. This is the most common grade used by contractors and is readily available. The phrase "No. 3 Common" is a designation given to a board by lumber graders. As you might

guess, there are also Nos. 1 and 2 and, believe it or not, a No. 4. Some of these grades are very hard to find. Stick with No. 3 Common, because it is of reasonable quality and is affordable. Also, it will probably be the only grade your lumber dealer carries.

When selecting your boards, try to avoid those that are warped, twisted, or have many small or sap. Knots are acceptable if they're tight, but if the board has many loose knots, leave it. Use your tape to measure how wide and long the board is. Always buy a board that is slightly longer and wider than needed, because some unseen portion of a board may be worthless. Take your time when selecting boards. Note the character and color of each board. Consider how it will look if you're planning to use a clear finish.

Wood dimensions, especially softwood dimensions, are misleading. The given dimensions, or the *rough-cut* or nominal size of a softwood board, are different from the actual dimensions, or the *true* or *planed* size of a board. This is because the board was sawed to one set of dimensions, but planed to another. For example, a 1 x 4-inch board is, in fact ¾ inch thick and 3½ inches wide. The nominal size of this board is 1 x 4. The actual dimensions are ¾ inch x 3½ inches. As another example, a 2 x 4 is actually 1½ inches thick and 3½ inches wide. Measure a few boards at the lumberyard and you'll quickly figure out how this system works. When measuring and planning a project, be certain to take these differences in width and thickness into account. Oddly enough, in most cases the stated length of a board is its actual length.

A different measuring system is used with hardwoods. Ask the dealer to clarify how hardwoods are graded and measured. Dealers are usually happy to explain these procedures and the pricing system for their wood. Remember that hardwood is expensive.

The backyard wood pile or nearby woods may supply some hardwood for gift projects. Small bird projects can be carved from logs or branches that are sufficiently dry. A slice of a log makes an excellent base for a shorebird, fish, and other gift projects. Look for hardwood in shipping pallets or any other place where it may be considered scrap. Ask around and you may find a source of hardwood pieces.

One of the pluses of woodworking is that it makes you more environmentally aware. For example, you will recognize that there are many different species of trees, with many different characteristics. Several gift projects use what is called spalted wood. Basically, this is wood that is often lying on the ground and beginning to decay. Fungi have invaded the cells of the wood and created a fascinating effect. With spalted wood, you encounter nature at work in a most interesting fashion.

Supplies

A wide assortment of supplies are needed to make these gift projects from wood. Supply lists are given for each project. Some of these supplies are mandatory. You may already have many in your shop or household. Others tend to make the gift project more useful, interesting, or attractive. These are usually items that you would have to purchase or order from a mail-order supplier. Following is a general discussion on the supplies that are needed or are helpful for making the projects in this book.

To assemble your gift projects, you will need wood glue. There are many excellent glues available. Buy one of the yellow glues that are advertised for woodworking. A number of projects require using a waterproof glue. In recent months, a new waterproof yellow glue has become available. Two-part epoxy glue will also be useful in crafting several projects. A bottle of standard white glue should also be available for use with projects. As with any product, read the label prior to use.

Another useful device for assembling some gift projects is a hot-melt glue gun. Hot glue has a long history in the furniture industry. Glue guns and sticks are a recent development, and are a more effective way of applying hot-melt glue than the traditional glue pot and hide-glue flakes. They provide a simple and effective way to assemble projects. Best of all, there are different types of glue sticks available.

Finishing nails of various sizes and wire brads will be needed for assembling projects. As indicated earlier, a nail set will prove useful with these nails. You may want to have a small tack hammer to drive in wire brads.

While several projects are best assembled with glue and wood screws, you may want to use the new drywall screws. They're very effective in wood, are available in a range of sizes, and are easy to use. A bit secured in an electric or cordless drill is an effective way to assemble projects with screws. Bits are available for use with both Phillips® and square-recess screw heads.

Dowels of varying diameters are used in many of the projects. Some large discount stores carry an excellent selection of dowels at reasonable prices. They are also available at lumber dealers, local hardware stores, and through mail-order suppliers. Walnut and oak dowels, should you want to use them, are often available from local hardwood dealers or from mail-order companies.

Most of the gift projects do not require commercial components. For other projects, commercial components are needed or are the better choice. For example, while you can make pegs from dowels rather than ordering commercial Shaker pegs, the commercial ones certainly look better. These have to be ordered from suppliers. Also, there are several desktop clock projects where clock movements are needed. Many mail-order suppliers handle a wide variety of clock movements. Again, national woodworking magazines will be helpful in giving you sources for these products.

The fun part of making gift projects is that you get to decide what will go into a project. For example, when making a desk pen set, you may decide to use a plastic pen set rather than a gold one. Items that will enhance your gift projects are available if you're willing to spend the extra money. Depending upon the person who is to receive the gift, you may or may not want to dress up the project.

Finishing Products

For most of the gift projects, you will decide which type of finish to use. There are several possibilities. The use of a woodburning unit to enhance a project with different designs was mentioned earlier. If you want to dress up a project, you may want to use some of the many stencils that are now available. In some cases, you will paint on a design. Even though you may not be very effective with a paintbrush, you will enjoy painting a fish or cat design.

There are a few basic finishing principles that should be addressed here. There are, generally speaking, two kinds of finishing products. One type is absorbed into the wood. These include lacquers, paint, polyurethane, and varnishes. The other type remains on the surface. These include oil and water stains, and oil finishes. With the exception of cutting boards and a few other gift projects, the decision on which type to use is up to you.

If you want a clear finish on a gift project, consider using one of the many lacquers or polyurethanes. The lacquers work well, are easy to use, and, best of all, dry quickly. After you have woodburned a design into a project, adding a clear lacquer finish will give it a great appearance. Deft® is an excellent product and easy to use. Read the labels on any of these products and be certain to use them in ventilated areas. After giving the project several coats of lacquer, rub the surface down with steel wool (0000). You will find Deft® to be an excellent product to use on both softwood and hardwood projects.

Painting the projects with one of the many latex gloss enamels available is both easy and fun. Don't paint the hardwood projects. Pine is the ideal wood for painting. Read the can directions and prepare the surface accordingly. After

using latex paints, clean the brushes and yourself with soap and water.

You can also decorate gift projects with stencils and latex paints. There are many commercial stencils available in metal, plastic, and even paper. Stencil designs include Americana, Christmas, and Halloween themes, and almost any other design you can imagine. Hobby and paint stores, mail-order catalogues, and discount stores carry stencils. Try stencilling a few projects and discover how easy it is to do.

With some of the gift projects, for example, the shorebirds and fish, you will have to paint an approximation of a creature or object. Be creative. Paint this creature or object the way you think it should appear. You will be impressed with the results, and so will the recipient of the gift.

Finishing products that are absorbed into the wood are excellent for use with pine projects. There are enough colors available to meet the needs of the most discriminating finisher. The lathe art projects provide the opportunity to use any number of different colored stains, if you're so inclined. Pine projects that are stained should also be covered with a surface finish. As with any chemical, read the labels and follow the various instructions for using the stains. A final rubbing of several coats of paste wax is an excellent way to finish your lacquered projects.

If you prefer an oil finish, especially on the hardwood gift projects, you may want to consider Watco® Danish Oil Natural. There are many excellent oil finishing products available. Most products provide complete information for their use on the can's label.

For cutting boards and other items that will be used with food, mineral oil is an excellent product. It is a pure oil that both preserves and enhances the wood. Some oils are toxic, while others become rancid on the wood. As a rule, warm the wood prior to applying the oil to it. This tends to encourage better absorption of the oil into the wood. Periodic reoilings may be necessary because of both use and washing.

PROJECTS

Before You Begin

The gift projects in this book are presented randomly. This approach exposes you to projects that you may not have otherwise considered for use as gifts. When wood projects are presented according to tools, methods, or their degree of difficulty, there is a tendency to consider only projects similar to ones made in the past. It limits the possibilities and challenges for you as a gift maker.

In addition to a photograph of a finished gift project, a list of materials is presented. It's important to note that this list contains *suggested* items to use. If a project's material list indicates the use of pine, you may prefer a hardwood instead. Your choice of accessories or finishes may also be different. Make each project according to your preferences, and the preferences of the recipient of the gift. This also applies to finishing techniques. Maybe the recipient doesn't like woodburning, and prefers an Early-American stencil design.

Drawings are provided with each of the gift projects. These drawings usually have the project's dimensions. As with the materials used, you may want to modify some or all of the dimensions of a given project. A shelf could be made longer or wider, depending upon the needs of the recipient. You may decide to make a project smaller than suggested because of the amount of wood available.

You will also note that each project has a suggested list of tools. Again, the rule here is to improvise if you lack a particular tool. Woodworking requires and encourages problem-solving, which is what makes it so interesting and challenging. As you read the instructions for a project, you may know a better way with different tools and methods to achieve the same results.

Step-by-step instructions are provided for each project to assist you in making the gift. To min-imize repetition of some detailed instructions, they will be given only once. For example, instructions on how to set up and use a table-mounted router will be given only once. Other projects requiring the same tool will have a reference to the earlier instructions.

Have fun!

1: Bagel Slicer (Illus. 44 and 45)

This gift will make it easier for bagel lovers to slice their bagels. It's the ideal gift for children like mine who, each day, must have a bagel with cream cheese and a slice of hard salami. While I would have preferred ending this gastronomical aberration, I gave each a bagel slicer for a Christmas gift. Check the local bagel market to be certain that the dimensions of the slicer will accommodate the bagels. The slicer should be made from hard maple so that it can be properly cleaned and maintained. Place the bagel in the slicer and, using a bread knife, cut down and through it.

MATERIAL:
- ¾" thick hard maple
- ⁷⁄₁₆" thick hard maple
- ½" diameter dowel
- 8 wood screws and waterproof wood glue
- Mineral oil

TOOLS:
- Band saw and radial arm saw, table saw, or sabre saw
- Drill press or electric drill (½" wood bit and ¹⁄₁₆" drill bit)
- Screwdriver or screw bit for electric drill

Illus. 44. Bagel slicer.

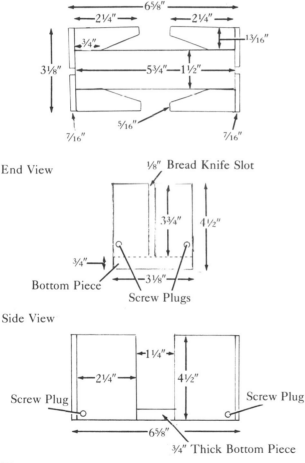

Illus. 45. Drawings of bagel slicer.

DIRECTIONS:

1. Read through all the directions before beginning the project. Study both Illus. 44 and 45, and note the project's various dimensions and how it is constructed. Using a band saw with a ½″ blade, resaw pieces of hard maple to the suggested thicknesses. Cut them longer than needed. Note how the end pieces are 7/16″ thick, the side pieces 13/16″ thick, and the bottom piece ¾″ thick. These thicknesses need not be exact.

2. Cut all pieces to their suggested lengths using a radial arm saw, table saw, or sabre saw.

3. Measure and mark the center of the end pieces. Mark the thickness of the bottom piece on each of the end pieces. Using a band saw or sabre saw, cut a slicing slot in each end. The slot should be at least ⅛″ wide or a thickness that will accommodate your bread knife. The slot should stop where the top surface of the bottom piece will join the end piece. This allows the user to cut through the entire bagel.

4. On the top edges of the four side pieces, measure and mark for the tapered cuts. Make dark saw lines on each piece that are easy to follow. Review Illus. 45 to note the various dimensions of the taper. The cut taper should begin at approximately ¾″ from the outside edge and taper to an approximate thickness of 13/16″. Note how the taper appears in both Illus. 44 and 45. The taper is best cut using a band saw. Take your time with this procedure.

5. Measure and mark for drill holes with which to assemble the project. Note in Illus. 45 how the slicer is assembled and where the screw holes should be placed. Using a ½″ diameter wood bit, drill holes approximately halfway through each piece. The ½″ diameter allows space for both the screw head and for a ½″ diameter plug to fill the hole. Drill the holes.

6. Prepare all surfaces for finishing using fine and extra-fine abrasive papers. Be sure to always sand with the wood grain.

7. Using wood screws and wood glue, assemble the project. The side pieces should be secured to the bottom piece before the end pieces are attached. You will need to drill small pilot holes or the screws will crack the wood. As you assemble each section, with the glue applied, drill a pilot hole and then secure the piece with a wood screw. A 1/16″ or smaller drill bit will work well for making the pilot holes. The pilot hole must be smaller than the diameter of the threaded screw shank for the screw to hold properly. Wipe off any glue that squeezes out during the assembly process. Glue tends to stain the wood. Be certain to wipe it off the various surfaces or it will show through the final finish.

8. After the slicer is assembled, cut plugs from a ½" diameter dowel to place in the screw holes. The plugs' length should be approximately the depth of the screw hole. Place a drop of glue on the wall of each hole and tap the plugs into the hole, flush with the surface.

9. Using fine and extra-fine abrasive papers, sand over the plugs and any other area that needs cleaning up. Also round the sharp corners on the project.

10. Finish the bagel slicer by applying several coats of mineral oil to it. Rub it on with a rag. If the wood is warm when the oil is applied, it will absorb it more quickly. The slicer can be washed and, on occasion, reoiled with mineral oil.

2: *Fish on a Stick*

(Illus. 46 and 47)

Making and painting fish to approximate the real thing is great fun. While it may not be immediately apparent, the two shown in Illus. 46 and 47 are a smallmouth bass and a rainbow trout. The fish are gifts for my son, Peter, whom I introduced to the joys of trout and bass fishing. Though they are not of museum quality, they are mighty fine gifts. Fish on a stick are fun to make, and the gift recipients are usually delighted with them. You don't have to be an accomplished painter to decorate a wooden fish profile.

MATERIAL:
- 1" x 6" pine
- ³⁄₁₆" diameter dowels
- Log slices
- Construction paper
- Variety of paints and small brushes

Illus. 46. Fish on a stick.

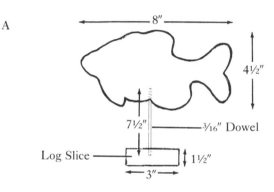

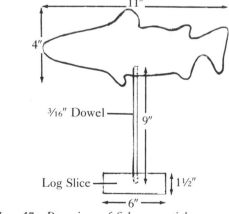

Illus. 47. Drawings of fish on a stick.

TOOLS:
- Band saw, scroll saw, or sabre saw
- Electric grinder and carbide burrs
- Finishing sander
- Electric drill and ³⁄₁₆" bit

24

OPTIONAL TOOLS:

- Rotary tool and burrs
- Flex-shaft tool and burrs
- Whittling knife
- Carving tools

DIRECTIONS:

1. Read through the directions and review both Illus. 46 and 47. Using construction paper, pencil, and a pair of scissors, draw and cut the fish patterns. If necessary, find a book on fish and copy some profiles. Another option is to draw the fish to approximate your idea of how they should look. This can be a fun family project. Make the fish as large or small as you want.

2. Trace the fish patterns on a pine board and cut them out using a scroll or sabre saw.

3. Using an electric grinder and carbide burr or a tool of your choice, shape the fish. The top and bottom edges of the fish should be tapered. The tail area should also be shaped to approximate a fish's tail. Spend time working on the various fins. Enjoy the process but be careful when using the various tools.

4. Final shaping can be accomplished using an electric finishing sander and a coarse-grit abrasive paper. You can also use small sanding sleeves on a rotary or flex-shaft tool to accomplish the same thing.

5. Using fine and extra-fine abrasive paper, prepare the surfaces for finishing.

6. Measure and cut pieces of ³⁄₁₆″ dowels to an appropriate length to support the fish.

7. Cut a slice from a fireplace log or a piece of branch from a fallen tree for the base. Be certain the piece is large enough to support the fish.

8. Center and drill ³⁄₁₆″ diameter holes in both the bottom of the fish and the top of the base. Be certain to center the hole on the bottom of the fish so that it won't tip over.

9. Use a variety of latex paints to finish the fish. If desired, paint an eye, mouth, and gills. You will find that small brushes that come with children's paint sets work fine for doing detail work on the fish. Remember, there is no such thing as a mistake. Each fish is one of a kind.

10. Do not paint the log base. Leave the bark in place, but sand the edges of it.

11. Insert the dowel in the appropriate fish and base holes. Now, admire what you've just created.

3: Christmas Candle Holder (Illus. 48 and 49)

People who receive one of these gifts look forward to another one the following year. There's something about having a date or year on a gift that makes it more memorable. The candles are a standard type that is available in red or white at most stores that stock candles.

MATERIAL:

- 1″ x 4″ pine
- 4¼″ long candles
- Construction paper
- Lacquer for finishing

TOOLS:

- Scroll or sabre saw
- Drill press or electric drill and ⁷⁄₁₆″ bit
- Finishing sander

DIRECTIONS:

1. Review the directions and Illus. 48 and 49. Using construction paper, draw and cut, with

Illus. 48. Christmas candle holder.

25

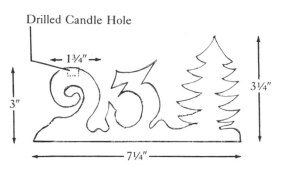

Illus. 49. Drawing of Christmas candle holder.

Illus. 50. Pasta forks.

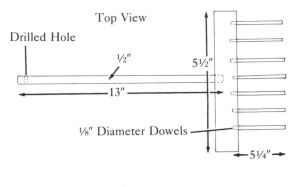

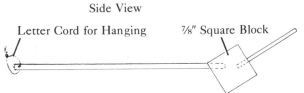

Illus. 51. Drawings of pasta forks.

scissors, a pattern of the project. The pattern does not have to include the fine cuts that can be made with a scroll saw.

2. Trade the pattern on the surface of the 1″ x 4″ material. You would be wise to make a bunch of these projects while you're doing it.

3. Using a scroll or sabre saw, cut the traced project from the board. If you're using a sabre saw, you may want to clamp the board to a workbench to make cutting easier and safer.

4. Drill the candle hole on the top of the number nine. If you prefer, drill it on the number three. Center the hole and drill it only sufficiently deep to hold the candle in place.

5. Sand the surface of the project using fine and extra-fine abrasive papers.

6. Finish the candle holder with a clear lacquer. Include a candle with the project when you give it as a gift.

4: Pasta Forks (Illus. 50 and 51)

For those who enjoy the art of making fettuccine Alfredo, pasta forks would be an ideal gift. Obviously, the forks can be used with spaghetti or other pasta, but they are designed for lightly stirring fettuccine dishes. They are made from hard maple and dowels. A buckskin hanging strap can be used to display the forks in the kitchen. This is a gift that anyone who enjoys cooking would be pleased to receive.

MATERIAL:
- ½″ diameter maple dowels
- ⅛″ diameter maple dowels
- 1″ (⁴/4's) thick hard maple
- Buckskin
- Waterproof wood glue
- Mineral oil

TOOLS:
- Band saw or sabre saw
- Drill press or electric drill and ½″ and ¼″ wood bits

DIRECTIONS:
1. Review the directions and Illus. 50 and 51 before beginning the project.

2. Measure and cut the handles for the two forks to length. While the project handles are 13″ long, you may want to lengthen or shorten the handles.

3. Measure and cut the tines for the forks. Each project fork has seven tines, thus there are a total of fourteen. Cut them to their suggested length or longer, if preferred.

4. Using a band saw or sabre saw, cut the maple blocks that will hold both the tines and the handle. The block should be cut to the desired or suggested length, and should be at least ⅞″ square.

5. On one surface of each block, measure and mark the location for the tines. Using a ⅛″ diameter drill bit, drill the tine holes to a depth of at least ¼″. The holes should all be the same depth.

6. Mark the center of the block on one edge and drill a ½″ diameter hole for the fork handle. Check Illus. 51 for the location of the handle. Repeat this process in the same location on the second block. The placement of the handle will determine the angle of the fork tines. This angle makes using the forks considerably easier. Take your time with this procedure. Drill the handle holes to a depth of at least ⅝″.

7. Spread a dab of waterproof wood glue in the tine holes and tap the tines in place. Wipe off any excess glue. Use waterproof glue because the forks, both in use and in washing, will be exposed to water.

8. Spread glue in the handle holes in the blocks and tap the handles in place on each fork. Remove any excess glue and allow it to dry.

9. Drill a ⅛″ diameter hole, near the top, through the handle for a buckskin hanging strap to pass.

10. Using a fine-grit abrasive paper, round the edges of the tines, the handles and the blocks. Lightly sand the surfaces.

11. Using a rag and mineral oil, finish the forks. Rub in several coats of oil. If possible, warm the forks slightly; this facilitates absorption of the oil into the wood.

12. Secure a length of buckskin to each handle.

5: *Hanging Letter Holder* (Illus. 52 and 53)

This functional gift project is of a size that could be placed in any kitchen or den. It's small enough to occupy a minimum of space, but large enough to hold a pile of bills or correspondence. If you want, custom-design it to fit an area or need of the recipient. This project also affords you a large enough surface on which to woodburn a design. If you prefer, stencil a design on the project.

MATERIAL:
- ½″ thick pine
- Finishing nails
- Wood glue and wood putty
- Construction paper
- Lacquer for finishing

Illus. 52. Hanging letter holder.

27

Front View

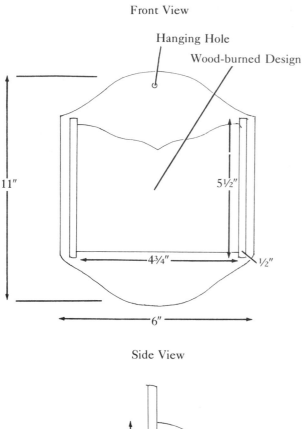

Hanging Hole

Wood-burned Design

11″

5½″

4¾″

½″

6″

Side View

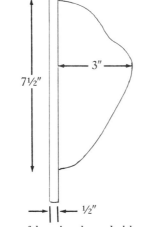

7½″

3″

½″

Illus. 53. Drawings of hanging letter holder.

TOOLS:

- Band saw, scroll, or sabre saw
- Electric drill and screw-sink or countersink and bit (¼″)
- Table-mounted router and roundover bit
- Finishing sander and nail set
- Woodburning set

DIRECTIONS:

1. Review the directions and Illus. 52 and 53 before beginning the project. Using construction paper, make patterns of the back, front and two side pieces. Make the patterns to the dimensions given. A good technique for making patterns is to fold the paper in half, draw the desired design on the paper, cut along the lines, and open the paper. The folded and cut paper is now a complete and exact pattern. Feel free to modify the designs for any piece of the holder. You may also want to change the dimensions.

2. Hopefully, you will have access to ½″ thick pine for the project. If not, possibly someone can plane some pine boards for you. Another option is to use a band saw and a ½″ blade to resaw standard thickness pine to the needed ½″. Place the rough, sawed surfaces on the back and inside of the project. If you want, you can sand the surfaces smooth with a belt sander. You can also skip the ½″ material and make the project from standard thickness 1″ pine. If you do, increase the size of the project to allow for the thicker material.

3. Trace the patterns on the pine boards and cut the various pieces using either a scroll or sabre saw.

4. With a roundover bit secured in the collet of a table-mounted router, rout all edges of the pieces. If you're using ½″ thick material, set the router to remove only a small portion of the edges. You can easily remove too much material.

5. Measure and drill a hanging hole in the top center of the back piece. Widen the hole by using either a screw-sink or a countersink. This procedure gives the hole a neater appearance.

6. Using fine and extra-fine abrasive paper and a finishing sander, prepare all surfaces for finishing. If you prefer, you can wrap a piece of abrasive paper around a block of wood and sand the pieces. Also lightly sand the routed edges.

7. Assemble the letter holder using wood glue and finishing nails. Wipe off any excess wood glue that is squeezed onto the surfaces. With a hammer and the appropriate-size nail set, tap the heads of the finishing nails under the surface of the wood. Fill the nail holes with wood putty or a plastic wood filler. This makes for a neater looking project. Sand off the excess filler.

8. Pencil a design on the surface of the front piece of the holder and woodburn it into the wood. The design shown in Illus. 53 is one that I created for the project. Try your own design. You may want to experiment on some scraps of pine with the burning unit prior to doing the finished design. After burning in the design, lightly sand the woodburned area with extra-fine abrasive paper. This cleans up the design and makes it appear sharper.

9. Finish the project with a clear lacquer finish.

6: *Flower Pot Holder*

(Illus. 54 and 55)

Designed to hang and display a small flower pot, this gift will look good in a kitchen. Best of all, the recipient may prefer using it to display some other decorative item. The design uses lots of scrolls which have become popular in recent years. If you have a floor-model scroll saw, you can really dress up this kind of project. A sabre saw will also accomplish the job. You may want to paint or woodburn a design on the surface of the back piece.

Illus. 54. Flower pot holder.

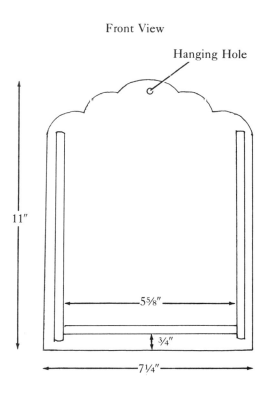

Front View

Hanging Hole

11″

5⅝″

¾″

7¼″

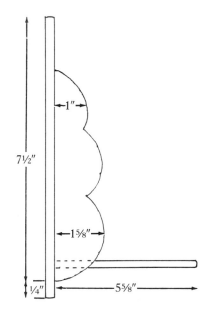

Side View

7½″

1″

1⅝″

¼″

5⅝″

Illus. 55. Drawings of flower pot holder.

29

MATERIAL:

- ½″ thick pine
- Construction paper
- Finishing nails
- Wood glue and wood filler
- Latex paint

TOOLS:

- Band saw and scroll or sabre saw
- Table-mounted router and roundover bit
- Electric drill, screw-sink or countersink, and ¼″ bit
- Finishing sander
- Nail set

DIRECTIONS:

1. After reviewing the directions and Illus. 54 and 55, make patterns from construction paper of the back, sides, and shelf piece. Make the patterns to the exact dimensions you want the project to be. As indicated earlier, fold the construction paper, draw the design on one of the folded halves, and cut it out with scissors. When the paper is unfolded, you will have a complete and exact pattern to use.

2. The project is made from ½″ thick pine. If you can't buy pine in this thickness, possibly someone can plane some for you. You may want to resaw your own using a band saw and a ½″ wide blade. Another option is to use standard 1″ material. If standard thickness pine is used, increase the size of the project accordingly.

3. Trace the patterns on the surface of the material and cut them out using either a scroll or sabre saw. The patterns should be traced *with* the grain of the wood.

4. Using a table-mounted router and roundover bit, lightly rout all edges of the various pieces.

5. Drill a hanging hole into the top center of the back piece. Use a screw-sink or countersink to widen the hole.

6. Using fine and extra-fine abrasive paper, finish-sand all the surfaces and the routed edges.

7. Assemble the holder using wood glue and finishing nails. Tap the nail heads under the surface using a nail set. Fill the nail holes with wood filler. When the filler is dry, sand the surfaces smooth.

8. If you want to wood-burn a design on the back surface, draw the design in pencil and then burn it in. Lightly sand over the design after the burning is complete. Finish the project with a clear lacquer finish to accentuate the wood-burned design.

9. You may prefer painting the holder with one of the many Early-American colors that are now available. An added touch would be a stencil design painted on the back surface. Another finishing option is to stain the holder to match the color of the recipient's cabinets or trim. Finish the stained piece with a clear lacquer.

7: Napkin Ring Caddy

(Illus. 56 and 57)

For those individuals or families who like to use linen napkins or high-quality paper ones, this may be the gift to give. The caddy is designed to serve as a holder for up to nine commercially made napkin rings, though you can make it to accommodate any amount you desire. As Illus. 56 indicates, the rings are placed over the dowels on the caddy when not in use. While the caddy itself can be lacquered, the rings can be painted different colors and with different designs. This is a fun family project. Each person can decorate his or her own napkin ring.

MATERIAL:

- 1″ (4/4's) piece of hardwood
- 1″ diameter dowels
- Napkin rings
- Wood screws
- Wood glue
- Lacquer and/or paint

TOOLS:

- Band saw or sabre saw
- Electric drill, screw sink, and ⅛″ bit
- Finishing sander
- Table-mounted router and roundover bit
- School compass

Illus. 56. Napkin ring caddy.

Side View   Top View

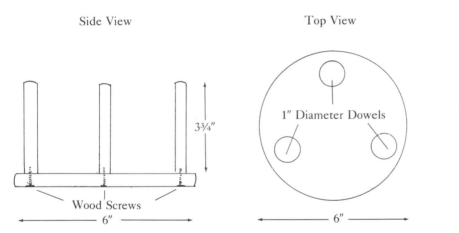

1" Diameter Dowels

3¾"

Wood Screws

6"   6"

Illus. 57. Drawings of napkin ring caddy.

DIRECTIONS:

1. With a school compass, make a 6″ diameter circle on the surface of a piece of hardwood. Using a band saw or sabre saw, cut out the circle. Take your time, so you have a perfect round shape for the base of the caddy.

2. Rout both edges of the base with a round-over bit.

3. Measure and cut the 1″ diameter dowels to length. An oak dowel was used for the caddy shown in Illus. 56. You may want to use a standard hardwood dowel or an oak one for the caddy posts. If you want the posts to accommodate more napkin rings, simply make them longer.

The standard commercial napkin ring is approximately 1¼″ wide. Another option is to add an additional post that will accommodate more rings.

4. Using abrasive paper, prepare the surfaces of the base and the dowels for finishing. The top edge of each dowel should be slightly rounded over with abrasive paper. This gives the project a more finished appearance.

5. Measure and mark the location of the posts on the bottom surface of the caddy base. Drill a pilot hole at each mark, and through the base. Insert the wood screws into the pilot holes until they extend just above the top surface of the base.

31

6. Spread wood glue on the bottom surface of a dowel, center the dowel over the point of the extending wood screw, and press down and turn the screw into it. Tighten the screw until glue squeezes out from under the dowel. Repeat the process for each post. If you have a problem getting the screws into the dowels, drill a pilot hole into the dowels. Center the dowels over the screws and press down and mark the center. Drill the pilot hole at the mark. Spread glue on the bottom surface of the dowel, place the dowel on the screw point, and secure it in place. Wipe off the excess glue that squeezes onto the surface of the base.

7. Finish the caddy with a clear lacquer. Paint and decorate the napkin rings or, if you prefer, finish them with a clear lacquer.

8: Owl Cutting Boards

(Illus. 58 and 59)

Hard maple cutting boards are always a popular and useful gift. Making a "parliament" of owls (the collective noun for more than one owl) is an extremely wise choice. The large board is very functional for the bigger cutting tasks. The pair of smaller boards is ideal for cheese and sausage or some other goodie that needs to be cut. As always, you can vary the size of this project to meet a specific need.

MATERIAL:
- 1″ (4/4's) thick hard maple
- Construction paper
- Mineral oil

TOOLS:
- Sabre or scroll saw
- Table-mounted router with roundover bit
- Finishing sander

DIRECTIONS:
1. Make patterns, to size, for both cutting boards. The folded construction paper method of making patterns is the best way to proceed (see Project 5).

Illus. 58. Owl cutting boards.

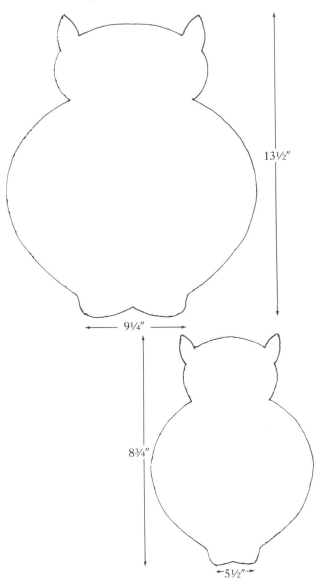

Illus. 59. Drawings of owl cutting boards.

2. Trace the patterns, with the grain, on the surface of hard maple. You may want to use a different hardwood, for example, birch or oak. I prefer hard maple because it is the perfect wood for a cutting board that can be used on a regular basis.

3. Cut out the traced owls using either a scroll or sabre saw. If you have a band saw with a ¼″ wide blade, use it. Maple is difficult to cut and burns easily if the blades are dull.

4. Rout the edges of the cutting boards using a table-mounted router and a roundover bit.

5. Using both fine and extra-fine abrasive paper and a finishing sander, prepare the surfaces and edges for oiling.

6. Before applying mineral oil to the boards, warm the wood. Apply the oil with a rag and allow it to soak into the wood. Several coats are recommended. The board should be reoiled occasionally.

9: *Porcupine Pull Toy*

(Illus. 60 and 61)

This project makes a fun and unusual pull toy for children, and an excellent gift for adults who like to display toys. It includes a North-American porcupine—a delightful forest critter—and its baby following behind. To give the toy that porcupine-like walk, the wheels have been squared. You will have a good time painting this gift because there are many options. The project shown in Illus. 60 is painted red, white and blue. The heads are painted yellow. By the way, in case you didn't know, the porcupine's original Italian name—*porcospino*—means thorny pig.

MATERIAL:

- 2″ x 10″ pine fir
- ¼″ diameter dowel
- ⅜″ diameter dowel
- Eye screws
- Wood glue
- 2″ diameter wheels
- 1″ diameter wheels
- String
- Paint

TOOLS:

- Band saw, scroll saw, or sabre saw
- Electric drill and ¼″, ⅜″, and ½″ bits
- Finishing sander

DIRECTIONS:

1. Review the directions and Illus. 60 and 61 before you begin crafting the project. You may want to draw the head and body of both porcupines, freehand, onto the surface of the wood. If not, make patterns from construction paper and trace them onto the board. Draw or trace the designs with the grain of the wood.

2. Cut the parts of both porcupines from the 2″ x 10″ material using an appropriate saw.

3. Mark the location of the wheel axles on both the large and small bodies. Place them as you see

Illus. 60. Porcupine pull toy.

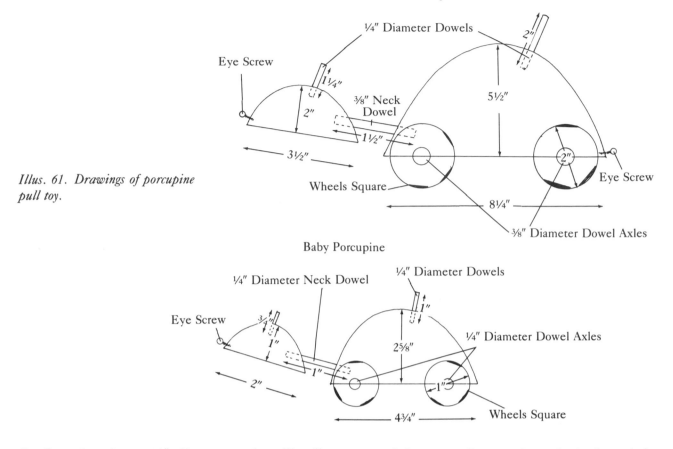

Illus. 61. Drawings of porcupine pull toy.

fit. In order that a ⅜″ diameter axle will roll smoothly, ½″ diameter axle holes should be drilled through the larger body. In that ¼″ diameter axles are to be used on the smaller porcupine, drill ⅜″ diameter axle holes through the smaller body. The axles should move freely, thus making the toys easier to pull.

4. Mark the location for the neck dowels on both the head and body of the mother and child. Drill ⅜″ diameter holes, ½″ deep, where marked on the mother. Note in Illus. 61 the angle of the head. Drill the two holes so that the head points upwards. In the smaller toy, drill ¼″ diameter holes, ½″ deep. Drill the holes at an angle so that this head also points upwards.

5. Measure and cut the neck dowels for both porcupines.

6. Wrap a piece of masking or duct tape ¼″ from the point of a ¼″ drill bit. The tape will serve as a stop to prevent you from drilling the porcupine quills or spines too deeply. The spines should

extend the same distance from the body and the head.

7. Along the top edge of the body and head of both toys, drill ¼″ diameter holes at different angles. Refer to Illus. 60 to note how the quills look when in place. Drill one hole for each quill.

8. Measure and cut two, 3″ long axles from a ⅜″ diameter piece of dowel. Using wood glue, glue a 2″ wheel on one end of each dowel piece. Insert the axles through the drilled holes in the body of the larger porcupine and glue on the other two wheels. Allow the glue to dry. Make sure that the wheels are not glued to the body of the toy.

9. For the small porcupine, measure and cut two, 2⅜″ long axles from a ¼″ diameter piece of dowel. Glue a 1″ diameter wheel to one end of both axles. Insert the axles through the body and glue the other two wheels to the axles. Allow the glue to dry.

10. Measure and cut ¼″ diameter dowels to the suggested lengths for the body and head of both critters. Count the holes drilled to determine how many dowels of each length you will need.

11. To reduce the sharpness of the dowels, round over the top edge of one end of all the dowels. This end should protrude.

12. Using various abrasive papers and a finishing sander, prepare the head and bodies for finishing.

13. Before gluing the dowels into the toys, paint everything, including the dowels. Use your imagination!

14. After everything has been painted, glue the dowel quills in place. Using the neck dowels, glue the head and body together on both toys.

15. Thread eye screws into the designated areas. Using string, tie the two porcupines together. Secure a longer string to the eye screw in the head of the larger porcupine, to pull the toys. You may want to tie a wooden bead, ball, or piece of dowel to the pulling end of the string. This makes it easier for a child to pull the toy.

Illus. 62. Napkin holder.

10: *Napkin Holder*

(Illus. 62 and 63)

A practical gift to give, the napkin holder is also easy to make. The design is simple yet attractive. While the napkin holder shown in Illus. 62 is made from pine, you may prefer making one from hardwood. You can dress up the holder by either wood-burning a design or painting a stencil on it. You may want to make several of these gifts.

MATERIAL:

- 1″ x 4″ pine
- ⅜″ diameter dowel
- Construction paper
- Wood glue
- Paint

TOOLS:

- Scroll or sabre saw
- Electric drill and ⅜″ bit
- Table-mounted router and roundover bit
- Finishing sander

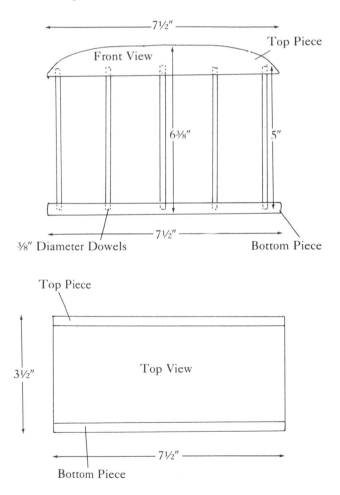

Illus. 63. Drawings of napkin holder.

DIRECTIONS:

1. Review Illus. 63 and decide if the dimensions are adequate for your needs. You may also want to modify the design. Using construction paper, make a pattern for the top piece of the holder.

2. Measure and cut the bottom piece to its dimensions.

3. Trace and cut the two top pieces.

4. Rout all edges on the base. Rout only the top edges on the top pieces of the holder.

5. Measure and mark the location of ⅜″ diameter dowels on both the base and the two top pieces. Drill ⅜″ diameter holes at the marked locations to a depth of ¼″. Wrap a piece of duct tape around the bit ¼″ up from the point. This will serve as a stop, so all the holes will be drilled to their exact depths.

6. Measure and cut the needed number of ⅜″ diameter dowels. The napkin holder shown in Illus. 62 and 63 requires ten dowel pieces 5″ long.

7. Glue the dowels in place in the drilled holes. Wipe off any excess glue.

8. Paint or finish the napkin holder as desired. If you decide to wood-burn a design on the top pieces, you may want to finish the holder with a clear lacquer. A small stencil would also look good on the top pieces.

11: *Lazy Susan* (Illus. 64 and 65)

A lazy Susan is the ideal functional centerpiece for a kitchen table. The swivel ball bearings located under the top piece of the lazy Susan allow the top piece an unrestricted smooth rotation. It's an excellent way to move salt and pepper shakers, condiments, or other food-support items around the table. Lazy Susan bearings are available in a range of sizes. This will allow you to design a lazy Susan to meet the specific table needs of the gift recipient. You may want to use sink cutouts that have a ceramic top surface already in place. If you prefer, you can laminate hardwood boards, for example, hard maple or oak. The lazy Susan shown in Illus. 64 and 65 was made from ⅜″ thick plywood.

MATERIAL:

- ⅜″ thick plywood
- ¾″ (¾'s) piece of hardwood
- 1¼″ (⁵⁄₄'s) piece of hardwood
- 6″ lazy Susan bearing
- Wood screws
- Wood filler
- Wood glue
- Paint

Illus. 64. Lazy Susan.

Illus. 65. Drawings of lazy Susan.

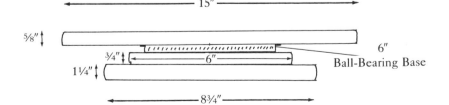

TOOLS:
- Band saw or sabre saw
- Electric drill, screw-sink, and ⅛" bit
- School compass
- Finishing sander

DIRECTIONS:

1. Review Illus. 65. Using a school compass or a nail-string-pencil compass, make a 15" diameter circle on a piece of ¾" thick construction paper or, better yet, plywood. With the nail-string-pencil compass, tie one end of a 15" long string, loosely, to a nail, and the other end to the bottom of a pencil, near the point. Drive the nail into the wood and use it as a pivot as you move and mark with the pencil at the other end of the taut string. This will give you a 15" diameter circle to cut.

2. Using either a band saw or sabre saw, carefully cut out the traced circle. Take your time, to ensure that you have a perfectly round circle. Any miscuts on the cutting edge can be cleaned up with a finishing sander.

3. Measure and cut a ¾" (¾'s) thick piece of hardwood to the same dimensions as the bearing. The piece for the lazy Susan shown in Illus. 64 and 74 is 6" x 6".

4. Using wood screws, the electric drill and a screw-sink, secure the lazy Susan bearing to the 6" x 6" piece of hardwood. You may want to drill pilot holes for the screws using a ⅛" bit.

5. Using a school compass or the nail-string-pencil device, make an 8¾" diameter circle on a piece of 1¼" (5/4's) hardwood. The hardwood base gives the lazy Susan stability. Cut the base using either a band saw or sabre saw.

6. Measure and mark on the bottom of the top section the exact location for the bearing plate. Turn the bearing and the attached hardwood piece so that you can access the screw holes in the bearing plate. Screw the bearing to the bottom of the top section using wood screws. Make sure that the screws do not penetrate through the top surface. Check the length of the screws before securing them in place.

7. With the top section lying face down on a flat surface, spread wood glue on the bottom surface of the 6" x 6" piece. Drill a pilot screw hole through the exact center of the 8¾" diameter piece. Place it on the glued surface and secure it with a large wood screw. Turn the assembly upright, test it, and then allow the glue to dry.

8. Paint or finish the project as desired. An occasional drop of a quality oil on a few bearings will protect all of the bearings and keep them working smoothly.

12: Flowers on Dowels
(Illus. 66 and 67)

This is the ideal bouquet of flowers for someone you truly care about. These flowers do not fade or wilt and never need watering. They do take time to make, but the project is well worth it. You will find yourself wanting to make an array of flowers from different species of wood. The ones shown in Illus. 66 are red and yellow with black seed pods. The woods are Osage orange (yellow), Indian padauk (red), and ebony (black). The leaves are light green and are pieces of poplar. Often, poplar will have a green streak that you can use. Scraps of hardwood work just fine. If you prefer, skip the hardwoods and make the

Illus. 66. Flowers on dowels.

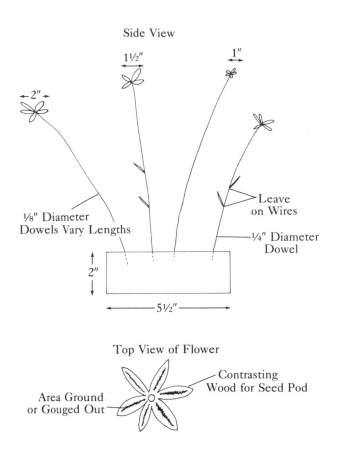

Side View

1½″

1″

2″

⅛″ Diameter
Dowels Vary Lengths

Leave
on Wires

¼″ Diameter
Dowel

2″

5½″

Top View of Flower

Contrasting
Wood for Seed Pod

Area Ground
or Gouged Out

Illus. 67. Drawings of flowers on dowels.

flowers from pine and paint them the desired colors. The stems are dowels that penetrate the underside of the flowers. The leaves are on pieces of wire that are drilled into the leaf and dowel. The base is a nice chunk of log. The Flowers on Dowels shown in Illus. 66 has a black walnut log for a base. You will find, once you begin making flowers, that there are all kinds of different ways to make this project.

MATERIAL:

- ¼″ thick pieces of hardwood (scraps)
- ¼″ diameter dowels
- ⅛″ diameter dowels
- Wire
- Chunk of firewood
- Wood glue and white glue
- Lacquer and/or paint

TOOLS:

- Band saw, scroll saw, or sabre saw
- Electric grinder, rotary tool, flex-shaft tool
- Carbide or high-speed steel burrs and sanding sleeves
- Carving tools
- Electric drill and ⅟₃₂″, ⅛″, and ¼″ bits
- Wire cutter (pliers)

DIRECTIONS:

1. Decide on how many and what kind of flowers you want in a bouquet. Draw a few designs to size until you come up with a design that you like.

2. Draw, freehand, a series of flowers on the surface of different hardwoods or, if preferred, pine. The wood should be at least ¼″ thick.

3. Using a band saw, scroll saw, or sabre saw, carefully saw the flower designs from the pieces of wood.

4. Depending upon the size of the flower, drill a ⅛″ or ¼″ diameter hole into the bottom center of the cut flower. The hole can penetrate through the flower because a seed pod will be glued over the hole. The dowel stems will be glued into these holes. If you prefer, the dowel can penetrate through the flower and its end be rounded over and painted to resemble a seed pod.

5. Cut small pieces of different hardwoods for use as seed pods. Use your imagination on both the size and shape of the pods.

6. If desired, make patterns for and cut out small leaves, approximately 1″ long and ¼″ thick. Before shaping the leaves, drill ⅟₃₂″ diameter holes into the ends of each leaf. This diameter is usually large enough to accommodate most small wires.

7. Cut ½″ long pieces of wire and, using white glue, glue them into the drilled holes in the leaves. A piece of wire at least ¼″ long should extend from the leaf. Allow the glue to dry.

8. Shape the flowers using burrs and carving tools. The bottom area of the flowers should be shaped to make the end of the petals look round. Remove wood from inside each petal.

9. After completely shaping or carving the flowers, glue a seed pod in the center of each flower unless you plan to use the end of the dowel stem as the pod. Allow the glue to dry.

10. Using burrs, sanding sleeves, and small power tools, shape the leaves.

11. Cut the dowel stems to varying lengths. Be certain to cut enough ⅛″ and ¼″ diameter dowels.

12. In that the holes for the leaf wires have to be drilled through the dowel stems, it's best to use only the larger ¼″ diameter dowels for the leaves. Decide where the leaves should be placed on the dowels and drill ¹⁄₃₂″ diameter holes through the dowels. Place a dab of white glue on the leaf wire and insert the wire into the drilled hole in the dowel.

13. Spread wood glue on the ends of the dowel stems and insert them into the drilled holes in the bottom of the flowers. Allow the glue to dry.

14. Cut a block from a firewood log that will serve as a base to hold the flowers. Drill holes for all the dowel stems. To properly display the flowers, drill a portion of the holes at an angle. Remember to drill holes for both the ⅛ and ¼″ diameter dowels.

15. Finish the flowers and leaves with a clear lacquer. If you prefer, paint the flowers, leaves, and stems.

13: Mirror (Illus. 77 and 78)

Everyone seems to like mirrors, especially small ones with a hardwood frame. This gift project is crafted from quarter-sawn red oak. You may want to increase the size of the mirror to meet the needs of the intended recipient. Best of all, once you learn how to make this kind of mirror, you can make as many as you want. The frame can be made from any hardwood or, if you want, pine.

MATERIAL:
- 1″ (4/4's) thick red oak, 5″ wide, 7″ long
- Mirror
- Construction paper
- Rubber bands (No. 105: 5″ long, ⅝″ wide)
- Wood glue and white glue
- Lacquer

TOOLS:
- Band or table saw
- Mitre saw
- Table-mounted router and roundover and rabbeting bits
- Electric drill and bit (⅛″)
- Finishing sander
- Small steel ruler
- Glass cutter

Illus. 68. Hardwood mirror.

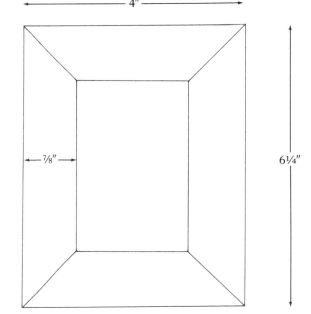

Illus. 69. Drawing of hardwood mirror.

39

DIRECTIONS:

1. After reviewing the directions and Illus. 69, measure and cut four oak strips approximately 1″ wide and 7″ long. While this will result in some waste, it is an easier way to make the frame. Use a band saw or table saw to cut these strips.

2. Rout a rabbet on one edge of each piece. Set the rabbeting bit to cut a depth of at least 1/8″. Most mirror glass is approximately 3/16″ thick. If you plan to use thicker and possibly a higher-quality mirror, cut the rabbet deeper. Select the best surface for the front of the mirror. Rout the rabbets for the other side.

3. With the roundover bit secured in the router, rout the remaining edges. Obviously, you do not want to rout the rabbeted areas with the round-over bit. Use a piece of scrap wood to test the depth-of-cut of the roundover bit. You don't want to remove too much wood.

4. Before cutting the mitres, make sure that the rabbeted edges will be on the inside bottom surface when the frame is assembled. Cut the two side pieces to the exact same lengths before mitring them. The bottom and top pieces should also be the same length.

5. Depending upon the type of mitre saw being used, set its angle to 45 degrees. Before making the mitre cuts, think through the process of how each piece will fit into the finished frame. Be certain that the rabbeted edges are on the inside. Mitre the two sides to the exact same lengths and mitre the top and bottom pieces to the exact same lengths. If you're using an electric mitre saw, be very careful. Take your time.

6. Large rubber bands work very well for holding together a glued frame. Clamp or nail a block to a flat surface. The block allows you to slide the frame against it while slipping the rubber band around the frames. Use a couple of rubber bands to hold the frame together.

7. Spread wood glue on all the mitred surfaces and assemble the frame. Slide the assembled frame against the block. It works best if you place the rubber band over the frame edge nearest to you and then stretch it until it surrounds all edges. The block holds the assembled frame in place while you're stretching the rubber band around it. Place a second band over the frame. After the rubber band is in place, you may have to realign each mitre. As you might guess, the rubber band applies equal pressure on all joints. Wipe away any glue that squeezes out. Leave the rubber bands in place until the glue is dry.

8. Prepare all surfaces for finishing using fine and extra-fine abrasive paper. Always sand with the grain.

9. Drill a small hanging hole in the center back of the top piece. The hole should be angled so that it will slip over a nail that is driven into a wall at an angle. Make the hole at least 3/8″ deep. Be careful that you don't drill through the mirror frame.

10. Remove any dust and apply several coats of a clear lacquer finish to the frame. Rub the finish with steel wool (0000) between coats. Wipe off the dust and wool hairs before applying another coat of lacquer.

11. If you prefer, take the frame to a local glass store and have a mirror cut to fit. You may want to cut your own. If you do, buy a piece of mirror tile from a local hardware store. Usually the tiles are 12″ x 12″.

To cut your own mirror, do the following: With a small steel ruler, measure the actual inside dimensions of the rabbeted area of the frame. Using a soft-tip pen and ruler, mark these exact dimensions on the mirror's reflective surface. With the ruler aligned on the inside of the line, run the glass cutter, applying even pressure on it, down and along the side of the ruler. Cut the full length of the mirror tile, even though there will be some waste. Align the scratch made by the cutter, faceup, on the sharp edge of a bench or board. While holding the mirror in place with one hand, press down on the section extending over the board or bench with your other hand. Wear gloves! The mirror should crack, evenly, along the line. Repeat the process to cut along the other marked lines on the mirror glass.

12. Place the mirror inside the rabbeted area of the frame to check its fit. If it fits, spread glue on the corner edges and along the sides. Spread glue on both the mirror and the rabbeted edges. Don't use too much glue, because it will squeeze out

on the front surface of the mirror. Allow the glue to dry with the mirror lying facedown.

13. Measure and cut a piece of construction paper that will cover the back of the frame. Glue it in place. If the hanging hole is covered by the backing, punch a hole through the paper to expose it.

14: Shaker Shelf with Hearts (Illus. 70 and 71)

For those who need an attractive, yet very functional, shelf in the kitchen, den, or bedroom, the Shaker shelf would be an ideal gift. You may want to change the dimensions to fit a specific need of the gift recipient. In addition to having a sizeable shelf surface, the project also includes three Shaker pegs for hanging items on. Shaker pegs, while great for hanging clothing, are also excellent for hanging decorative or collectible items. The heart cutouts give the shelf a country look. You may want to paint this gift.

MATERIAL:
- 1″ x 8″ pine
- 1″ x 4″ pine
- Shaker pegs
- Construction paper
- Wood glue
- Paint

Illus. 70. Shaker shelf with hearts.

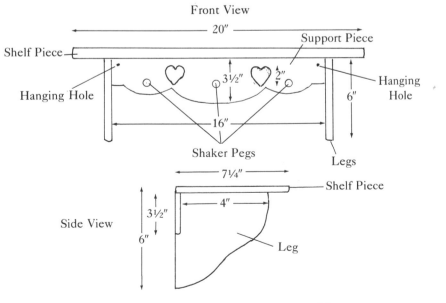

Illus. 71. Drawings of Shaker shelf with hearts.

41

TOOLS:

- Sabre saw
- Electric drill, screw-sink, and ½″ wood bit
- Table-mounted router and roundover bit
- Finishing sander

DIRECTIONS:

1. Review both Illus. 71 and the directions before beginning. Make a pattern for the shelf legs and for the heart cutouts from construction paper.

2. Measure and cut the shelf top from 1″ x 8″ pine.

3. Trace and cut the legs from 1″ x 8″ pine. Lay the pattern, with the grain, in such a way that you use a minimum of wood. Use a finishing cut blade in the sabre saw. If you prefer, use a scroll saw.

4. Measure and cut the support piece to length. Design and cut the support piece as shown in Illus. 70. You may want to change the design to meet your tastes.

5. Measure and mark the location of the Shaker pegs on the support piece. Drill ½″ diameter holes to accommodate the peg's tenon.

6. Drill hanging holes, using a screw-sink, into the support piece. Illus. 71 shows their location.

7. Trace the heart pattern on two locations on the support piece. Drill a ½″ hole inside the traced heart in which to insert the sabre-saw blade through. Cut out the heart areas.

8. Trace the ends of the support piece on the side surface of each leg. Note the side view of the project in Illus. 71. Cut out the traced area on the legs. This is the area where the support piece will be secured to the back of each leg.

9. Using a roundover bit in a table-mounted router, rout the edges of the shelf top, the legs and the bottom, and the exposed edge of the support piece. Rout also the front edge of the hearts.

10. Spread glue on the cut-out area on the back of one leg. Nail one end of the support piece to the leg using finishing nails. If you prefer, use wood screws. Repeat the procedure for the second leg. Allow the glue to dry. You may want to paint the various parts before assembling them.

11. Spread a bead of glue on the top edge of the legs-support piece assembly and nail the shelf top to it, using finishing nails. Wipe away any excess glue.

12. Glue and tap the Shaker pegs into the drilled holes in the support piece.

13. Using fine and extra-fine abrasive paper and a finishing sander, prepare all surfaces for finishing.

14. Paint or finish the project as desired.

15: Sock and Mitten Drying Rack (Illus. 72 and 73)

This drying rack can be very practical in a snowy climate where the children are in constant need of dry mittens and socks. The rack is designed with removable dowels, so more space can be provided if needed. It also has a large hanging hole if the user wants to hang the drying items near a heat source.

MATERIAL:

- 1″ x 8″ pine
- ⅜″ diameter dowels
- Lacquer

Illus. 72. Sock and mitten drying rack.

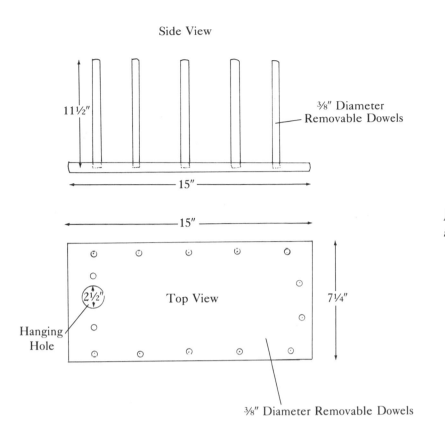

Side View

11½"

⅜" Diameter
Removable Dowels

15"

15"

Top View

7¼"

2½"

Hanging
Hole

⅜" Diameter Removable Dowels

Illus. 73. Drawings of sock and mitten drying rack.

TOOLS:

- Sabre saw
- Electric drill and bit (⅜")
- Table-mounted router and roundover bit
- Finishing sander

OPTIONAL TOOLS:

- Drill press
- Circle cutter

DIRECTIONS:

1. Review Illus. 73 before beginning the project. You may want to modify the size of the rack.
2. Measure and cut a 15" long piece of 1" x 8" pine.
3. Cut a 2½" diameter hole in the center of one end of the board. The hole allows the user to hang the rack or carry it. The hole can be cut with a sabre saw after a small hole has been cut for penetration of the blade. If you have a drill press, make the hole with a circle cutter.
4. For placement of the dowels, mark a location

every 2" around the entire board. Place the holes at least ¼" from the edges of the board. Drill ⅜" diameter dowel holes at the marked location. The holes should be at least ⅜" deep.
5. Cut twenty ⅜" diameter dowels to a length of 11½". Using a finishing sander, sand the end edges of the dowels slightly round. This makes placing and removal of the dowels from the drilled holes easier. It also gives them a more finished appearance. Place the dowels into the drilled holes. There is no need to glue the dowels into the holes.
6. Rout all edges of the rack board using a roundover bit.
7. Prepare the board for finishing with fine and extra-fine abrasive paper. The dowels should be ready for finishing.
8. Finish the dowels and board with a clear lacquer finish. Apply several coats, to make the wood more water-resistant. To protect the wood further from moisture, apply several coats of paste wax to the dowels and rack board.

43

16: Thimble Holder

(Illus. 74 and 75)

This project is a large, black walnut "thimble" which serves as a means of displaying real thimbles. It was designed by the late Leanne DeLaurenti, a devoted collector, and turned by Andy Matoesian. It has provisions for six rows of pins and a single pin on top, permitting the display of 25 thimbles. You may want to modify the design to increase or decrease the number of thimbles displayed. A close examination of the thimble shown in Illus. 74 reveals the systematic indentations given to the project by Matoesian. The display pins are spiral-grooved dowel pins, better known to some as furniture pins.

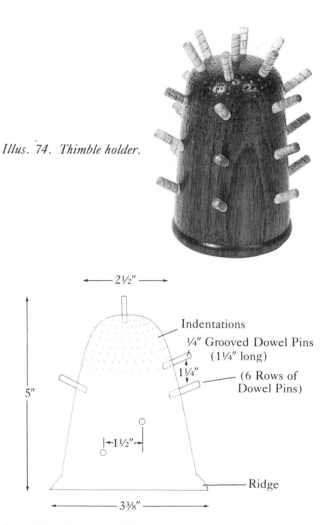

Illus. 74. Thimble holder.

Illus. 75. Drawing of thimble holder.

MATERIAL:
- 3½" (1⁴⁄₄'s) thick black walnut
- ¼" diameter dowel pins
- Wood glue and white glue
- Lacquer

TOOLS:
- Band saw
- School compass
- Clamp
- Wood lathe and turning tools
- Electric drill and ¼" wood bit
- Awl

DIRECTIONS:

1. Review Illus. 75 and note the dimensions of the project. While you may want to spindle-turn the project on a lathe, the faceplate method may be better for some. Prepare a turning block of black walnut that is at least 3½" (1⁴⁄₄'s) thick and 5½" long. The turning block should run with the grain. After cutting a block to length, using a school compass, make a 3½" diameter circle on the end grain of the block. Cut out the turning block using a band saw. You may prefer to make the project from wood other than black walnut.

2. Prepare a round glue block that is at least 4" in diameter. Using white glue and wood clamps, secure the glue block to the turning block. When the turning is completed, cut the glue block off with a band saw. Clamp the assembly until the glue is dry.

3. Attach a faceplate to the assembly and thread it on the lathe. You may want to bring the tailstock forward, revolving center in place, to make the block more secure during the turning process.

4. Some turners are more traditional; others are eclectic in their choice of turning tools. If you prefer gouges, by all means use them. If you want to use scrapers, do so. Some of us are inclined to use both. In any event, shape the project. Refer to Illus. 74 and 75 periodically. Be certain that the holder slightly tapers from bottom to top. Prepare the surface for finishing.

5. While the project is still on the lathe, measure, mark, and drill the dowel pin holes. Allow at least 1¼″ between dowels. There are six rows of pins, with four pins per row. A single pin can be placed in the middle of the top. Don't drill the holes too close to one another. The distance between the rows of pins will be reduced as you move from bottom to top. While there is 1¾″ between rows on the holder shown in Illus. 74 and 75, this distance will vary based on the overall diameter of the holder. In other words, your project may be larger or smaller, after turning, than the project presented here. Use a ruler and pencil to lay out and mark the location of the drilled holes. Remember to sand away the pencil marks prior to finishing.

6. Use an electric drill and a ¼″ diameter wood bit to drill the angled dowel pin holes. Wrap the bit about ¼″ up from its point with a piece of duct tape. This will serve as a stop so the holes are drilled to a uniform depth. As you drill the pin holes, keep the angle as uniform as possible. Don't drill at too drastic an angle. Rest your hand on the project as you align the bit and actually drill the hole. This will provide some stability as you drill. When one row has been drilled, rotate the holder on the lathe and drill the next row. Remember to drill a final hole in the middle of the top of the holder.

7. Use an awl to make small indentations in the surface of the upper third of the holder. This is to make the project look more like an actual thimble. The indentations should be somewhat uniform and ordered. Note how they appear on an actual thimble. If no awl is available, use a large nail and a tack hammer to make the marks.

8. Clean up the surface with extra-fine abrasive paper. Be sure the pencil marks have been removed.

9. Place a drop of wood glue in each of the drilled holes and tap the dowel pins in place. Remove any excess glue from the surface of the holder.

10. Finish the project with several coats of clear lacquer. Avoid using too much lacquer or it will run under the dowel pins. Give the holder a good finish so it will hold up under use.

17: Shorebird I (Illus. 76 and 77)

Whether carved from a block of basswood or cut from a piece of pine, shorebirds are fun to make, decorate, and give as gifts. They are an ever-popular item, and most people can't seem to get enough of them. This project is cut from a piece of pine. The design is of a common shorebird. The detailed painting on the bird might make an ornithologist squirm, but most people will be impressed. It's fun to make these birds and then paint them in a way that you want them to appear.

MATERIAL:
- 1″ x 8″ pine
- ⅜″ diameter dowel
- Construction paper
- Small piece of firewood
- Paint

TOOLS:
- Scroll or sabre saw
- Finishing sander
- Electric drill and ⅜″ bit

DIRECTIONS:
1. Draw a design of the shorebird on construction paper and cut it out for use as a pattern. On a piece of 1″ x 8″ pine, trace the shorebird pattern.

2. Using either a scroll or sabre saw, cut the shorebird pattern from the board.

3. Measure and cut a slice of log approximately 5″ long and 2½″ wide to serve as a base.

4. Drill a ⅜″ diameter hole in the bottom center of the shorebird and also in the middle of the log base. The holes should be at least ½″ deep.

5. Cut an 8″ long piece of ⅜″ diameter dowel. Place one end of the dowel into the drilled hole in the bird and the other end into the log hole. Make sure that the base will adequately support the bird without tipping over. If necessary, cut a larger piece of log for the support base.

6. Using the finishing sander, prepare the surfaces of the bird for finishing. You may want to

Illus. 76. Shorebird I.

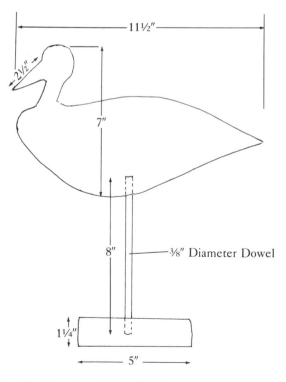

Illus. 77. Drawing of shorebird I.

round the edges of the log base using the sander. It tends to give it a more finished appearance.
7. The project bird is painted white, black, and blue-grey. Paint yours in any color or design desired. Then give it an appropriate Latin-sounding name.

18: Business Card Holder (Illus. 78 and 79)

Interesting and different desk-top pieces always make excellent gifts. Every desk should have some type of business card holder. This project is actually one of two pieces that make up a desk set. Project 19, a clock, is the second item in the desk set. Both are crafted from a piece of red, Indian padauk. If you do not have access to padauk, consider using black walnut, cherry, or oak. A piece of adhesive felt is attached to the bottom of these projects so that they do not scratch the surface of a desk.

MATERIAL:
- 1¾" (¾'s) thick hardwood
- Wood glue
- Adhesive felt
- Danish oil or lacquer

TOOLS:
- Radial arm or table saw
- Band saw
- Clamps
- Finishing sander

DIRECTIONS:
1. Review Project 19 and decide if you prefer to make both the business card holder and the desk clock. If so, follow the directions given with Project 19 for cutting the block to be used for the business card holder. If you prefer to make just the card holder, measure and cut a piece of hardwood 1¾" (¾'s) thick, 4½" wide, and 3¼" long.
2. Draw a diagonal cutting line from one bottom corner to one top corner of the block. Refer to

Illus. 78. Business card holder.

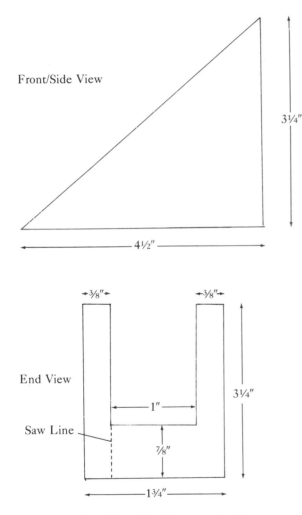

Front/Side View

3¼″

4½″

⅜″   ⅜″

End View

3¼″

1″

Saw Line

⅞″

1¾″

Illus. 79. Drawings of business card holder.

Illus. 78 and 79. Cut the piece as marked. Be certain to make a straight cut.

3. One the wide edge of the project piece, mea-

sure and make two lines that are ⅜″ from each side. The lines should run vertically from the top edge to the bottom edge. Make another line ⅞″ from the bottom edge that runs horizontally from one side to the other. Note the end view of the project shown in Illus. 79.

4. Align the band-saw fence with the blade and one vertical line so that a ⅜″ thick slice can be cut from the piece. Note again Illus. 79 and the marked saw line. Cut the slice, being careful to keep it even at both the top and bottom. Handle the slice carefully, because it will be glued back on shortly.

5. Realign the band-saw fence and cut down the other ⅜″ vertical line; this time, however, at the ⅞″ line that runs from one side to the other.

6. Readjust the band-saw fence to make a cut along the ⅞″ line. Stop this cut when the blade intersects with the existing cut. You don't want to cut into the side of the holder. Basically, what you're doing is cutting out a chunk of wood from the center of the piece.

7. Using wood glue, reassemble the side slice back onto the piece. Clamp the assembly until the glue is dry. Be certain to put scraps between the clamp's metal parts and the surfaces of the holder. Clamps tend to mark even the hardest of woods. Wipe off any glue that squeezes onto the surface.

8. Prepare the surface for finishing, using extra-fine abrasive paper and, if needed, a finishing sander. Wipe off any dust.

9. Finish the holder with either an oil or lacquer finish. Be sure to read and follow the directions supplied with the product. If you plan on making the desk clock (Project 19), use the same type of finish on both projects.

10. Cut and apply a piece of felt to the bottom of the holder. As indicated, this helps prevent the piece from scratching the desk.

19: *Clock I* (Illus. 80 and 81)

This desk clock is a companion piece to the business card holder described in Project 18. As indicated, the business card holder can be made

Illus. 80. Clock I.

sive to make a very classy gift. This project is made from Indian padauk, an imported hardwood, but can just as easily be made from black walnut, oak, cherry or some indigenous wood. If the recipient has a walnut desk, a walnut clock and/or business card holder would look great. Clock movements of all sizes, types, and prices are available from numerous mail-order suppliers. You will need a wood bit of sufficient size to drill a hole in the hardwood that will accommodate the clock movement.

MATERIAL:
- 1¾″ (¾'s) thick hardwood
- Quartz clock insert (2⅜″ rear mounting)
- Adhesive felt
- Danish oil or lacquer

TOOLS:
- Band saw
- Table or radial arm saw
- Drill press and Forstner bit (2⅜″)
- Finishing sander

DIRECTIONS:
1. Review the directions for this project and Project 18, the companion business card holder. If you prefer, the angled piece cut from the clock project can be used for the business card holder.
2. Measure and cut a piece of 1¾″ (¾'s) thick hardwood so that it is 6¼″ long and 4½″ wide. Though the wood does not have to be exactly 1¾″ thick, it must be at least 1¼″ (⁵⁄₄'s) thick, in order to accommodate the clock insert.
3. Measure and mark a point on one side that is 2⅞″ from the bottom edge. Draw a line from this point to the opposite top corner of the block. Cut this section off, along the line, being careful to make a straight saw line.
4. Measure and mark the location of the clock insert hole on the piece. In the design shown in Illus. 81, the center of the hole is 2¾″ from the bottom edge and at the exact midpoint of the block.
5. If following the design indicated in Illus. 81, use a 2⅜″ diameter Forstner bit and a drill press to drill the clock insert hole 1″ deep. Clamp the

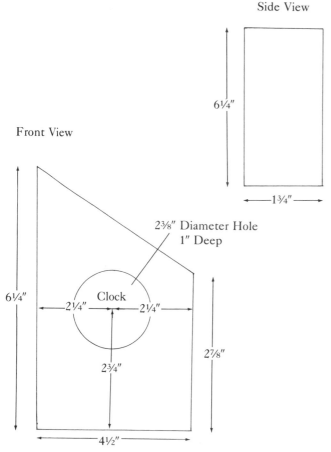

Illus. 81. Drawings of clock I.

from the same piece of hardwood used for the clock. Given the availability of clock movements for the gift maker, it's easy and rather inexpen-

piece while drilling the hole. If you are using a clock insert with a different diameter, drill a hole that corresponds to it. After the hole has been drilled, place the clock in the hole to check its fit. The clock should fit snugly in the hole, so that it does not fall out. On the other hand, it shouldn't fit too tightly, because you will have to periodically remove it to change its battery.

6. Prepare the surfaces for finishing. You will have to spend some time and energy removing the saw marks on the angled cut. Use a finishing sander with fine and extra-fine abrasive papers.

7. Remove any dust from the project. Finish it with either an oil or lacquer finish. If lacquer is used, rub the surfaces down between coats with steel wool (0000). Remove the wool hairs before applying the next coat. A final coat of paste wax will add more luster to the finish and better protect the project.

8. Measure and cut a piece of adhesive felt and secure it to the bottom of the project. Install the clock's battery, set the time, and insert it into the drilled hole.

20: Skis and Ski Pole Rack (Illus. 82 and 83)

Whether a skier prefers downhill or cross country skiing, finding a place to put skiis and poles is always a problem. This rack will serve the skier well both during ski season and in the off-season. It is designed to accommodate four pairs of skis and four sets of poles. A center hook is provided for a special piece of apparel, sunglasses, or another item used for skiing. The tips of the skis fit between the two dowels. Straps should be used to secure the skis together while they are hanging on the rack. The ski pole straps are hung over the dowels designed for the poles.

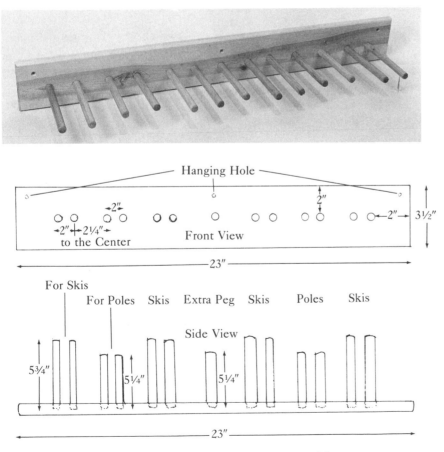

Illus. 82. Skis and ski pole rack.

Illus. 83. Drawings of skis and ski pole rack.

49

MATERIAL:

- 1" x 4" pine
- ½" diameter dowels
- Wood glue
- Lacquer

TOOLS:

- Sabre saw, table saw, or radial arm saw
- Electric drill, screw sinks, and wood bit (½")
- Table-mounted router and roundover bit
- Finishing sander

DIRECTIONS:

1. Review the dimensions for the project shown in Illus. 83. If its size is adequate, measure and cut a piece of 1" x 4" pine, 23" long.

2. Measure and mark the location for the dowel holes. All measurements extend to or from the center of the dowel holes. The dowels should be placed 2" from either end and 2" from the top edge. All dowels should be exactly 2" apart. The pairs of dowels, with the exception of the center dowel, should be 2¼" apart. The single center dowel hole is 11½" from either end. It is 2" from the dowels on either side of it. This is all indicated in Illus. 83. If you want, measure and mark the locations of the dowels in a way that's easiest for you.

3. Drill the dowel holes through the board. Use a ½" diameter wood bit and an electric drill to make the holes. If a drill press is available, use it.

4. Measure and cut ½" diameter dowels to length. The ski dowels should be 5¾" long. The ski pole dowels and the single center dowel should be 5½" long.

5. Measure and mark for three hanging holes. Using an electric drill and screw sink, drill the hanging holes.

6. Rout the edges and ends of the board with a roundover bit.

7. Using a finishing sander, round over the edges of the dowels. Prepare the surfaces of the board for finishing.

8. Spread a dab of glue in each dowel hole and tap in a dowel. The dowels should be driven to the back surface of the board. Be certain you use the longer dowels for skis and the shorter ones

for poles and the center dowel. Wipe off any excess glue.

9. Finish the project with several coats of clear lacquer. Rub in a few coats of paste wax to further protect it from moisture. Rub the finish with steel wool (0000) between the coats of lacquer. Be certain to remove the steel "hairs" from the wool that get caught on the finish.

21: *Farmer Match Holder* (Illus. 84 and 85)

For those who like country designs and long wooden matches, this will make a fine gift. The holder accommodates the entire box of what I call "farmer" matches. The box simply slips inside the holder, the sliding cover is pulled up, and matches spill on the lower portion of the box. The user can reach in this area and pick one or several loose matches. You will sometimes see these holders made from tin. The matches in this holder can prove tempting to children, so it's important that you hang the holder high, far from their reach. The holder is made from ½" thick pine and lends itself to either a wood-burned design or a painted stencil. A clear lacquer finish will showcase the woodburning.

Illus. 84. Farmer match holder.

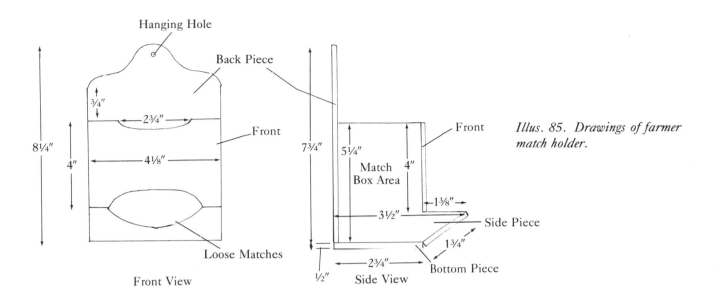

Illus. 85. Drawings of farmer match holder.

MATERIAL:

- ½″ thick pine
- Wire brads
- Wood glue
- Wood filler
- Construction paper
- Lacquer

TOOLS:

- Scroll or sabre saw
- Band, radial arm, or table saw
- Table-mounted router and roundover bit
- Finishing sander
- Wood-burning set
- Electric drill and screw sink

DIRECTIONS:

1. Review Illus. 85 and these directions prior to beginning the project. To use the suggested dimensions, it is necessary that you have ½″ thick pine. If you don't have a planer, possibly a friend can plane it for you or you can resaw standard-thickness pine to ½″ on a band saw with a ½″ wide blade. On occasion, a lumberyard may stock ½″ thick pine or will plane it for you. This could prove expensive.

2. Make a pattern of the top area of the back piece from construction paper. Measure and cut

the back piece of the project. Trace the pattern for the top area and cut it out using a scroll or sabre saw.

3. Measure and mark the top center of the back piece and drill a hanging hole using an electric drill and screw sink.

4. Measure and lay out the various cuts on the side pieces. Cut one side piece as shown in the side view drawing of the project contained in Illus. 85 and use it as a pattern for the second side piece. Cut it to length using a sabre, radial arm, or table saw. The other cuts on the side pieces are best made using, if available, a band saw.

5. Measure and cut the front piece to length. Using a can, some other round object, or, if you have one, a circle template, draw the rounded lines on the bottom and top of the front piece. Cut out these areas using a sabre or scroll saw.

6. Measure and cut the bottom piece. It is a rectangle that is 4⅛″ long and 2¾″ wide. Note the dimensions on the drawings contained in Illus. 85.

7. The bottom front piece is also 4⅛″ long, but 1¾″ wide. Measure and cut this piece. Using something round as a pattern, trace a rounded line on the top edge of the front piece and cut it out.

8. Using a table-mounted router and roundover

bit, rout all outer edges of the various parts. Portions of an edge that will be joined to another piece should not be routed. Use your own judgement as to what edges will look better if routed. If you are using ½" thick material, be careful not to set the router bit too high. Just roll the edges slightly.

9. After reviewing Illus. 85, assemble the holder using wood glue and finishing nails. Drive the nail heads in using a nail set. Fill the holes with a wood filler, and allow the filler to dry.

10. If you plan to use lacquer on the holder, you may want to first wood-burn a design on the front piece. Note Illus. 84 for an example of a design. If you will be using paint as a finish, you may want to consider putting a stencil on the front piece. Another option is to wood-carve a small design on the surface.

11. Prepare the surface for finishing using various abrasive grits and, if available, a finishing sander. Be sure to wipe or blow off all the sanding dust prior to applying any finishing product. If you have wood-burned a design, lightly sand over the finished design to clean it up. Remove the dust and then apply several coats of a clear lacquer.

12. Buy a box of farmer matches, insert the box inside the holder, and present the gift. The recipient will be delighted.

22: *Bench* (Illus. 86 and 87)

A bench, by definition, is a long seat. It can be designed to any length, width, or shape. Best of all, it can be made to meet the specific needs of the user—as a coffee table, plant stand, seat, magazines holder, foot rest, and even as something to stand on. Depending upon how they're finished, benches can be used inside or outside, in the kitchen or on the deck. This project bench started out to be a rather small seat to be used on a deck. It ended up as a rather large coffee table and plant stand for a deck. The change was orchestrated by the person who asked for a bench as a gift. You may encounter a similar design change from the person for whom you're crafting the gift. Buy some extra pine just in case.

Illus. 86. Bench.

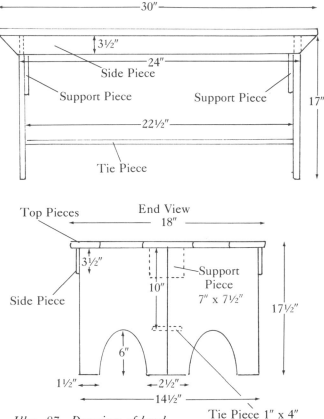

Illus. 87. Drawings of bench.

MATERIAL:

- 1" x 8" pine
- 1" x 4" pine
- Finishing nails and wood screws
- Wood glue
- Wood filler
- Paint

52

TOOLS:

- Sabre saw
- Radial arm or table saw
- Electric drill, screw sink, and bit (⅜″)
- Nail set
- Table-mounted router and roundover bit
- Finishing sander

DIRECTIONS:

1. Review Illus. 87 and these directions. Decide how large or small you want to make the bench. It can be modified to suit the needs of the gift recipient. The following directions describe how to craft the project bench as presented in Illus. 86 and 87.

2. Measure and cut the four leg pieces to length. The width of each leg is 7¼″, the exact width of a 1″ x 8″ pine board.

3. On one leg, design and cut out, using a sabre saw, the round, decorative area on the bottom of the leg. Trace the design onto the surface of the remaining three legs and cut it out.

4. Using a 1″ x 4″ pine board, cut the tie piece to a length of 22½″.

5. For securing the legs together, cut two support pieces 7″ long from a 1″ x 8″ board.

6. Measure and cut two side pieces from a 1″ x 4″ pine board. Each piece should be 30″ long and the width of the 1″ x 4″, which is 3½″.

7. Measure and cut an angle on the ends of both side pieces. The angled cut should make the side pieces 24″ long on the bottom edges. If confused, check Illus. 87. Find the midpoint of the pieces and measure for the angles from there. Use a sabre saw to make the cuts.

8. Using 1″ x 4″ boards, cut the top pieces to a length of 30″. If you allow a small space between the 1″ x 4″ top boards when assembling them, you will need five boards. The spacing will need to account for ½″. Note Illus. 87. The top is 18″ wide, but five 3½″ wide 1″ x 4″ boards measure 17½″. Actually, the spacing adds a nice touch to the top of the bench.

9. Rout all the edges using a table-mounted router and roundover bit. Don't rout edges that will not be exposed, for example, the bottom edges of the top pieces. Rout the ends of the top edges, because they will be exposed. Also, don't rout edges or that portion of an edge that will be joined to another piece.

10. Using wood glue and finishing nails or wood screws, attach the 7″ support pieces to the top back surfaces of both pair of legs. Be certain the legs are flush at the top and tight together at the center joint. Refer to Illus. 87.

11. Nail and glue the side pieces to both leg panels. Be certain the top edges are flush and that the outer surfaces of the legs align with the bottom corners of the angled cut on the side pieces.

12. Nail or screw and glue the tie piece to both leg panels. The top surface of the tie piece should be 10″ from the top edge of both leg panels. If needed, refer to Illus. 87.

13. Center one top piece on the assembly. Be certain its overhang is aligned with the side pieces. Nail and glue it in place. Align and secure the remaining top pieces. Remember to space each piece.

14. If a hand area for picking up the bench is desired, cut it out in the middle of the top piece. Measure and draw on the board's surface an area that is approximately 6″ long and 1½″ wide. Be certain to center the hand area on the board.

15. Drill a ⅜″ diameter hole through the traced area to allow the sabre saw blade to penetrate and make the cut. Cut out the area. With the finishing sander, round the edge.

16. Cut off the corners of the outer top pieces. This eliminates any sharp corners that someone could walk into. The corner cuts should end at the top corner of the side pieces. Round over the edges using a finishing sander.

17. Drive in the heads of the finishing nails using a nail set. Fill the nail holes with a wood filler and allow it to dry.

18. Using fine and extra-fine abrasive papers, prepare all surfaces for finishing. Remove any sharp corners. Also, sand any excess filler over the nail holes.

19. Before applying any finishing products, be certain to wipe or blow away all dust from the project's surfaces. Paint the bench as desired. The bench shown in Illus. 86 was painted a light-grey.

23: Hanging Window

Box (Illus. 88 and 89)

The hanging box is an ideal gift for that person who collects items but has no way of displaying them. It can be designed to accommodate and display small or large items effectively. There is sufficient surface on the top section of the box for you to add an attractive and relevant stencil. The box is crafted from ½″ thick pine but, if you prefer, use oak or some other hardwood.

MATERIAL:

- ½″ thick pine
- Wood glue
- Wood filler
- Finishing nails
- Stencil
- Paint

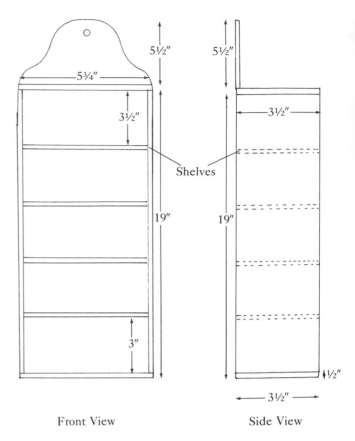

Illus. 89. Drawings of hanging window box.

TOOLS:

- Sabre saw
- Radial arm or table saw
- Table-mounted router and roundover bit
- Electric drill and screw sink
- Nail set
- Finishing sander

DIRECTIONS:

1. Review Illus. 89 and note the project's dimensions. Unless you want to modify the design, measure and cut the top piece of the box to length. The project design is based on using ½″ thick pine. You may want to modify the suggested dimensions if thicker material is being used.

2. Draw and cut the rounded area on the top

Illus. 88. Hanging window box.

piece. You may want to make a pattern for this cut. Rout the edges using a roundover bit.

3. Measure and drill, using a screw sink or bit and countersink, the hanging hole in the top piece. Be certain it's centered, so the box hangs properly.

4. Measure and cut to length the two side pieces. If you plane 1" x 4" pine to a thickness of ½" for the project, the side pieces will be 3½" wide. Remember, 3½" is the standard width of a 1" x 4" pine board.

5. Measure and cut the top and bottom rectangular pieces of the box. Both are 3½" wide and 5¾" long. Don't rout these pieces or the side pieces. Sharp edges look good on this project. The exception is the rounded portion of the top piece.

6. To ensure accuracy of the individual shelves, assemble all of the project pieces before measuring and cutting the individual shelves. The shelves should fit tightly between the sides. Given the variability in thickness of planed materials, the shelves could be cut too long or too short.

7. Using wood glue and finishing nails, assemble the box portion of the project, for example, the sides, the rectangular top, and the bottom pieces. Drive the nail heads under the surface and fill the hole with wood filler.

8. Glue and nail the top piece to the back surface of the top of the box. Nail it from the bottom surface of the rectangular top piece into its bottom edge.

9. Measure and cut the 3½" wide shelves to length. Four shelves were used for the hanging window box shown in Illus. 88.

10. The location of the shelves should be laid out on the surfaces of the side pieces. You may want three shelves that have an equal distance between them, and one that is smaller. If you prefer, make all the shelves so that they have an equal distance between them.

11. Using wood glue and finishing nails, secure the shelves to the side pieces of the box. Nail from the outer surfaces of the side pieces. Take your time with this task, so you get the shelves straight. If a nail misses a shelf, pull it out and renail. Patch the extra hole with some wood filler.

12. Set all the nails and fill the holes in with wood filler. When the wood filler and glue are dry, prepare all surfaces for finishing using fine and extra-fine abrasive paper.

13. Paint the box and decorate the top piece with an appropriate stencil.

24: *Doll Cradle* (Illus. 90 and 91)

Here is the perfect gift for your daughter or granddaughter. You can, as I have done, customize the design to accommodate that favorite doll. As you will note from Illus. 90, the cradle has rockers. While the project can be painted and then decorated with a stencil, you may prefer to wood-burn a name or design on it. It could then be finished with a clear lacquer finish, to set off the burned design. However you decide to finish this project, it is enjoyable to make and to give.

MATERIAL:
- 1" x 10" pine
- 1" x 8" pine
- Finishing nails or wood screws
- Wood glue
- Wood filler
- Stencil
- Paint

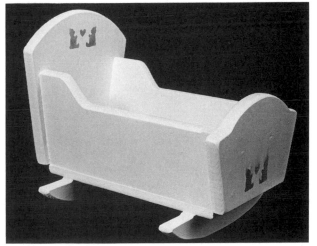

Illus. 90. Doll cradle.

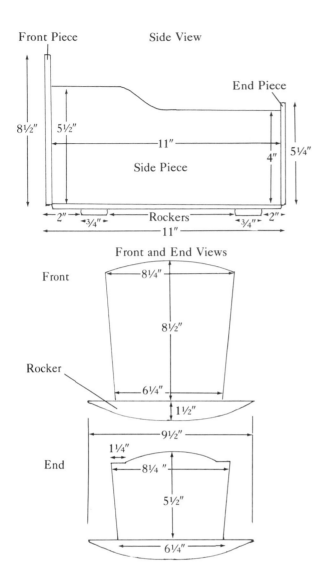

Illus. 91. *Drawings of doll cradle.*

TOOLS:

- Scroll or sabre saw
- Radial arm or table saw
- Table-mounted router and roundover bit
- School compass
- Nail set
- Finishing sander

DIRECTIONS:

1. Review Illus. 91 and the suggested dimensions. As suggested, you may want to modify the dimensions to accommodate a particular doll. Be sure to make the cradle large enough for the doll, possibly a small pillow, blankets, and whatever else may be required.

2. From a piece of 1″ x 10″ pine, design, measure, and cut the front piece. A school compass can be used to make the large, curved top edge. Note how the piece tapers on both sides. Use a sabre or scroll saw to make the curved cut.

3. Measure, design, and cut the end piece using a piece of 1″ x 10″ pine. Check the angle, design and dimensions of the end piece. A sabre or scroll saw works well for cutting this piece.

4. Measure and design a side piece on a 1″ x 8″ board. Note the design and different widths of the piece. Cut the designed side piece and trace the second side piece using the first for a pattern. Cut the second piece. Use a scroll or sabre saw to cut these pieces.

5. Measure and cut the bottom piece of the cradle. The piece should be 11″ long and 6¼″ wide.

6. You may want to make a pattern for the rockers. If not, draw one freehand after noting how it is designed in Illus. 91. The rockers should be 9½″ long and 1½″ wide at their center. Cut the first rocker and use it as a pattern for the second one. Cut the second rocker from the pattern.

7. Rout all edges other than those that will be joined to another piece. For example, the top edges of the bottom piece and the bottom edges of the side pieces should not be routed.

8. Before assembling the pieces, prepare all surfaces for finishing using fine and extra-fine abrasive paper and a finishing sander. Wipe off or vacuum any dust from the surface.

9. Prior to assembling the cradle using finishing nails or wood screws and wood glue, review Illus. 90 and 91. Note how the side pieces are secured at an angle to the front and end pieces.

10. Assemble the side pieces to the front and end pieces. Wipe away any excess glue.

11. Secure the two rockers to the bottom piece. Note the placement of the rockers in Illus. 91.

12. Attach the bottom piece with rockers to the other assembly. Be certain that no nails or wood screws are jutting out. You don't want little fingers to get cut.

13. Drive the nail heads under the surface and

fill the holes with wood filler. When the filler has dried, sand off any excess. Using a finishing sander, sand any pointed corners to round them. You may want to round the ends of the rockers. Remove any dust prior to applying any finishing product.

14. Paint and stencil the project or, if you prefer, wood-burn a design and finish it with a clear lacquer.

25: *Boot Jack* (Illus. 92 and 93)

The boot jack is truly a back-saving device for the person who wears boots but doesn't like to stoop over to pull them off. It is especially practical in a home where children like to roam through the house after playing in the snow or the mud. It's also a good gift for someone who likes pieces with country or Americana designs. You can wood-burn or stencil on the project, because it has a large surface. To use the boot jack, place the back of the boot to be removed in the V shape and pull the boot while standing on the jack with your other foot. Reverse the process to remove the other boot.

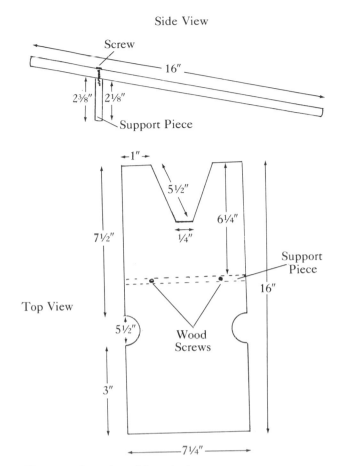

Illus. 93. *Drawing of boot jack.*

Illus. 92. Boot jack.

MATERIAL:

- 1″ x 8″ pine
- Wood screws
- Wood glue
- Lacquer

TOOLS:

- Scroll or sabre saw
- Band saw
- Electric drill and screw set
- Table-mounted router and roundover bit
- Finishing sander

DIRECTIONS:

1. Measure and cut a 1″ x 8″ piece of pine 16″ long.

2. Using a ruler and coffee can or some other round object, lay out the V shape and the curved

57

areas of the jack. Refer to Illus. 92 and 93. Cut out these areas using a scroll, sabre, or band saw.

3. Measure and cut the support piece. Note that Illus. 93 shows that the support piece has an angled cut on the top. The piece should be 7¼″ long, 2⅜″ wide on the front edge, and 2⅛″ wide on the back edge. Use a band saw or scroll saw to make this angled cut or, if necessary, use a sabre saw by adjusting the shoe or base of the saw. If you're unfamiliar with your scroll saw parts, check the owner's manual.

4. Rout all edges using a table-mounted router and a roundover bit. Do not rout the top edges of the support piece.

5. Glue and screw the support piece to the bottom surface of the boot jack. Note Illus. 93 for the approximate location.

6. Prepare the surfaces for finishing using abrasive paper and a finishing sander. Remove any sharp edges in the V-shaped area, so a rubber boot cannot be punctured.

7. If you want, wood-burn a design on the surface and add a clear lacquer finish. Remember, always sand over the burned design before adding a finish, to clean it up. You may prefer painting the jack, or painting it and applying a country stencil. Whatever product you finish it with, give the jack several coats so that the finish holds up under use.

26: *Box with Fish Lid*
(Illus. 94 and 95)

Here is an unusual gift for the person who likes boxes or for someone who likes fish. It's a fun project to make and to paint. The box is large enough to provide useable storage space. The sides of the box are made from ¼″ thick batting, which is usually available at a local lumber dealer. You will find it useful for making boxes of all sizes. The fish can be carved or shaped with power tools. Best of all, you'll get a chance to try your hand at painting a fish.

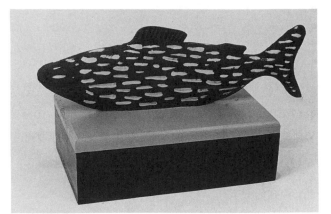

Illus. 94. Box with fish lid.

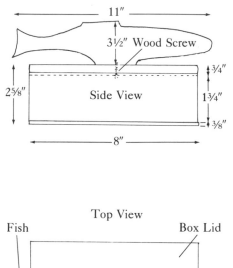

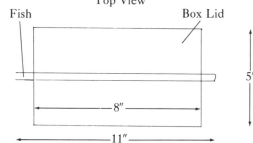

Illus. 95. Drawings of box with fish lid.

MATERIAL:
- 1″ x 8″ pine
- ⅜″ thick pine
- ¼″ thick batting
- Wood glue
- Wood screw
- Paint

TOOLS:
- Table or radial arm saw

- Band saw
- Mitre saw
- Scroll or sabre saw
- Table-mounted router and roundover and rabbeting bits
- Electric grinder, rotary tool, or flex-shaft tool
- Carbide or high-speed steel burrs and sanding sleeves
- Carving tools or whittling knife
- Large rubber bands
- Electric drill and screw set
- Finishing sander

DIRECTIONS:

1. Review the project directions and Illus. 94 and 95. Note how the lid is rabbeted to fit inside the box, and how the bottom piece of the box is attached to the edges of the side pieces.

2. Using ¼″ thick batting, cut pieces for the sides and ends. Cut them at least ¾″ longer than their final mitred length. This extra length allows for the mitre cuts.

3. Set up your mitre saw to cut the side pieces and end pieces to the suggested lengths or the dimensions needed. Take your time and think before making the cuts, so they're done correctly and safely.

4. Using wood glue and large rubber bands for clamps, assemble the mitred side and end pieces. Make sure that the mitres fit well, and allow the glue to dry before removing the rubber bands.

5. Measure and cut the bottom piece for the box from ⅜″ thick pine. You may have to resaw a piece of 1″ x 8″ pine to achieve this thickness. Use a band saw and a ½″ wide blade. The sawed surface can be used as the outside bottom of the box. It can be sanded smooth or, if you prefer, covered with adhesive felt. Glue the bottom piece to the box frame. Clamp the assembly until the glue is dry.

6. Measure and cut the lid piece from 1″ x 8″ pine to the exact length and width of the box.

7. Rout the top edges of the box lid using a roundover bit.

8. Secure a ¼″ rabbeting bit in the router and set it to cut a ¼″ wide and ¼″ deep rabbet. Rout the rabbets into the bottom edges of the lid. You may want to make two ⅛″ passes. This is a safer way to rabbet, and it also will often prevent splintering.

9. After the lid has been rabbeted, check its fit inside the box. If it's too tight, lightly sand the lid rabbet until you achieve a good fit. Do not sand the inside of the box, because it will affect the box's appearance. No one looks at the lid tenon.

10. While you can draw the fish freehand on the surface of a piece of 1″ x 8″ pine, you may want to make a pattern from construction paper. Make the pattern to the exact length and width of the fish. Draw the fins and any other details you want on your fish. Leave at least 3″ on the bottom edge of the fish flat. This is the area that will be attached to the top surface of the box. Trace the pattern onto the board's surface and cut it out using a scroll or sabre saw.

11. Carve or shape the fish to approximate a real one. If you prefer, use an electric grinder, rotary, or flex-shaft tool and carbide burrs and sanding sleeves. Some woodworkers like to use a sloyd knife and carving tools to shape and detail the fish. Whichever tools you use, take your time. You may want to go over the surface of the fish with a finishing sander and several grits of abrasive paper. Some final shaping can be done with the sander.

12. Glue and screw the fish to the top surface of the lid. The wood screws should penetrate through the lid and into the bottom of the fish. Make sure your screws are long enough to adequately penetrate the fish.

13. Prepare the box surfaces for finishing. Wipe off all the dust prior to applying any finishing products.

14. Paint the fish prior to adding a finish to the lid of the box. Give it lots of details, including a mouth and eyes. Use your imagination.

15. After the fish has been painted, paint the box and lid in matching colors. The green and yellow fish shown in Illus. 94 is mounted on a light-blue lid and a dark-blue box. If you prefer, wood-burn some detail into the fish and lacquer both the fish and the box.

27: Clock II (Illus. 96 and 97)

This would make a special gift for someone who enjoys a fine, black walnut clock with a quartz movement. As you will note from Illus. 96, the walnut has an interesting flaw that appears in the front surface of the piece that adds character. The block used was actually a piece of scrap that was discarded at a hardwood dealer. The quartz movement can be ordered from any number of mail-order suppliers. For this size movement, you will need a 2⅜″ diameter Forstner bit to drill a hole in the block. Most clock suppliers also carry bits. While the movement and bit are expensive, the bit can be used for many other projects, especially clock projects. By the way, the clock is ideally suited for either a shelf or a desk.

MATERIAL:
- 2″ (8⁄4's) thick black walnut
- 1″ (4⁄4's) thick black walnut
- Clock movement
- Wood glue
- Adhesive felt
- Lacquer

TOOLS:
- Radial arm or table saw
- Band saw
- Drill press and Forstner bit (2⅜″)
- Clamps
- Table-mounted router and roman ogee bit
- Finishing sander

DIRECTIONS:
1. Measure and cut a 2″ (8⁄4's) thick piece of walnut to a length of 7⅝″. If you prefer, make the clock from another hardwood, for example, red oak.
2. Mark the location of the clock movement hole on the front surface of the block. The hole for the clock shown in Illus. 96 was drilled to one side in order to showcase the flaw in the wood. Unless you have a block of wood with a similar flaw, locate the hole in the upper center portion.

Illus. 96. Clock II.

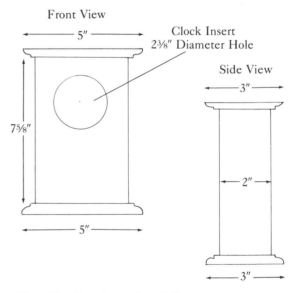

Illus. 97. Drawings of clock II.

3. Clamp the block on the drill press and drill a 2⅜″ diameter hole at least 1″ deep. Place a scrap of wood between the clamp and the block so the surface isn't damaged by the clamp. Reduce the speed of the drill press before drilling.
4. Measure and cut the top and bottom pieces from a 1″ (4⁄4's) thick piece of walnut or whatever hardwood you're using. Note Illus. 96 for the dimensions of these pieces.
5. With a roman ogee bit or, if you prefer, a roundover bit, rout the top edges of the bottom

and top pieces. The bottom edges should not be routed.

6. Prepare all surfaces for finishing using a sander and fine and extra-fine abrasive paper. Make sure you sand with the wood's grain. Be careful not to round the sharp routed edges on the top and bottom pieces. Wipe off the sanding dust.

7. Using wood glue and clamps, glue the top and bottom pieces in place. Put scraps of wood between the clamps and the surfaces of the parts. Make sure they are aligned perfectly on the top and bottom of the block. Wipe away any excess glue and leave the clamps in place until the glue is dry.

8. Use a clear lacquer finish on the project. Rub the surface, between coats, with steel wool (0000). Wipe off or vacuum the wool hairs before applying another coat of lacquer.

9. Cut a piece of adhesive felt to the proper dimensions and attach it to the bottom surface of the project. This will prevent the clock from scratching the top surface of a desk or wherever else it may be placed.

10. Install a battery, set the movement, and place it in the drilled hole.

28: *Speaker Stands*
(Illus. 98 and 99)

For the person who is tired of having his or her high-quality speakers sitting on the floor, this may be the gift to give. The stands shown in Illus. 98 and 99 are designed to accommodate my Boston Acoustic speakers. With the tall back on the stands, the speakers cannot tip over rearwards. There is sufficient space on the top of the stand to prevent them from falling forward. A hole is drilled through the back piece where the connecting wires can be run. You should design the stands to accommodate the type and size of speakers that will be placed on them. The stands shown in Illus. 98 have been stained and finished with a clear lacquer. By the way, remember you are making two stands, one for each speaker.

MATERIAL:
- 1″ x 10″ pine
- 1″ x 8″ pine
- Wood screws
- Finishing nails
- Wood glue
- Wood filler
- Danish walnut stain
- Lacquer

TOOLS:
- Radial arm or table saw
- Band saw
- Scroll or sabre saw
- Electric drill and 1¼″ multi-spur bit
- Table-mounted router and roundover bit
- School compass
- Nail set
- Finishing sander

DIRECTIONS:
1. Review the project design and dimensions as indicated in Illus. 98 and 99. Change the dimensions to accommodate specific size speakers. You may also want to change the leg or back design. A clear lacquer finish may be preferred over the

Illus. 98 Speaker stands.

61

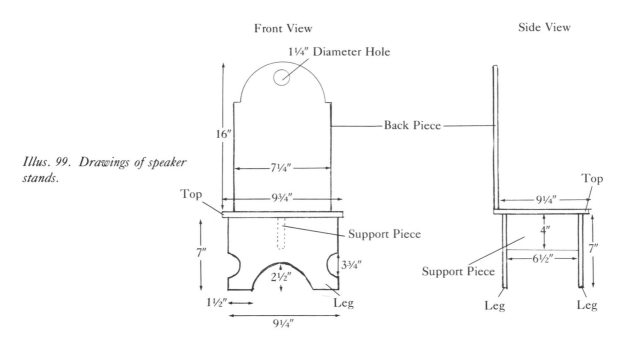

Front View   Side View

1¼" Diameter Hole

Back Piece

16"

Illus. 99. Drawings of speaker stands.

7¼"

Top   Top

9¾"   9¼"

Support Piece

7"   4"

Support Piece

3¾"   6½"   7"

2½"

1½"   Leg   Leg   Leg

9¼"

stain and lacquer. Design and finish the project to meet the needs and tastes of the gift recipient. Remember, you will be making two stands. Double the number of pieces.

2. Measure and cut the back piece from a 1" x 8" board. Make a pattern for the top curved area or, if you prefer, draw it freehand. Cut the top area using a scroll or sabre saw.

3. Drill a 1¼" diameter hole or one that the connecting wires can be slipped through in the top center of the back piece.

4. Measure and cut the top piece or seat from a piece of 1" x 10" pine.

5. Measure and design a leg on a piece of 1" x 10" pine. A school compass can be used to make the cutout area in the front of the leg. Draw the cutout area on the sides. Cut the leg using a scroll or sabre saw.

6. Use the cut leg as a pattern for the second leg. Trace the leg onto the surface of a piece of 1" x 10" pine and cut it out.

7. Measure and cut the support piece to a length of 6½" and a width of 4".

8. Rout the edges of the various pieces using a table-mounted router and a roundover bit. Don't rout those edges that will be joined to another piece. Be sure to rout the drilled hole in the back piece.

9. Using wood glue and wood screws, attach the

back piece to the top or seat. The screws should enter from the bottom surface of the top piece and into the end of the back piece.

10. Glue and nail the support piece to the two legs. Make sure that all the pieces are flush on the top edges. The support piece should be in the center of the two legs.

11. Glue and nail the top piece or seat to the leg assembly. The top piece should overlap each leg an equal distance.

12. Prepare all surfaces for finishing using a finishing sander and fine and extra-fine abrasive paper. Wipe away all the dust.

13. If you prefer, stain the project with a stain that will suit the tastes of the gift recipient. Apply a lacquer finish when the stain is dry. You may want to paint the stands or finish them with a clear lacquer.

29: *Mirror Shelf*
(Illus. 100 and 101)

This is a decorative yet functional piece that will be appreciated by the gift recipient. Best of all, the hanging piece has a mirror to reflect whatever item may be displayed on the shelf. While the shelf shown in Illus. 100 is stained and lacquered,

Illus. 100. Mirror shelf.

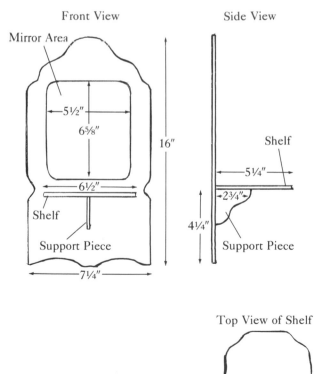

Illus. 101. Drawings of mirror shelf.

you may want to leave the gift natural or even consider painting it. Try to get a sense of what finish the gift recipient would enjoy most. If you want, the dimensions can easily be modified.

MATERIAL:

- 1″ x 8″ pine
- Mirror glass
- Construction paper
- Finishing nails
- Hanger
- Danish walnut stain
- Lacquer

TOOLS:

- Radial arm or table saw
- Sabre or scroll saw
- Electric drill and 3/8″ bit
- Glass cutter
- Table-mounted router and roundover, cove, and rabbeting bits
- Finishing sander

DIRECTIONS:

1. Review Illus. 100 and 101. Make patterns of the back piece, the area to be cut out for the mirror, the shelf, and the support piece. Make the patterns to actual size from construction paper. This way, if you want to make shelves at some point in the future, you will have the patterns to use.

2. Measure and cut a piece of 1″ x 8″ pine to length for the back piece. Trace the back piece pattern on the board and cut it out using either a sabre or scroll saw.

3. Cut a piece of 1″ x 8″ pine for the shelf to its recommended length and width. Trace the shelf pattern onto its surface and cut it out using a scroll or sabre saw.

4. On a piece of scrap pine, trace the support piece pattern. Cut it out with an appropriate saw.

5. Place the mirror cutout area pattern on the back piece and trace it. Make sure you have it centered on the mirror area of the back piece. Note how the area appears in Illus. 100.

6. Drill a 3/8″ diameter hole through the traced mirror area and cut it out using a scroll saw. The saw blade can be threaded through the drilled hole to begin the cut. Take your time with this cut, especially when cutting the round corner areas. Keep the straight lines straight.

7. Secure a cove bit in the router and rout the front edges of the back piece and the top edges of the shelf. Do not rout the back edge of the shelf where it will be joined to the back piece. Also, do not rout with a cove bit the front edges of the mirror area.

8. With a roundover bit in the router, rout the back edges of the back piece and the bottom edges of the shelf. Also, rout the front edges of the mirror area and the nonjoined edges of the support piece.

9. Use a rabbeting bit to rout the back surface of the mirror area. Most mirror glass is approximately ³⁄₁₆″ thick. Thus, the rabbeted area must be at least ³⁄₁₆″ deep. Set the bit to the proper depth of cut and rout out this area. Take your time with this procedure, to ensure that it is done safely and without splintering.

10. Prepare all surfaces for finishing using an electric sander and fine and extra-fine abrasive paper. Wipe off the dust from all surfaces.

11. Using glue and finishing nails, secure the shelf to the back piece. Make sure it's straight. Wipe off any excess glue.

12. Glue and nail the support piece to the bottom of the shelf and the front of the back piece.

13. Measure the inside rabbeted area where the mirror glass will fit. Note the rounded corners. Using a ruler and soft-tip pen, mark the dimensions on the reflective surface of the mirror glass. For specifics on cutting glass, review the directions in Project 13.

14. When the glass piece has been cut, use the chipping area of the cutter to round the four corners of the mirror. Take your time with this procedure. Chip only a little bit of glass at a time. If you try to chip too much, you may break the mirror, Check the mirror for fit in the rabbeted area.

15. Secure a hanger to the top back surface.

16. Before gluing the mirror in place, finish the shelf. It's a lot easier to do the finishing work before the mirror is in place. If you prefer, stain the shelf and then apply a clear lacquer finish.

The shelf could also be painted or left natural with a clear lacquer finish.

17. After the project has been finished, place the mirror in the rabbeted area. Apply white or wood glue to the corner areas so it is on both the wood and the glass. Place a drop or two along the sides also. Leave the project lying facedown until the glue is dry.

18. Measure and cut a piece of construction paper to place over the mirror area on the back of the shelf. Spread glue on the surface of the paper near the edges and press the paper onto the back of the shelf. Rub your finger over the glued area and allow the area to dry.

30: Candle Box (Illus. 102 and 103)

This country piece can be used to hold candles, as in an earlier era, or hung as a decorative piece. It can even be used as a planter. If it will be used as a planter, include a plastic liner or a pot to protect the wood from water damage and leakage. Better yet, the candle box can be used as a catchall for pencils, pens, and all those items that are small and need to be put someplace. If you want a clear finish, consider wood-burning a design on the front piece. The project can also be painted and, if desired, a stencil applied.

Illus. 102. Candle box.

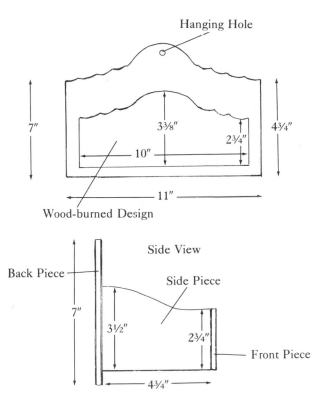

Front View

Hanging Hole

7″

3⅜″

2¾″

4¾″

10″

Wood-burned Design

11″

Side View

Back Piece

Side Piece

7″

3½″

2¾″

Front Piece

4¾″

Illus. 103. Drawings of candle box.

MATERIAL:
- 1″ x 8″ pine
- Construction paper
- Finishing nails
- Wood filler
- Wood glue
- Lacquer

TOOLS:
- Radial arm or table saw
- Scroll or sabre saw
- Electric drill and screw-sink
- Table-mounted router and roundover bit
- Wood-burning set
- Nail set
- Finishing sander

DIRECTIONS:
1. Review Illus 103. In order to make the scrolls uniform on both the back and front pieces, make patterns.

2. Measure and cut the back from a piece of 1′ x 8″ pine to a length of 11″. Trace the scroll pattern on the top part of the back piece. Note that the sides should be 4¾″ high. Cut the back piece using either a scroll or sabre saw.

3. Measure and drill a hanging hole in the back piece using the electric drill and screw-sink.

4. Measure and cut the front piece from a piece of 1″ x 8″ pine. It should be 10″ long. Measure and mark the height of the sides of the front piece and then trace the scroll pattern on the board. Cut it out using an appropriate saw.

5. Measure and cut the side pieces to the suggested dimensions. If a pattern was made, trace and cut the angle on the top edges of the side pieces.

6. Rout all edges, except those that will join other pieces, using a roundover bit.

7. Before assembling the candle box, prepare all the surfaces for finishing using fine and extra-fine abrasive paper and a finishing sander. Wipe off the sanding dust.

8. Using glue and finishing nails, assemble the front piece to the two sides pieces. Next, assemble the side pieces to the back piece. Note how this assembly should be at least ⅜″ from both side edges and the bottom edge of the back piece. Wipe off any excess glue.

9. Measure the inside dimensions of the project, to determine the exact size of the bottom piece. Cut the bottom piece from 1″ x 8″ pine to the exact dimensions indicated in Illus. 103.

10. Glue and nail the bottom piece in place.

11. Using a nail set, drive the nail heads under the surface. Fill each hole with wood filler. When the filler is dry, sand over the nail areas with the finishing sander.

12. Wood-burn in a design on the surface of the front piece. The candle box shown in Illus. 102 has a flower design. The flowers are on stems with some leaves. Try a design of your own making. Pencil it on the surface and then, using the wood-burning set, follow the lines with the hot point. Sand over the burned design with the finishing sander and extra-fine abrasive paper. Remove all dust.

13. Finish the candle holder with several coats of clear lacquer.

65

31: Hanging Magazine/Phone Book Rack (Illus. 104 and 105)

While the rack may not hold the White Pages of an urban area, it can accommodate most telephone books. The gift recipient may prefer using it for a magazine holder. Either way, it's a functional gift that can be hung at the end of a kitchen cabinet or any place else the user may prefer. You may want to redesign it to make it hold either a larger or smaller telephone directory. The project looks good with a wood-burned design on the top piece and finished with a clear lacquer. The front strips are ¼" thick batting that is 2½" wide. This kind of batting is generally available at a local lumberyard. Generally, it's used for trim in houses.

MATERIAL:
- 1" x 6" pine
- ¼" thick batting
- Finishing nails and wire brads
- Construction paper
- Wood glue
- Wood filler
- Lacquer

TOOLS:
- Radial arm or table saw
- Band saw
- Scroll or sabre saw
- Electric drill and screw-sink
- Table-mounted router and roundover and rabbeting bits
- Nail set
- Finishing sander
- Wood-burning set

DIRECTIONS:
1. Review the project design and dimensions shown in Illus. 104 and 105. You should make a pattern for cutting the top piece of the project. This will make for a more accurate rounded top area.

Illus. 104. Hanging magazine/phone book rack.

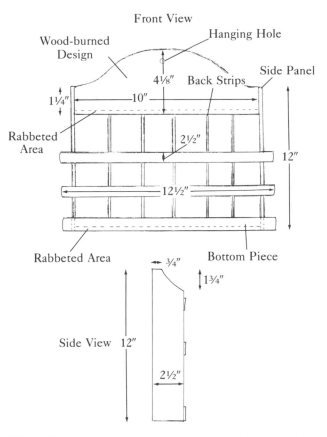

Illus. 105. Drawings of hanging magazine/phone book rack.

2. Measure and cut the top piece from 1″ x 6″ pine to a length of 10″. The ends of the top piece should be 1¼″ wide. Trace the pattern onto the piece and cut the rounded area using a scroll or sabre saw.

3. Measure, mark and drill with a screw-sink the hanging hole. Be certain the hole is centered in the upper area of the top piece.

4. Measure and cut the two side pieces from 1″ x 6″ pine to a length of 12″. Using a table saw or band saw, rip the side pieces to a width of 2½″.

5. Design the rounded area on the top of one side piece. Refer to Illus. 105 for help with dimensions. Cut out the area. Using the finished side piece as a pattern, trace the cutout rounded area onto the surface of the second side piece. Cut out the area.

6. Measure and cut the bottom piece from 1″ x 6″ pine to a length of 10″. Using a band saw, table saw or, if necessary, a scroll saw, rip the bottom piece to a width of 2½″.

7. With a rabbeting bit in the router, make a ¼″ rabbet ¼″ deep in the back bottom edge of the top piece. Strips of batting will eventually be secured in the rabbet.

8. Rabbet one edge of the bottom piece ¼″ deep using a ¼″ rabbet. Batting strips will eventually be secured in this rabbet.

9. Rout the top edges of the top piece with a roundover bit.

10. Glue and nail the bottom piece with the rabbeted area facing the back. Batting strips will be glued and nailed into the rabbeted area to serve as the back of the holder.

11. Glue and nail the top piece to the top portion of the side pieces. Use two finishing nails in each side so the top piece doesn't twist. Allow the glue to dry on the assembly.

12. Measure and cut three 2½″ wide batting strips to a length of 12½″.

13. Glue and nail one piece of batting flush with the bottom piece. It should overlap the side pieces equally. Wire brads should be used to nail the strip.

14. Glue and nail a second batting strip ¾″ down from the bottom edge of the curved area of the side pieces.

15. Glue and nail the third batting strip between the other two strips. You should have an equal distance between the strips.

16. Measure the length between the top rabbeted area and the bottom rabbeted area on the back of the holder. Cut four 2½″ wide pieces of batting to this length.

17. Glue and nail the batting strips in the rabbeted areas. Place the strips so there will be approximately ¼″ between them. Use small wire brads to nail the strips.

18. Drive all finishing nails under the wood's surface using a nail set. Fill the holes with wood filler.

19. Using a finishing sander, prepare all surfaces for finishing using fine and extra-fine abrasive paper. Round over any sharp edges. Remove any excess wood filler.

20. Draw a design on the surface of the top piece. Note the design on the rack shown in Illus. 104. Wood-burn the design by following the pencil lines with the hot point. Sand over the burned area.

21. Wipe off all the finishing dust. Apply several coats of lacquer to the holder.

32: Child's Coat Rack
(Illus. 106 and 107)

This coat rack makes a simple yet very attractive and useful gift. Best of all, the size and number of Shaker pegs can be easily varied. While the gift may be used in a child's bedroom, it can be made for the parent of the child who usually hangs up the child's coats, clothes, etc. The coat rack shown in Illus. 106 is painted white with alternating green and red Shaker pegs. It has ample surface to add a stencil or some other decorative touch. You may want to paint the child's name on the rack. Wood-burning a name or design is another option.

MATERIAL:
- 1″ x 8″ pine
- Shaker pegs
- Construction paper
- Wood glue
- Paint

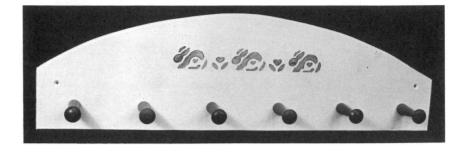

Illus. 106. Child's coat rack.

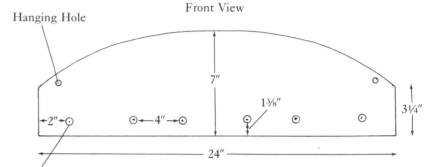

Illus. 107. Drawing of child's coat rack.

TOOLS:
- Sabre saw
- Electric drill, screw-sink, and ½″ wood bit
- Table-mounted router and roundover bit
- Finishing sander

DIRECTIONS:
1. Measure and cut a 1″ x 8″ pine board to a length of 24″.
2. Each end should be 3¼″ wide. Measure and mark the ends.
3. Make a pattern for the rounded top area of the rack. Trace the pattern from the 3¼″ end marks. Using a sabre saw, cut out the traced area.
4. Measure and mark the location of the hanging holes. Drill the holes using a screw-sink or ¼″ bit and countersink.
5. Measure and mark the locations of the Shaker pegs. On the rack shown in Illus. 106, the pegs are all 1⅜″ from the bottom edge. The end pegs are spaced 2″ from each end to the center of the peg hole. The remaining pegs are spaced 4″ to the center of each peg hole. Drill the peg holes using a ½″ diameter wood bit. It is assumed that

the Shaker pegs have a ½″ diameter tenon. The holes should be drilled through the board.
6. Rout all edges using a roundover bit.
7. Prepare the surfaces and edges for finishing using a sander and fine and extra-fine abrasive paper. Wipe off all the dust.
8. If you plan to paint the project, paint the pegs and the board before gluing the Shaker pegs in place. This will make the job a lot easier. Any other design work should also be done before the pegs are in place.
9. Place a dab of wood glue in each drilled hole and tap the Shaker pegs in place.

33: Open Cabinet/Shelf
(Illus. 108 and 109)

This project has lots of space to display some large pieces or collectibles. The shelf is sufficiently deep so that it will truly showcase any items that are placed on it. The basic design can be modified or made to different dimensions. For example, you may want to add more shelves in

68

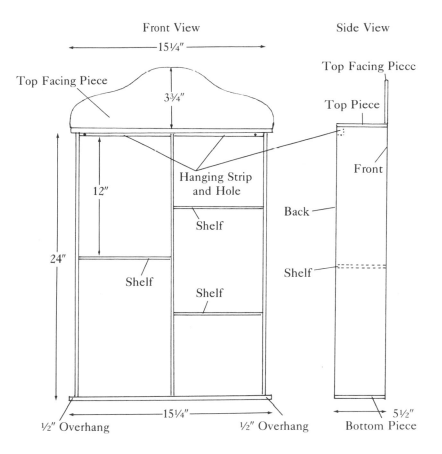

Front View · Side View

15¼″

Top Facing Piece · Top Facing Piece

3¾″

Top Piece

Hanging Strip and Hole

Front

12″

Shelf

Back

24″

Shelf

Shelf

Shelf

Shelf

15¼″

½″ Overhang · ½″ Overhang

5½″

Bottom Piece

Illus. 108 (above). Open cabinet/ shelf. Illus. 109 (right). Drawings of open cabinet/shelf.

order to display more items. While the shelf shown in Illus. 108 is finished with a clear lacquer, you may want to paint it. It is crafted from ½″ thick pine, but could be made from oak or some other hardwood.

MATERIAL:
- ½″ thick pine
- Construction paper
- Finishing nails
- Wood glue
- Wood filler
- Lacquer

TOOLS:
- Radial arm or table saw
- Band saw
- Sabre or scroll saw
- Electric drill and screw-sink
- Nail set
- Finishing sander

DIRECTIONS:

1. Review the project design and dimensions as indicated in Illus. 108 and 109. Make a pattern of the entire top facing piece. The project is made from ½″ thick pine. Hopefully, you can obtain some at the local lumberyard or have a friend plane it to thickness. If not, you can resaw standard thickness pine with a band saw and a ½″ saw blade.

2. Measure and cut the top facing piece to length. Trace the prepared pattern on the board and cut it out using a sabre or scroll saw. Make sure that the dimensions correspond to the dimensions shown in Illus. 109.

3. Measure and cut the two side pieces and one middle piece to a length of 24″ and a width of 5½″. The pieces can be cut to width on a band saw or table saw using a ½″ wide saw blade.

4. The top and bottom pieces should be measured and cut. They should be 15¼″ long and 5½″ wide.

5. Before cutting the shelves, assemble the project. Do some measuring before gluing and nailing. Using wood glue and finishing nails, assemble the side pieces and middle piece to the top and bottom pieces. There should be a ½″ overhang on each side of the top piece and the bottom piece. Note the overhang in Illus. 108 and 109. Make sure that the middle piece is secured in the center of the top and bottom pieces. Nail and glue the top facing piece to the top, front edge of the top piece.

6. To hang the cabinet, secure hanging strips with holes drilled in them to the cabinet. Measure the distance between the side pieces and the middle piece. Cut two strips 1¼″ wide to this length. Drill a hanging hole in each strip. Glue and nail the strips to the back, bottom surface of the top piece. Note their placement in Illus. 109.

7. Measure between the side and middle pieces to determine the length of the shelves. Cut three shelves to this length and to a width of 5½″.

8. Measure and mark the location of the shelves on the side and middle pieces. Spread glue on the ends of the shelves and nail them in place. Wipe off any excess glue that squeezes out.

9. Drive the nail heads under the surface using a nail set. Fill the holes with wood filler.

10. Go over all surfaces with a finishing sander using fine and extra-fine abrasive paper. Leave the edges sharp. Wipe off all sanding dust.

11. Finish the cabinet/shelf with a clear lacquer finish. Rub the finish with steel wool (0000) between coats. Be sure to wipe off the steel hairs before applying another coat of lacquer.

34: *Desktop Pen Set*
(Illus. 110 and 111)

This pen set makes an attractive and functional gift for the person with an office or home desk. While the project holds two pens, one with red ink and the other with black, you could use a pencil-and-pen combination. Pen-and-pencil sets with funnels are available from a variety of mail-order suppliers. By the way, the funnel is that item that is secured to the wood and holds

Illus. 110. Desktop pen set.

Top View

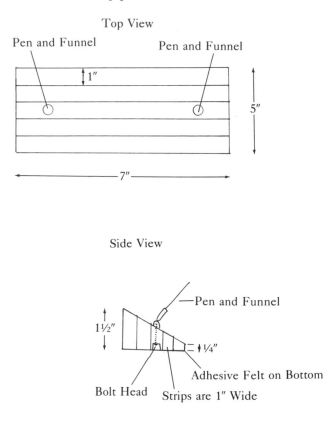

Illus. 111. Drawings of desktop pen set.

the pen or pencil. You may want to add a calendar or a large, note-holding paper clip between the writing instruments. The pen set shown in Illus. 110 is made from scraps of walnut and cherry that were lying around my shop. An adhesive felt has been attached to the bottom of it to prevent it from scratching the desktop.

MATERIAL:

- 1½″ (6/4's) thick hardwood scraps
- Pen-and-pencil set with funnels
- Wood glue
- Adhesive felt
- Lacquer

TOOLS:

- Radial arm or table saw
- Band saw
- Electric drill and ⅛″ and ¼″ bits
- Clamps
- Finishing sander or belt sander

DIRECTIONS:

1. While hardwood scraps are suggested, you may have to buy a few pieces of hardwood. As indicated, scraps of walnut and cherry that were approximately 1½″ (6/4's) thick and 1″ (4/4's) wide were used for the desktop set shown in Illus. 110. Review Illus. 111 prior to beginning.

2. Measure and cut hardwood strips to the suggested dimensions. They can vary slightly in thickness and width because the pen base is cut to the finished angle on the band saw.

3. Glue and clamp the strips of hardwood together. Assemble the strips so that they are all flush on what will be the bottom surface of the pen base. Alternate the two woods so that you will have a walnut strip, a cherry strip, a walnut strip, etc. Leave the clamps in place until the glue dries.

4. If needed, trim the sides using a radial arm or table saw. The ends on both sides should be neat and clean. Don't remove too much wood.

5. Adjust the band-saw table to cut the base at the desired angle. Align the fence for making the cut. If it will help, measure and mark ¼″ up from the bottom on one edge of the base and 1½″ up on the other edge. The marks should be made on one side of the base. Draw a straight line between the two marks. Note Illus. 111. Align the band-saw blade to cut along this line.

6. Measure and mark the location of the pen funnels on the top surface of the base. Drill a ⅛″ diameter hole straight down and through the base. It is assumed that the funnel bolts are not larger than ⅛″. If they are, use a larger-diameter bit.

7. Note the length of the funnel bolts. From the bottom surface, drill a ⅜″ diameter hole into the previously drilled hole. The hole should be deep enough to allow the funnel bolt to extend through to the top surface. As you might guess, the hole needs to be ⅜″ in diameter in order to accommodate the head of the funnel bolt. There should be enough thread exposed to screw the funnel securely in place. Keep the hole straight with the ⅛″ diameter hole and don't make it too deep.

8. Using a finishing sander and coarse, fine, and extra-fine abrasive paper, remove the saw marks from the top surface of the base. Keep all edges sharp. Don't round them over with the sander. Sand the front and back edges along with both sides. Prepare all the surfaces for finishing. The bottom surface will be covered with adhesive felt, so it does not have to be sanded. You may have to remove some hard glue from the bottom surface, however.

9. Finish the base with several coats of lacquer. Rub the surface with steel wool (0000) between coats. Make sure you remove any steel hairs that are on the surface before applying another coat. You may also want to apply several coats of paste wax to the project. Don't apply wax to the bottom surface.

10. Secure the pen funnels in place with their bolts. Apply the adhesive felt to the bottom surface.

35: Salt and Pepper Shakers (Illus. 112 and 113)

Shakers made from black walnut are a stylish and functional gift. You can also make them from cherry, oak, ash, or some other hardwood. Avoid using any of the toxic exotic woods, for obvious reasons. While the shakers are designed to withstand daily use, they may more appropriately be used for more formal occasions. The salt-and-pepper storage areas are secured from the bottom

Illus. 112. Salt and pepper shakers.

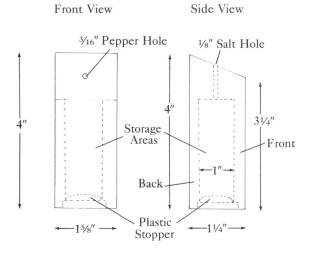

Illus. 113. Drawings of salt and pepper shakers.

with 1″ diameter plastic stoppers. The stoppers are available from mail-order and craft stores. As you will note from Illus. 112 and 113, the shakers have only one hole in their top. As you will discover from using the shakers, one hole is adequate. To minimize salt flow, the salt shaker's hole is ⅛″ in diameter. To allow more flow, the pepper shaker's hole is ³⁄₁₆″ in diameter. Feel free to change either the design or the dimensions of the project.

MATERIAL:

- 1¾″ (⁶⁄₄'s) thick black walnut
- Plastic stoppers
- Lacquer

TOOLS:

- Radial arm or table saw
- Band saw
- Drill press, 1″ and 1¼″ Forstner bits, and ⅛″ and ³⁄₁₆″ bits
- Drill press vise
- Finishing or belt sander

DIRECTIONS:

1. Measure and cut the hardwood blocks to their suggested lengths and widths, as indicated in Illus. 113.

2. Using a band saw and a ½″ wide blade, saw the blocks to their suggested or desired thickness.

3. Set the desired angle on the band-saw mitre gauge and cut the top sections of both shakers. Mark the front and back lengths of a shaker on its side surface and draw a straight line between the points. This will give you the angle of cut needed. Check the side-view drawing for these dimensions presented in Illus. 113.

4. On the bottom end of each shaker, draw lines from one corner to the other. Where the lines intersect is the exact center.

5. Secure a 1¼″ diameter Forstner or multi-spur bit in the drill press. Clamp a shaker in a drill press vise, bottom edge facing up. Align the marked center of the shaker under the point of the bit. Drill a hole no more than ¼″ deep. The hole needs to be deep enough to accommodate the top flange of the plastic stopper.

6. While the shaker is still clamped into the vise, secure a 1″ Forstner or multi-spur bit into the drill chuck. Drill a 1″ diameter hole into the shaker, stopping where the front surface ends and the upward angle cut begins. Note the side-view drawing in Illus. 113 detailing where the drilled hole should end. If you drill any further into the shaker, the bit will break through the angled top surface.

7. Repeat the drilling tasks on the second shaker.

8. On the angled top surfaces of the shakers, draw lines from one corner to the other. Where the lines intersect is the center point.

9. Drill a ³⁄₁₆″ diameter hole at the marked centerpoint of what will be the pepper shaker. The hole should be drilled straight down so that it meets the 1″ diameter storage hole.

10. On the salt shaker, drill a ⅛″ diameter hole, where marked, into the storage area.

11. Using coarse, fine, and extra-fine abrasive papers on a belt or finishing sander, remove the saw marks from all the surfaces. Also prepare the surfaces for finishing. Leave the edges sharp.

12. Finish the shakers with a clear lacquer. Rub the finish with steel wool (0000) between coats. Remove the steel hairs before applying more lacquer. Apply and polish the shakers with some paste wax. Secure the plastic stoppers in place.

Illus. 114. Elephant bank.

36: *Elephant Bank*

(Illus. 114 and 115)

This gift project is for the child who likes to save money, enjoys music, and has a preference for red elephants covered with white spots. Cut from a piece of 2″ x 10″ fir, the bank has clear-plastic ovals covering the money area. Whenever money is deposited into the bank it has to pass through a slot melody movement. The coin activates the movement to play a tune. To remove the money from the bank, remove the music movement slot or one of the plastic sides. In order to make the elephant more stable, a base is secured to it. You will especially enjoy the opportunity to paint this project.

MATERIAL:
- 1″ x 10″ fir
- 1″ x 6″ pine
- Clear-plastic side plates and nails
- Bank slot melody movement
- ⅜″ diameter dowel
- Construction paper
- Wood screws
- Wood glue
- Paint

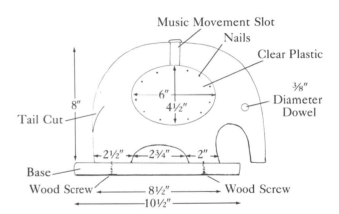

Illus. 115. Drawing of elephant bank.

TOOLS:
- Radial arm, table, or band saw
- Scroll or sabre saw
- Table-mounted router with roundover bit
- Electric drill, screw-sink, and ⅜″ bit
- Finishing sander
- Hammer

DIRECTIONS:
1. Review Illus. 114 and 115. Measure and cut a piece of 1″ x 10″ stock to a length of 11″. Using

construction paper, make a pattern, to size, of the project elephant.

2. Trace the elephant pattern on the 11″ piece of 1″ x 10″ material. Cut the elephant using an appropriate saw. Given the thickness of the wood, you may want to cut it with a band saw and a ¼″ wide blade. A good scroll saw should also work. Don't forget to cut in the tail.

3. Measure and mark the length and width of the melody movement to be used. Note its placement in Illus. 114 and 115. The movement should fit snugly in the cut slot. Using a band saw, cut out the slot.

4. Place an oval clear-plastic side plate on the side of the elephant. The top edge of the plastic should touch the bottom edge of the music movement slot. Trace the oval onto the surface of the elephant. Draw another oval approximately ¼″ inside the first oval. You will have to draw the second oval freehand. It is the second oval that needs to be cut. The ¼″ between the first traced oval and the second is the area where the plastic oval is nailed to the side of the elephant.

5. Using a band saw or scroll saw, cut down through the movement slot and cut out the marked oval. When the oval is cut, saw away any remaining wood in the melody slot. Take your time when cutting the oval. The money area should have a nice, round appearance.

6. Locate where you want the elephant's eye. Mark and drill a ⅜″ diameter hole through the elephant. Measure and cut a piece of ⅜″ diameter dowel that will extend ⅜″ on each side of the elephant. Paint the dowel the desired eye color before it's glued in place. The elephant shown in Illus. 114 has green eyes.

7. Measure and cut a piece of 1″ x 6″ pine to a length of 8½″. The width of a 1″ x 6″, which is 5½″, is adequate for the base.

8. Rout the edges of the elephant using a round-over bit. Do not rout the oval areas. You should also rout all edges of the base piece.

9. Prepare all surfaces and edges for finishing using an electric sander and several different grits of abrasive paper. Wipe away the dust created by the sanding process.

10. Paint the base and the elephant in colors of your choosing. You may want to decorate the elephant with different-colored dots, stripes, etc. Remember to paint the eye dowel an appropriate color. Allow the paint to dry.

11. Center the elephant on the bottom of the base and mark the location of the feet. Using wood screws, an electric drill, and a screw bit, drive the screws through the center of each marked foot area. Do not drive the screws all the way through. The screws should extend approximately ¼″ above the top surface of the base.

12. Spread glue on the bottom of each foot and center them on the point of the screws. Force the elephant down to the top surface of the base piece. Tip the assembly upside down and drive the screws in the rest of the way. Let the screw heads penetrate the bottom surface, so they won't scratch any surface the bank is set on.

13. Place the melody movement in the slot. If it's too loose, use a dab of white glue to hold it in place. Allow the glue to dry.

14. Nail the plastic side plates in place. Don't hammer too hard or you will shatter the plastic. Also, be careful not to scratch the side plates. Place something under the nailed side when you are going to nail the other plate in place.

15. Glue the eye dowel into the drilled hole.

16. Deposit a coin and listen to the tune.

37: *Bowl Mirror*
(Illus. 116 and 117)

For those who enjoy turning projects from wood, this one is unusual. A block of black walnut is faceplate-turned into a bowl. The bowl is re-aligned on the faceplate and a hole is turned, off-center, into the top of the bowl. A quality mirror with a bevelled edge is glued into the bottom of the off-center hole. The bowl mirror can adorn an end table or, if preferred, hang on a wall. You may prefer using a hardwood other than walnut. The mirror can be purchased from any number of mail-order suppliers or, possibly, a local mirror/glass store.

Illus. 116. Bowl mirror.

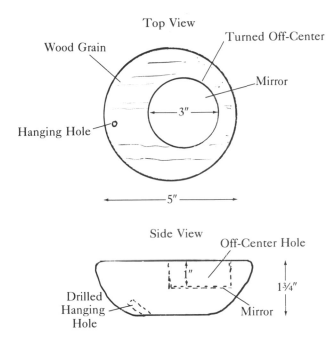

Illus. 117. Drawings of bowl mirror.

MATERIAL:

- 1¾″ (7/4's) thick black walnut
- 3″ diameter bevelled mirror
- White glue
- Lacquer

TOOLS:

- Wood lathe
- Turning tools
- Band saw
- Clamp
- School compass and vernier caliper
- Electric drill and ¼″ bit

DIRECTIONS:

1. Using a school compass, make a 5½″ diameter circle on a 1¾″ (7/4's) thick piece of hardwood that is at least 6″ wide and 6″ long. If you prefer, glue-up several pieces of hardwood to achieve the necessary thickness. You may even want to laminate the block with strips of veneer or some other type of hardwood. Cut the block round, as traced, using a band saw.

2. Make a 3½″ diameter glue block from a piece of scrap pine. Use a school compass to make the circle. Cut the block using a band saw.

3. Spread glue on the pine block and place it at the center of the bottom of the hardwood turning block. Clamp the assembly until the glue is dry.

4. Secure a 3″ faceplate to the glue block and thread the assembly onto the lathe. With a revolving center in the tailstock, bring the tailstock forward and into the front surface of the turning block. This will help support the block during the initial parts of the turning process. It also helps prevent the turning block from flying off the glue block or being ripped from the faceplate screws.

5. Turn the block to shape using either scraping tools or gouges. Note the final shape of the bowl shown in Illus. 116. If necessary, use fine and extra-fine abrasive paper to prepare the bowl's surface for finishing.

6. Remove the assembly from the lathe. Remove two screws from the faceplate and realign it on the bottom of the turning. Directly above the final placement of the faceplate is where the off-center mirror-hole will be. Resecure the faceplate at its new location with the removed screws. You should retighten the third screw as well. Thread the assembly back onto the lathe.

7. Slow the lathe down when turning off-center. Align the tool rest to face the front surface of the bowl. Set the vernier caliper to measure a 3″ diameter hole. Use a 1″ square-nose scraper to turn the mirror hole. The hole should be at least 1″ deep, with a clean, straight wall. Check the diameter of the hole frequently with the caliper to be certain that it is precisely 3″ in diameter. Take your time with this procedure and watch the bowl carefully as it rotates off-center.

75

8. While the bowl is still on the lathe, check the fit of the piece of mirror glass in the off-center hole. Don't drop the mirror on the lathe. If necessary, make the hole a bit larger. You want a good fit, but not a tight fit.

9. Realign the tool rest to the side of the bowl. With a cut-off tool, begin removing the glue block. Do this by cutting ever so slightly into the bottom surface of the bowl. Keep the cut straight. Before the tool cuts all the way through, place your hand not holding the tool by the bowl and be ready to catch it. If this procedure worries you, cut the final area that's holding the glue block and bowl together with a band saw.

10. Drill an angled ¼" diameter hanging hole into the bottom of the bowl. The hole should be opposite the mirror hole and approximately ½" deep. Protect the top surface of the bowl as you turn it over to drill the hanging hole. Lay it on some paper or a cloth.

11. Prepare the bottom and top surface for finishing. Use a finishing or belt sander on the bottom surface. Extra-fine abrasive paper should be used to prepare the top surface for finishing. Remove all the sanding dust from the bowl.

12. Finish the bowl and the side of the mirror hole with lacquer. Rub the surfaces with steel wool (0000) between coats. Wipe off the steel hairs that result from using the wool.

13. Spread a bead of white glue on the bottom surface of the mirror hole and set the mirror in place. Press down on the mirror. Allow the glue to dry. Clean the mirror.

38: Oil and Vinegar Caddy (Illus. 118 and 119)

This is a difficult but worthwhile project for the individual who likes to make and give turned pieces. The caddy is designed to fit oil and vinegar cruets that were purchased as part of the gift. As you might guess, there is little uniformity in either the diameter or height of cruets. Find the cruets you want to use and then design the caddy to accommodate them. It's unlikely that the recipient of the caddy would have cruets that would fit. The caddy is made from black walnut. You will need a 2⅜" diameter multi-spur bit to drill the various parts of the caddy that support and hold the cruets.

Illus. 118. Oil and vinegar caddy.

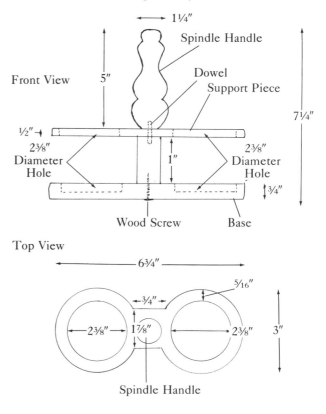

Illus. 119. Drawings of oil and vinegar caddy.

MATERIAL:

- 1½″ (6/4's) thick black walnut
- 1″ (4/4's) thick black walnut
- ⅜″ diameter dowel
- Construction paper
- Wood glue
- Wood screw
- Lacquer

TOOLS:

- Wood lathe
- Radial arm or table saw
- Band saw
- Scroll or sabre saw
- Turning tools
- School compass and vernier caliper
- Plastic circle template
- Drill press, screw-sink and ¹⁄₁₆″, ⅜″, and 2⅜″ multi-spur bits
- Drill press vise
- Clamp
- Finishing sander

DIRECTIONS:

1. Review Illus. 118 and 119 before you start the project. Make a pattern of the caddy base and the support piece. The same pattern can be used for both pieces. Measure and mark the center of the pattern where the 2⅜″ diameter holes should be drilled. The school compass will be of help in making the pattern.

2. Resaw on the band saw, using a ½″ wide blade, a ½″ (2/4's) thick piece of walnut. The piece should be at least 7½″ long and 4″ wide.

3. Trace the caddy base/support piece pattern onto the surface of the ½″ (2/4's) piece of walnut. Mark on the surface where the holes should be drilled.

4. Before cutting out the traced support piece, drill the 2⅜″ diameter holes where marked. Clamp the traced support piece onto the drill press table with a scrap board underneath it. Align the multi-spur bit point over the marked location of the hole. Drill a hole through the piece. Repeat the drilling process to make the second hole in the support piece.

5. Using a scroll or sabre saw, cut out the traced support piece. By drilling the holes before cutting the piece, there is less chance of breaking the narrow walls of the support piece.

6. Measure and cut a piece of ¾″ (3/4's) thick walnut for the caddy base. The wood can be thicker if that's what you have available. The piece should be cut to a length of 7½″ and a width of 4″.

7. Trace the caddy base/support piece pattern onto the surface of the ¾″ (3/4's) thick piece. Mark the exact location of the two drilled holes.

8. Clamp the traced caddy base to the drill press table and drill, where marked, the two 2⅜″ diameter holes. The holes should be drilled to a depth of approximately ⅜″.

9. Cut the caddy base, as traced, using a scroll or sabre saw.

10. For turning the spindle handle, measure and cut a piece of walnut 2″ square and 9″ long. At the same time and from the same spindle block, also turn the post that separates the caddy base and support piece.

11. Secure the block between the drive center in the headstock and the revolving center in the tailstock. After bringing the spindle to roundness, mark a 5″ long area for the handle. On another part of the spindle, mark a 1″ long area for the round piece that will be placed between the support piece and the caddy base. Refer to Illus. 128.

12. Spindle-turn the handle as desired and turn round the 1″ long piece. The spindle handle should have a diameter of at least 1¼″ at the bottom end. When the turning is complete, separate the pieces using a band saw. You want a flush end on the bottom of the spindle handle and two flush ends on the 1″ round piece.

13. Drill a ⅜″ diameter hole through the center of the support piece. This hole will have a ⅜″ diameter dowel pass through it and into the spindle handle and the 1″ round piece.

14. Drill a ⅜″ diameter hole into the bottom center of the spindle handle. The hole should be at least ½″ deep. Hold the spindle straight and steady when drilling it, so the hole will be straight.

15. In the top of the center of the 1″ piece, drill a ⅜″ diameter hole to a depth of at least ½″.

16. Cut a piece of ⅜″ diameter dowel to a length of ⅞″. Place the dowel in the ⅜″ diameter hole in the support piece. The dowel piece should extend equally on both sides of the support piece.

17. Spread wood glue in the hole in the bottom of the spindle handle and also on the bottom surface of the spindle. Tap the spindle onto the dowel extending from the support piece. The bottom of the spindle should be flush with the top surface of the support piece. The resawed surface of the support piece should be used as the bottom surface.

18. Spread glue in the drilled hole in the 1″ piece and also on its top surface. Tap it onto the ⅜″ diameter dowel piece extending from the bottom of the support piece. Make sure that the surfaces of the support piece and the 1″ piece make good contact. Allow the glue to dry.

19. In the middle of the bottom of the caddy base, drill a pilot hole with a screw-sink. The screw-sink should drill a pilot hole through the base, but also make an area for the screw head.

20. Using a 1/16″ bit, drill a pilot hole in the middle of the bottom of the 1″ piece. This pilot hole will prevent the wood screw from splitting the piece when it penetrates it.

21. Spread wood glue on the bottom surface of the 1″ piece and around the hole in the caddy base. Start to thread the wood screw into the bottom of the 1″ piece and, before it is tight, align the drilled holes of the support piece exactly over the drilled holes in the caddy base. Tighten the screw and wipe off any wood glue that squeezes out.

22. Prepare all surfaces and edges for finishing using fine and extra-fine abrasive paper. Be careful when sanding the support piece, to ensure that the rings aren't broken. Wipe off the sanding dust. Finish the project with several coats of lacquer. Place the cruets in the caddy and you will have one fine gift.

39: *Scrap Box with Lid*
(Illus. 120 and 121)

The box shown in Illus. 120 is made from a piece of scrap red oak found at a hardwood lumber

Illus. 120. Scrap box with lid.

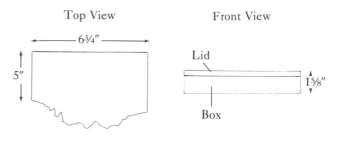

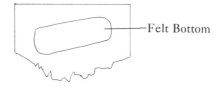

Illus. 121. Drawings of scrap box with lid.

dealer. Portions of the bark remain in place, along with the material that is under the bark. The rough, jagged surface of the oak tree also remains intact. This kind of material makes for a fine box, and one that will be a treasured gift. Unlike most boxes that have hinged lids, this one has a lid that must be lifted off. Inside the box, a storage area has been drilled and ground-out with a carbide burr. The bottom is covered with a piece of adhesive felt. Look through the scrap piles at hardwood dealers and in the back-yard log pile. You may be able to cut a chunk from a log that can be used as a gift box. Somewhere, there's a piece of scrap hardwood waiting for you to find and use as a box.

MATERIAL:

- 1¾″ (⅞'s) thick piece of scrap red oak
- Adhesive felt
- Lacquer

TOOLS:

- Radial arm or table saw
- Band saw and ½″ wide blade
- Drill press and multi-spur or Forstner bit
- Electric grinder, rotary tool, or flex-shaft tool
- Carbide burrs and sanding sleeves
- Finishing and belt sander

DIRECTIONS:

1. Measure and cut a piece of scrap hardwood to the approximate dimensions indicated in Illus. 121.

2. Set the band-saw fence to saw a ⅝″ thick slice of the scrap piece for the lid.

3. Sand away the band-saw marks on the bottom surface of the lid and the top surface of the box. Use a coarse-grit abrasive paper on a belt or finishing sander.

4. Draw a storage area on the top surface of the box. Using a Forstner or multi-spur bit, drill out as much of the area as possible. Set the drill so that the depth is uniform.

5. Using carbide burrs in an electric grinder, rotary tool, or flex-shaft tool, remove more wood from the storage area. Shape the hole, and its side wall, so that it looks like an oval. Make the bottom of the storage area as flat as possible. Remove any bit marks from the surface and wall of the storage area.

6. Prepare all surfaces for finishing using fine and extra-fine abrasive paper and a finishing sander. Remove the dust created by the sander.

7. Finish the box and lid with several coats of lacquer. Rub with steel wool (0000) between coats of lacquer. Wipe away the steel wool hairs before applying additional coats of lacquer.

8. Measure and cut a piece of adhesive felt to fit into the storage area. Apply it to the bottom surface of the storage area.

40: Tic-Tac-Toe Game

(Illus. 122 and 123)

Everybody likes to play tic-tac-toe, especially when going on a family vacation. It's also a fun game that will keep your kids away from the television set for awhile. One of the game boards

Illus. 122. Tic-tac-toe game.

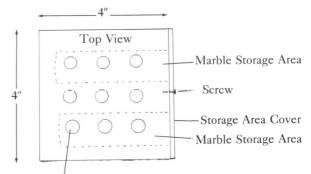

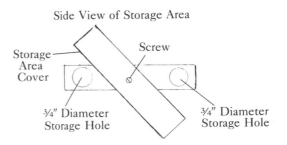

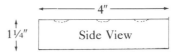

Illus. 123. Drawings of tic-tac-toe-game.

79

shown in Illus. 122 is made from wild cherry and contains two storage areas where the marbles can be placed when not in use. This game is a good gift for a child or an adult. Most discount stores sell marbles. The other game board shown in Illus. 122 is made from thinner stock and does not contain storage areas for the marbles. Both game boards are fun to make and to give as gifts.

MATERIAL:
- 1¼" (6/4's) thick hardwood
- Marbles
- Screw
- Lacquer

TOOLS:
- Radial arm or table saw
- Drill press and ¹⁄₁₆", ½", and ¾" bits
- Drill press vise
- Table-mounted router and roundover bit
- Finishing and belt sander

DIRECTIONS:
1. You may want to make some games with both the storage area and without it. The length and width of the game without a storage area are the same. This game is ¾" (¾'s) thick.
2. To make the game with the storage area, cut a piece of 1¼" thick hardwood to a length of 4" and a width of 4".
3. Sand the sawed edges smooth using a belt or finishing sander.
4. On one side (avoid the ends, where you would be drilling into the wood grain), measure and mark the location of the ¾" diameter storage holes. Place the block in a drill press vise and drill the ¾" diameter holes to a depth of at least 2¾". Each storage area should hold four marbles.
5. Measure and mark the location of the nine indentations where the marbles can be placed. With a ½" diameter steel bit, drill the indentations deep enough to hold a marble in place. Set the drill press so that all the indentations are drilled the same depth.
6. Rout all edges, except the top and bottom edges of the storage area side, with a roundover bit.

7. Measure and cut a storage area cover to a thickness of ¼" and to the exact length and width of the storage side.
8. Measure and mark the center of the storage area cover. While holding the cover in place, drill a ¹⁄₁₆" diameter pilot hole through the cover and into the game block. Thread a small wood screw through the cover pilot hole and into the block's pilot hole. This should allow the user to move the cover for access to the marble storage areas.
9. Prepare all surfaces for finishing. Slightly round the outside edges of the storage cover. Wipe away the dust.
10. Finish the project with several coats of lacquer. Purchase two sets of marbles that are different colors.

41: Two-Storey Birdhouse (Illus. 124 and 125)

Given the new status and upward mobility of many of our feathered friends, two-storey birdhouses are the in-thing. The person you make this gift for will be delighted; certainly the birds in his or her yard will appreciate it. Many people are now displaying painted birdhouses in the kitchen or other rooms where collectibles can be showcased. This is a fun project to make and paint. You may prefer a bit more decoration than that displayed on the birdhouse in Illus. 124.

MATERIAL:
- ½" thick pine
- ¼" diameter dowel
- Eye screw
- Wood screws
- Finishing nails
- Wood glue
- Paint

TOOLS:
- Radial arm or table saw
- Band saw
- Electric drill, screw-set, and ¼" and 2" or smaller wood bits
- Finishing sander

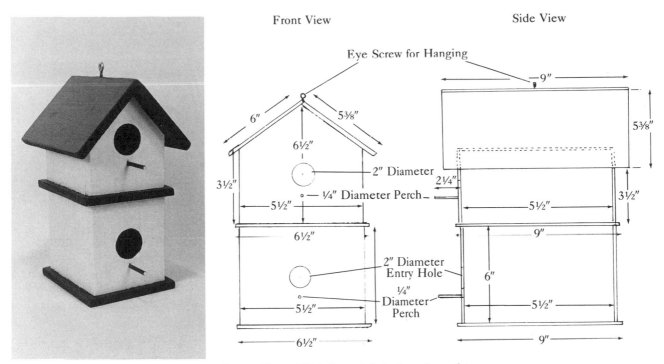

Illus. 124 (above left). Two-storey birdhouse. Illus. 125 (above right). Drawings of two-storey birdhouse.

DIRECTIONS:

1. Review Illus. 124 and 125 to note the dimensions and construction of the birdhouse. The birdhouse is best made from ½″ thick pine. If you can't find any at the local lumberyard and no one will plane some for you, resaw standard 1″ (¾'s) thick pine using a band saw and a ½″ wide blade.

2. Measure and cut the various parts of the birdhouse. The front and back of the top storey are the same length and width. The top and back of the bottom storey are also the same width and length. The sides of the top storey are the same dimensions; so are the sides of the bottom storey. The two roof pieces are the same length, but different widths. This is necessary, because one overlaps the other. The floors for both stories are exactly the same.

3. Drill entry holes in both the top and bottom of the front pieces. The holes should be drilled to a diameter that is appropriate for the birds you would like to live in the house. Measure and mark the center of both pieces. Drill the holes to the desired diameter. The birdhouse shown in Illus. 124 has 2″ diameter holes, which are rather large.

4. Measure and drill ¼″ diameter holes below the entry holes. A ¼″ diameter dowel will be inserted to serve as a perch.

5. Measure and cut two pieces of ¼″ diameter dowel to a length of 2¼″.

6. Using wood glue and finishing nails, assemble the birdhouse. Screw the floor onto the first storey, and the back piece onto the second storey. This will allow the owner to clean both storeys at the end of each season. Birds, too, prefer a clean house.

7. In the middle of the roof, thread in an eye screw for hanging the house.

8. Glue the ¼″ dowel pieces in place.

9. Go over all surfaces with a finishing sander and a variety of abrasive papers. Round the sharp edges and, if you prefer, give the birdhouse a "used" look. Wipe off all the dust.

10. Paint the birdhouse and, if you want, decorate it. Why not paint some windows and window boxes on it?

81

42: *Pig Mirror* (Illus. 126 and 127)

Animal mirrors have become popular in recent years. Once you understand how this type of mirror is made, you can make mirrors of any animal you want. This project can be easily redesigned to meet both the interests and needs of a child. While the mirror shown in Illus. 126 is stained and lacquered, you may want to paint and decorate your gift mirror. You also may want to increase the size.

Illus. 126. Pig mirror.

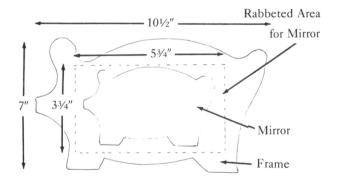

Illus. 127. Drawing of pig mirror.

MATERIAL:
- 1″ x 8″ pine
- Mirror glass
- Construction paper
- White glue
- Hanger
- Stain
- Lacquer

TOOLS:
- Radial arm, table, or scroll saw
- Sabre saw
- Electric drill and ⅜″ bit
- Table-mounted router and roundover and rabbeting bits
- Glass cutter
- Finishing sander

DIRECTIONS:
1. While reviewing Illus. 127, decide whether you prefer a pig or another animal. Either way, two patterns should be made. Make a pattern, to size, of the animal frame. Make a second pattern, of the animal that will be cut out for the mirror area. Make the patterns from construction paper.

2. Cut a piece of 1″ x 8″ pine to length and trace the frame pattern onto it. Using a sabre, or, if you prefer, a scroll saw, cut the frame as traced.

3. Align the mirror pattern on the center of the frame and trace it onto the surface. Drill a ⅜″ hole through the pattern area to permit penetration of a sabre-saw blade. Carefully cut out the traced area with a sabre saw.

4. Remove the bearing from the top of a rabbeting bit and secure the bit in a table-mounted router. You have to rabbet the area for the mirror on the back of the frame. The area is rabbeted so that you can cut a rectangular piece of mirror glass to fit into the frame. Mirror glass is approximately ³⁄₁₆″ thick. Check the thickness of the mirror glass that you are using and rabbet an area that will accommodate this thickness. It's more efficient and safer to set the router bit so that not too much wood is removed in each pass. Make several passes to achieve the desired depth. Be very careful when doing this kind of routing. You may want to clamp a guide board on top of the router table where the frame will be placed and moved over the bit. Think safety and concentrate on what you're doing.

5. Rout all the edges, except the back of the rabbeted area, with a roundover bit.

6. Measure and cut a piece of glass to fit in the frame. You may want to refer to Project 13 for some ideas on cutting glass. Do not glue the glass in place until the frame has been finished.

7. If you prefer, stain and lacquer the frame. You may want to paint and even decorate it.

8. Nail a hanger to the back of the frame. This should be done before the mirror glass is in place. Hammering on the frame can crack the mirror.

9. Place the mirror glass in the rabbeted area and dab white glue along its edges. Make sure that the glue is on the rabbeted frame surface and on the mirror. Let the mirror lie facedown until the glue dries.

10. Measure and cut a piece of construction paper to glue over the back of the frame and mirror. Spread white glue on the edge of the paper and press it in place.

Illus. 128. Desk barometer.

43: *Desk Barometer*

(Illus. 128 and 129)

This is the ideal gift for anyone interested in knowing weather conditions. It is designed for the desk, but could be redesigned to fit anywhere, including on a wall. The barometer shown in Illus. 128 is placed in a block of white oak. The barometer itself can be purchased from mail-order suppliers or local craft shops. You need only drill a hole in the block and then insert the instrument.

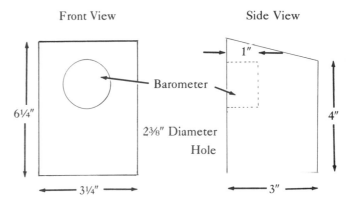

Illus. 129. Drawings of desk barometer.

MATERIAL:
- 3″ (12/4's) thick hardwood
- Barometer
- Adhesive felt
- Lacquer

TOOLS:
- Radial arm or table saw
- Band saw
- Drill press and 2⅜″ Forstner bit
- Clamp
- Finishing or belt sander

DIRECTIONS:

1. Find or purchase a sufficiently large block of hardwood for the project. While white oak was used for the desk barometer, shown in Illus. 128,

you may prefer black walnut, red oak, or some other wood. You may want to use a log from the backyard wood pile. Make sure it's good and dry.

2. Measure and cut a hardwood block to the suggested or desired dimensions. The top angle cut can be made using a band saw and mitre gauge.

3. Measure and mark the location for the hole that will accommodate the barometer. While the barometer shown in Illus. 128 requires a 2⅜″ diameter hole, yours may be different. Normally, instructions will accompany the instrument indicating the size hole needed.

4. When drilling large blocks, it's best to clamp them to the drill-press table. Put a piece of scrap between the clamp and the block's surface to protect it. Align the drilling mark under the bit and drill the hole to a depth of at least 1″.

5. Using belt and finishing sanders, remove any saw marks from the block's surface. Prepare all surfaces for finishing using fine and extra-fine abrasive papers.

6. Finish the project with a clear lacquer or a finish of your choice.

7. Measure and cut a piece of adhesive felt and secure it to the bottom. This prevents any possible scratching of the desktop by the wood.

8. Set the barometer to your local setting and insert into the drilled hole. Check the accompanying directions on how to set the barometer.

44: Rabbit Shelf

(Illus. 130 and 131)

While an adult may enjoy this project, it is ideal for a child. The shelf has a smiling rabbit head on both ends. It also has a support piece that sprouts three Shaker pegs for hanging fun things or, if necessary, clothes. The actual shelf can be used to display small treasures or to store a comb and brush. As always, you may want to custom-design the project to fit a particular spot in a room. It's also a fun project to paint and, if you want, detail the rabbit head with eyes, whiskers, a nose and anything else you think a rabbit should have.

MATERIAL:
- 1″ x 8″ pine
- 1″ x 4″ pine
- Shaker pegs
- Construction paper
- Wood glue
- Finishing nails
- Wood filler
- Paint

TOOLS:
- Radial arm or table saw
- Scroll or sabre saw
- Electric drill, screw-sink, and ½″ bit
- Table-mounted router and roundover bit
- Finishing sander

Illus. 130. Rabbit shelf.

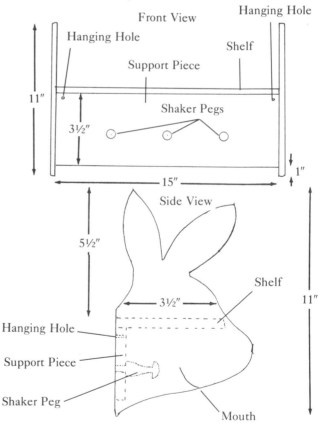

Illus. 131. Drawings of rabbit shelf.

DIRECTIONS:

1. Review Illus. 131 and decide on final dimensions to be used. Make a pattern for the rabbit head with construction paper. Remember, the

84

pattern has to be the actual size of the rabbit head.

2. Trace the pattern on a piece of 1″ x 8″ pine cut to length. Cut out the traced rabbit using either a scroll or sabre saw. If you want, draw and cut a smile into the rabbits.

3. If the project dimensions are being used, cut two pieces of 1″ x 4″ pine to a length of 15″. One piece will be used for the shelf, while the other will be the support piece.

4. If three Shaker pegs are to be used, measure and mark their location on the 1″ x 4″ support piece. Also, mark the location of the two hanging holes.

5. Using an electric drill and ½″ diameter bit, drill the three marked holes for the Shaker pegs. With a screw-sink, drill the two hanging holes. It is assumed that you are using Shaker pegs with a ½″ diameter tenon. If not, change the bit size.

6. Rout all the edges, except those that will be joined together, using a roundover bit.

7. Using wood glue and finishing nails, secure the shelf to one edge of the support piece. With a nail set, drive the nail heads under the surface and fill the holes with wood filler.

8. Glue and nail the rabbit heads to the assembly. Make sure they are placed evenly on both ends of the shelf assembly. Set the nails and fill the holes with filler.

9. Prepare the surfaces for finishing using fine and extra-fine abrasive paper and a finishing sander. Remove all dust.

10. If the Shaker pegs are going to be painted or finished in the same color as the support piece, they can be glued and tapped in place. If not, glue them in after the pegs and support piece have been finished.

11. Paint and decorate the project. Again, you may want to paint or even wood-burn details of the rabbit's face. The shelf shown in Illus. 130 is painted a light-blue and white. Use some creativity in finishing the project.

45: *Pasta Measurer*
(Illus. 132 and 133)

How much spaghetti do you cook for three people? With a pasta measurer, you will know ex-

Illus. 132. Pasta measurer.

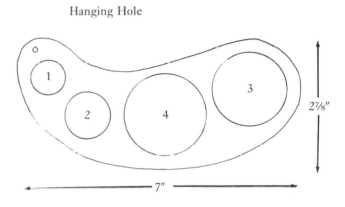

Hanging Hole

2⅞″

7″

Illus. 133. Drawing of pasta measurer.

actly. The measurer allows you to consistently fix the same amount. It is designed with four holes through it. If you want to cook pasta for one person, use enough to fill the hole marked 1. For three people, a handful of pasta that fits into the hole marked 3 should be adequate. It's a clever item, and makes a great gift. By the way, a piece of buckskin in the hanging hole adds a final touch to the project. The project should be made from hard maple.

MATERIAL:
- ¼″ thick hard maple
- Construction paper
- Buckskin
- Mineral oil

TOOLS:
- Band saw
- Sabre or scroll saw
- Drill press, 7/8", 1¼", 1½", and 1¾" Forstner or multi-spur bits, and screw-sink
- Finishing or belt sander

DIRECTIONS:

1. Note from Illus. 132 and 133 the dimensions and how the project is designed. You may want to make a pattern from construction paper.

2. Hard maple is preferred because you may want to wash the measurer on occasion. However, it could also be made from oak or any other hardwood. Use a band saw and a ½" wide blade to cut a piece of hardwood to an approximate ¼" thickness.

3. Trace the pattern or draw the design of the measuring device on a ¼" thick piece of hardwood. Cut out the project using either a scroll or sabre saw.

4. Measure and mark the location of each hole. Also, mark a location for the hanging hole. Hopefully, you will have the needed Forstner and/or multi-spur bits to drill the different holes. If not, you may want to use a circle cutter secured in a drill press. In that the circle cutter has graduations for setting the size of the hole cut, it should work well. Hole saws, again with a drill press, could also be used. This is one of those projects where you may have to improvise when making the measuring holes.

5. Prepare all surfaces for finishing. You may want to sand away the saw marks left by the band-saw blade using either a belt or finishing sander. Remove the sharp edges from the top and bottom of the project with a fine abrasive paper.

6. Remove all the dust and rub in several coats of mineral oil. If the wood is warmed, the oil is absorbed better.

7. Cut the length of buckskin and thread it through the hanging hole and tie.

46: *Woodcocks* (Illus. 134 and 135)

For those who enjoy displaying or collecting birds, a covey of woodcocks—a mother and two

Illus. 134. Woodcocks.

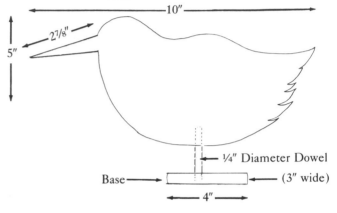

Illus. 135. Drawing of woodcock.

chicks—is a rather nice gift. The woodcocks shown in Illus. 134 are made from pine and painted slate-blue and black. They are shaped like woodcocks, but their chosen colors are slightly off. In any event, this is a fun project to make and a nice one to receive.

MATERIAL:
- 1" x 6" pine
- ¼" diameter dowel
- Construction paper
- Paint

TOOLS:
- Radial arm or table saw
- Scroll or sabre saw
- Table-mounted router and roundover bit
- Electric drill and ¼" bit
- Finishing sander

DIRECTIONS:

1. Illus. 135 depicts the dimensions for the larger bird. Design the smaller ones to your own specifications. The best way to make any bird is to design and cut an actual pattern. Using construction paper, make a pattern of both the larger and smaller birds. You may want to make several large birds and any number of smaller ones.

2. Trace the patterns on 1″ x 6″ pine and cut them out using either a scroll or sabre saw.

3. Measure and cut bases for the birds. The project bases are cut from scraps of 1″ x 6″ pine. The bases are 3″ wide and 4″ long.

4. Measure and mark the location of dowel holes in the middle of the bottom of each bird. Also, mark the middle of each base.

5. Drill ¼″ diameter holes where marked both on the birds and the bases. The holes should be at least ⅜″ deep.

6. In that woodcocks have short legs, the support dowels should be approximately 2″ to 3″ long, at most.

7. Rout, using a roundover bit, the edges of the base pieces only. Do not rout the edges of the birds.

8. Prepare all surfaces for finishing using fine and extra-fine abrasive paper and a finishing sander. Remove all dust when done.

9. Paint the woodcocks the way you want them to look. Be imaginative! You will enjoy painting and decorating them. By the way, remember to give them eyes.

47: *Scroll Mirror*

(Illus. 136 and 137)

This gift project is both functional and decorative. Crafted from pine, it is easy to make once you have a pattern. You can make this rather traditional design into a collage of small mirrors or, if you prefer, several larger ones. The mirror looks good when finished in a variety of ways. A clear lacquer finish with a small wood-burned design in one corner looks very nice. The mirror also looks attractive when painted with a single stencil. The mirror shown in Illus. 136 is stained dark and finished with lacquer. Try your hand at varying both the size of the mirror and the finishes.

Illus. 136. Scroll mirror.

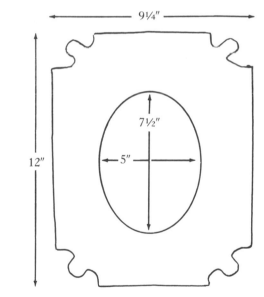

Illus. 137. Drawing of scroll mirror.

MATERIAL:

- 1″ x 10″ pine
- Mirror glass
- Construction paper
- Hanger
- White glue
- Stain and lacquer

87

TOOLS:

- Radial arm or table saw
- Scroll or sabre saw
- Electric drill and ⅜″ bit
- Table-mounted router and roundover and rabbeting bits
- Glass cutter
- Finishing sander

DIRECTIONS:

1. Note the dimensions of the project indicated in Illus. 137. You may prefer a larger or smaller version of the scroll mirror. In order that all four corners of the frame will be exactly the same, make a pattern using construction paper. You should also make a pattern of the oval center of the frame. This pattern can, with some modification, also be used for cutting the glass. If you prefer oval picture mats, they can be purchased in the size needed.

2. Measure and cut a piece of 1″ x 10″ pine to length. Trace the frame pattern on the wood. The oval center area of the frame should also be traced onto the piece. Be certain to center the oval on the frame.

3. Using a scroll or sabre saw, cut out the frame.

4. Drill a ⅜″ diameter hole in the traced oval area. Insert the blade of the sabre saw in the hole and cut out the oval area.

5. With a roundover bit secured in the router, rout the edges of the frame. Rout also the front edge of the oval. Do not rout the back edge of the oval.

6. Secure a rabbeting bit in the router. The back area of the oval must be rabbeted in order to accommodate the mirror. Most mirror glass is approximately ³⁄₁₆″ thick. Rout the mirror area to a depth that will accommodate the mirror glass. You may have to make several passes to rabbet the area safely.

7. Using a finishing sander with fine and extra-fine abrasive paper, prepare all surfaces and edges for finishing. Remove all the dust prior to applying any finishing products.

8. You may want to stain the frame and then finish it with a clear lacquer. If you prefer, paint it and then do some tole painting or stencilling. A wood-burned design with a clear lacquer finish also looks good.

9. Nail a picture hanger on the back upper part of the frame.

10. Using the oval template as a guide, trace an oval on a piece of mirror glass with a soft-tip pen. The traced line will need to be approximately ¼″ larger than the original pattern. Check its size against the rabbeted area in the frame.

11. Remove sections of the mirror glass that are near the oval with a glass cutter. Follow the traced line, applying an even, downwards pressure on the cutter all the way around the oval. While holding the oval piece, tap along the scratched mark so the glass will break away from the oval. Take your time with this procedure. Use the chipping areas of the glass cutter to chip away any excess from the oval. Check to be certain the oval fits properly in the rabbeted area of the frame. If not, chip away some of the mirror until it fits.

12. Place the mirror in the rabbeted area of the frame. Using white glue, periodically place a spot on the edge of the mirror and on the edge of the rabbet. Don't use too much glue or it will run onto the front of the mirror. Leave the frame lying facedown until the glue is dry.

13. Measure and cut a piece of construction paper to cover the mirror area on the back of the frame. Spread white glue on the edge of the paper and press the paper in place.

48: Recipe Box (Illus. 138 and 139)

While this project may seem a bit complicated, once you study how it is made and assembled, you'll realize it isn't that difficult. With a clear lacquer finish covering the box and an appropriate wood-burned design, it makes a fine gift. The inside of the box is 5¾″ long, 3½″ deep and 3¾″ wide. This is ample space for most recipe cards and other items, if preferred. The box is made from ½″ and ¾″ thick pine. The knob is wooden and can be purchased in most local stores. You may prefer a fancier lid knob. The box can be hung or placed on a countertop.

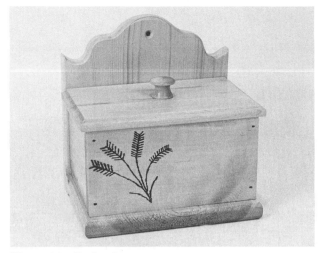

Illus. 138. Recipe box.

Front View

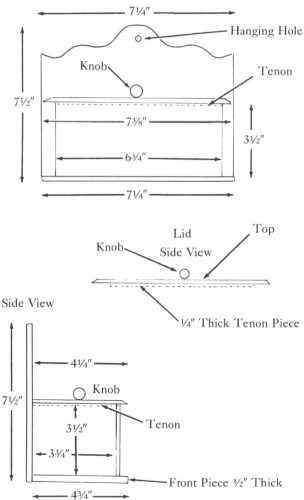

Illus. 139. Drawings of recipe box.

MATERIAL:

- 1″ x 8″ pine
- 1″ x 6″ pine
- Wooden knob
- Construction paper
- Finishing nails
- Wood glue
- Wood filler
- Lacquer

TOOLS:

- Radial arm or table saw
- Band saw
- Scroll or sabre saw
- Electric drill, screw-sink and ⅛″ bit
- Table-mounted router and roundover and cove bits
- Wood-burning set
- Nail set
- Finishing sander

DIRECTIONS:

1. Review Illus. 138 and 139. You may want to modify the design of the back piece or some other part of the project. From construction paper, make a pattern of the top scroll area of the back piece. As indicated, you will need both ½″ and ¾″ thick pine for the project. As you may recall, ¾″ is standard thickness for pine. If you can't buy or have ½″ thick pine planed, resaw your own using a band saw and a ½″ wide blade.

2. Measure and cut the back piece from a 1″ x 8″ pine board. Trace the scroll area on one end of the piece and cut it out using either a scroll or sabre saw. The back piece should be 7½″ long.

3. Measure and cut the bottom piece from a 1″ x 8″ board. As you will note, it should be 4¾″ long and 7¼″ wide, the standard width of a 1″ x 8″ board.

4. Cut the front piece from ½″ thick pine. It is 6¾″ long and 3½″ wide.

5. Cut the two side pieces from ½″ thick stock. As you will note in Illus. 139, the side pieces are 3¾″ long and 3½″ wide.

6. Make the lid from ½″ pine. It should be 7⅜″ long and 4¼″ wide. Don't cut the lid tenon yet.

7. Drill the hanging hole using a screw-sink or

bit and countersink, in the top center of the back piece.

8. Rout the edges of the back and bottom pieces using a roundover bit. Do not rout the edges of the other box pieces.

9. Using a cove bit, rout the top front and side edges of the lid.

10. Glue and nail the bottom piece to the back piece. Note Illus. 139 for placement of the pieces.

11. Nail and glue the front piece to the two side pieces.

12. Secure the box area to the back and bottom pieces using wood glue and finishing nails. Place the assembly so that the overlap is the same on both sides on the bottom piece. Don't let it slide out of place when nailing it.

13. Drive all the nail heads under the surface using a nail set. Rub wood filler in all the nail set holes and allow it to dry.

14. Measure the inside dimensions of the box. These are needed for making the lid tenon. The tenon should fit neatly into the box area, but not too tightly.

15. Using a band saw and a ½″ blade, resaw a piece of pine to a thickness of ¼″. Cut the piece to the length and width needed for the lid tenon. Test the piece for fit in the box area.

16. Center the tenon on the bottom surface of the lid. Glue and nail it, with brads, in place. Check again for fit in the box area.

17. Secure the knob to the middle of the lid.

18. Prepare all the surfaces and edges for finishing using a sander with fine and extra-fine abrasive paper. Wipe off the dust.

19. Draw and wood-burn a design on some location on the box. Note the one on the recipe box shown in Illus. 138. Sand over the design after it is burned into the wood.

20. After wiping the surfaces and edges clean, finish the project with a clear lacquer.

49: Ring Toss Game

(Illus. 140 and 141)

This is a game that people of all ages can play. Rubber rings—the type used for canning

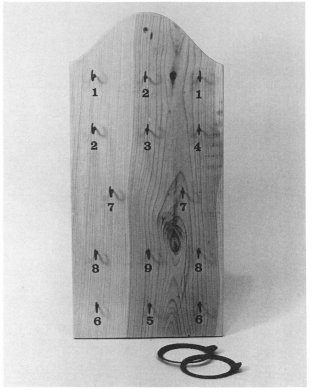

Illus. 140. Ring toss game.

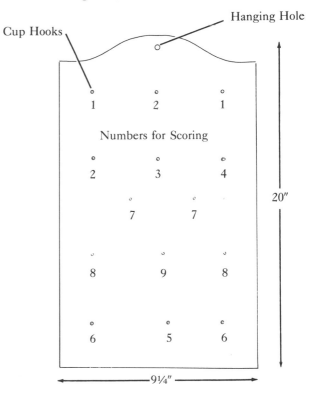

Illus. 141. Drawing of ring toss game.

purposes—are tossed in an attempt to snare them on one of the cup hooks. Each cup hook is worth a certain number of points. Each player begins the game with five rings. Cup hooks are available in hardware or discount stores, as are canning jar rubber rings. The numbers for scoring under each hook are stencilled on. You can assign any value you wish to the hooks. The game is a great gift for the office or shop, and for the young or old. It can be hung up on a wall or leaned against a chair.

MATERIAL:

- 1″ x 10″ pine
- Cup hooks
- Number stencils
- Construction paper
- Stencil paint
- Lacquer

TOOLS:

- Radial arm or table saw
- Scroll or sabre saw
- Electric drill and screw-sink
- Table-mounted router and roundover bit
- Finishing sander

DIRECTIONS:

1. You may want to make a pattern for the top, curved portion of the board. This helps make both sides even.
2. Measure and cut a piece of 1″ x 10″ pine to length. Trace the pattern on the top portion of the board and cut it out. A sabre saw will work fine cutting this project.
3. Measure and mark the locations of the cup hooks. With an awl or sharp nail, make a slight indentation at each mark. This will make it easier to thread the cups into the wood.
4. Drill a hanging hole in the top middle of the board.
5. Rout the edges of the board.
6. Prepare the surfaces and edges for finishing using fine and extra-fine abrasive paper and a sander. Wipe off the dust.
7. Apply several coats of lacquer to the board. Rub the surface with steel wool (0000) between

coats of lacquer. Remove the wool hairs before applying the next coat. By the way, you may prefer painting the board. Finish it the way you want it to look.
8. Thread the cup hooks in place at each indentation.
9. Stencil numbers for points under each hook. Take your time with this task, so the numbers are straight and neat.
10. Using five rubber rings per player, begin the game. Enjoy!

50: *Birds on a Log* (Illus. 142 and 143)

This is a great gift for someone who likes carved birds. It should be made by someone who likes to carve or shape small critters from a piece of hardwood. One bird is shaped from a piece of black walnut, and the other from wild cherry. Scrap pieces of hardwood and a log from the wood pile are all the materials you need for this project. Bent wires, inserted into the birds and a log slice, serve as legs. When properly bent, the wire makes very realistic legs. If you prefer, detail can be carved into each of the birds. A clear lacquer finish makes the birds and log look very professional.

MATERIAL:

- 1″ (4/4's) hardwood scraps
- Fireplace log
- Construction paper
- 1/32″ wire
- White glue
- Lacquer

TOOLS:

- Band saw
- Carving tools or sloyd knife
- Electric grinder
- Rotary or flex-shaft tool
- Carbide burrs
- Sanding sleeves
- Electric drill and 1/32″ bit
- Needle-nose pliers
- Finishing sander

Illus. 142. Birds on a log.

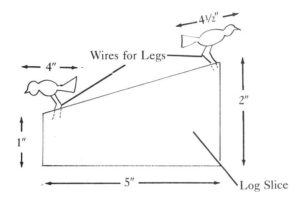

Illus. 143. Drawing of birds on a log.

DIRECTIONS:

1. Make patterns of the birds. You can do better design work with pencil and paper. You may want to increase the size of the birds. Trace the patterns on scrap pieces of hardwood. The scraps should be at least 1″ (4/4's) thick, for the birds.

2. Cut out the traced birds and rough-shape them using a band saw and a ¼″ blade. The band saw is a good tool to remove some of the excess wood. It makes the carving or shaping job much easier. Be careful when using the band saw.

3. Carve or shape the birds using tools of choice. I tend to use an electric grinder with a carbide burr and either a rotary or flex-shaft tool with sanding sleeves. These tools and accessories permit fast removal of wood and easy shaping. You may want to use a sloyd knife or carving tools. Use whatever tool gives you the most satisfaction.

4. If you like, give the birds detail. For example, you may want to carve in a wing area, feathers, eyes, or details of the beak. A finishing sander and extra-fine abrasive paper work well for any final shaping and for surface preparation for finishing.

5. Slice a piece of log that is at least 5″ in diameter and 2″ thick. You may want to use the entire piece or split it in half.

6. Drill angled ¹⁄₃₂″ diameter holes into the body of each bird. The holes should be at least ¼″ deep. These holes will receive the wire that needs to be bent for the legs. Holes should also be drilled into the top of the base where the birds will be placed.

7. Using needle-nose or similar pliers, cut pieces of ¹⁄₃₂″ diameter wire and shape them into bird legs. Allow enough length so that each wire can penetrate the ⅜″ deep holes in both the birds and the base.

8. Remove any dust from the birds and the log base. Finish them with a clear lacquer. Rub the birds with steel wool (0000) between coats. Wipe off the steel hairs before applying more lacquer.

9. Place a dab of white glue on the ends of the leg wires and insert them into the drilled holes on both the birds and base. Allow the glue to dry.

51: *Laminated Cutting Board* (Illus. 144 and 145)

Cutting boards are great gifts. They're not only very functional but, when well-made, can be very attractive. The cutting board shown in Illus. 144 is made from hard maple with strips of green veneer running through it. You may want to change the shape of the board and also the color or type of laminate used. Use waterproof glue on the project, because cutting boards are washed frequently. If you want, a hanging hole to accommodate a piece of buckskin can be drilled through the board. Mineral oil should be used to finish the board.

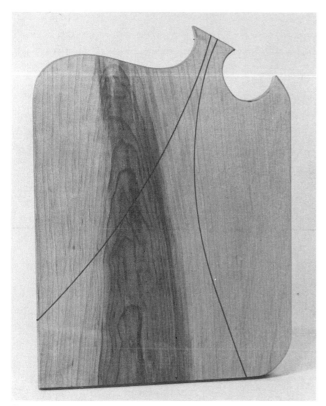

Illus. 144. Laminated cutting board.

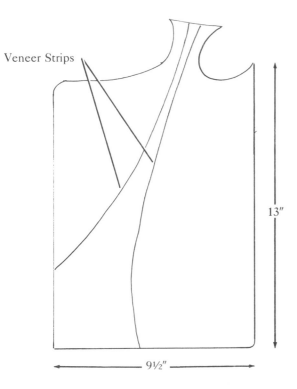

Illus. 145. Drawing of laminated cutting board.

Veneer Strips

13″

9½″

MATERIAL:

- 1″ (4/4's) hard maple
- Green veneer
- Waterproof wood glue
- Mineral oil

TOOLS:

- Band saw or scroll saw
- Table-mounted router and roundover bit
- Clamps
- Finishing and belt sanders

DIRECTIONS:

1. Cut a piece of 1″ (4/4's) thick hard maple to a length of at least 14″ and a width of 9½″.

2. Draw pencil lines on the surface where the veneer will be placed.

3. Cut through the board, following one line. Do not cut on the other line yet.

4. Cut a piece of veneer to a length and width that will fit between the cut pieces of maple. The piece should be a bit wider and longer than needed.

5. Spread waterproof wood glue on the sawed edges of the maple and also on both sides of the piece of veneer. Using several clamps, clamp the assembly tightly together. Make sure that the pieces do not slide apart when being clamped. You may have to maneuver the assembly and the clamps to accomplish this. Wipe off the excess glue that squeezes onto the surface. Allow the glue to dry.

6. Remove the clamps and break or cut off the excess veneer. Also sand away any dried glue that's on the surfaces.

7. Cut through the board along the second pencil line. Cut a piece of veneer to fit into this area. Apply the glue and clamp the veneer until the glue dries.

8. After removing the clamps, clean up the board by removing any excess veneer and glue. You may have to use a coarse-grit abrasive paper to get it all off. Always sand with the wood grain.

9. Draw on the board how you want it shaped. You may want to refer to Illus. 144 to note how that board was shaped. Using either a band or scroll saw, cut the board to shape.

10. Rout all edges of the cutting board using a roundover bit.

11. Using a finishing or belt sander, or both, prepare the surfaces and edges for finishing. Fine and extra-fine abrasive paper should be used to give the board a nice finish. Remove all dust.

12. Apply several coats of mineral oil, with a rag, to a warm board. Let the board sit in the sun or by a heat register, to warm it up. This allows the oil to be absorbed more quickly and more deeply into the board. An occasional reoiling is recommended.

13. If you want, drill a hanging hole through the board.

52: *Sliding Book Rack* (Illus. 146 and 147)

This unusual project is geared for the young student or for someone who wants to display a few special books. As with other projects, you may want to increase or decrease the length of this book rack. Also, the project provides ample surface for any kind of decoration. The rack shown in Illus. 146 has a wood-burned design on its large end piece. You may prefer a painted rack with a stencil or some other decoration. The centerpiece of the rack slides to either accommodate more books or to provide support for those placed on the rack. The end pieces secure the dowels.

MATERIAL:
- 1″ x 8″ pine
- ½″ diameter dowels
- Construction paper
- Wood glue
- Lacquer

TOOLS:
- Radial arm or table saw
- Scroll or sabre saw
- Drill press and ½″ wood bit
- Rotary tool and sanding sleeves
- Table-mounted router and roundover bit
- Wood-burning set
- Finishing sander

Illus. 146. Sliding book rack.

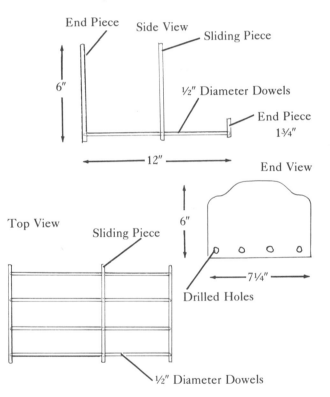

Illus. 147. Drawings of sliding book rack.

DIRECTIONS:

1. Review Illus. 147. As suggested, you may want to modify the size of the project. Using construction paper, make patterns of the large end piece and the sliding piece.

2. Measure and cut the two pieces to the desired length from a 1″ x 8″ pine board.

3. Trace the pattern on the two large pieces and cut them out using either a scroll or sabre saw.

4. Measure and cut the small end piece. The piece should be 7¼″ long and at least 1¾″ high.

5. Cut four ½″ diameter dowels to a length of 12″ unless you are modifying the project's suggested dimensions.

6. Measure and mark the location of the dowel holes on the two end pieces and the centerpiece. Review Illus. 146.

7. With a ½″ diameter bit, drill holes into the two end pieces to a depth of approximately ½″.

8. Drill ½″ diameter holes through the centerpiece. The dowels need to pass through this piece.

9. Using sanding sleeves and a rotary tool, widen the centerpiece holes so that the centerpiece can slide easily on the dowels.

10. Rout the edges of the pieces using a round-over bit.

11. If you plan to wood-burn a design on the surface of the two large pieces, do it before assembling the rack.

12. Prepare all the surfaces for finishing using fine and extra-fine abrasive paper. Remove the dust, especially from the drilled holes.

13. Finish the various pieces with a clear lacquer. It's best to finish everything before assembling the project.

14. Spread glue into the drilled holes in the large end piece and tap the dowels in place. Allow the glue to dry.

15. Slide the centerpiece onto the dowels. You may have to scrape excess lacquer from the drilled holes. The piece should slide easily along the dowels. If necessary, rub some paste wax on the dowels and polish them.

16. Spread glue into the drilled holes in the small end piece and tap the dowels in place. Allow the glue to dry.

53: *Foot Stool* (Illus. 148 and 149)

A traditional foot stool is always an enjoyed and much-used gift. The stool described and shown here is the traditional Early American eight-board stool that can be made in any size. If you're so inclined, design can be transformed into a bench

Illus. 148. Foot stool.

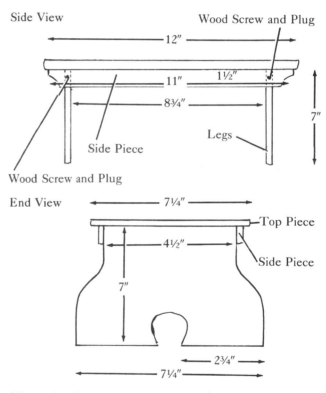

Illus. 149. Drawing of foot stool.

design. While the stool can be used to stand on, it is best used as a place to rest feet or for sitting. Stools that are stood on have a tendency to tip over. The stool shown in Illus. 148 is stained and finished with lacquer. You may prefer a clear finish or, better yet, a painted finish with several stencils painted on the top surface.

MATERIAL:

- 1″ x 8″ pine
- Wood glue
- Wood screws
- Screw plugs
- Construction paper
- Stain and Lacquer

TOOLS:

- Radial arm or table saw
- Scroll or sabre saw
- Table-mounted router and roundover bit
- Electric drill, screw bit, and ½″ wood bit
- Finishing sander

DIRECTIONS:

1. Review Illus. 149. To ensure uniformity of parts, it's best to make a pattern for the legs and the side pieces. Make the patterns to size using construction paper.

2. Measure and cut the top piece from 1″ x 8″ pine.

3. Trace two legs from the leg pattern on a 1″ x 8″ board and cut them out with a radial arm or table saw. Use a scroll or sabre saw to cut the circle area on the bottom of the legs.

4. Using the side piece pattern, trace two side pieces onto the surface of a 1″ x 8″ board. Cut the pieces out using a scroll or sabre saw.

5. Rout the edges of the stool parts using a round-over bit. Do not rout those edges that will be attached to another part. For example, do not rout the back edges or the top edges of the side pieces because they will be attached to the top piece and the legs. You want as much surface as possible for the joint.

6. Measure and mark the location of the screw holes in the two side pieces. The screws will attach the side pieces to the two legs. You may want to refer to Illus. 149 to note how the side pieces and legs relate to one another. The screw holes should be drilled with a ½″ diameter wood bit and should be at least ⅜″ deep. This assumes that you will be using ½″ diameter screw plugs that have a ⅜″ long tenon. Drill two holes in each side piece.

7. Assemble the side pieces and legs using wood screws and glue. Make sure that the legs are straight in the assembly.

8. Place the assembly on the top surface of the top piece and mark the location of the screw holes using the top end of the legs as a guide. Also, mark the location of one screw hole for each side piece. Drill two ½″ diameter holes ⅜″ deep for each leg, and one hole for each side piece.

9. Spread wood glue on the top ends of the legs and the top edges of the side pieces. Center the top piece on the legs–side piece assembly. Thread wood screws in place and allow the glue to dry. You may want to use an electric drill and screw set to drive in the wood screws.

10. Place a drop of wood glue in each of the screw holes and tap a wooden screw plug in place. Allow the glue to dry.

11. Using a finishing sander and fine and extra-fine abrasive paper, prepare all surfaces and edges for finishing. Wipe off all dust.

12. Stain the stool. When the stain is dry, apply a clear lacquer finish to the stool. If you prefer, omit the stain and finish the stool with a clear lacquer finish or paint the stool and decorate it with stencils.

54: *Lath Art Owl* (Illus. 150–152)

This is one of those very special gifts that requires some extra time and effort, but is well worth it. The recipient of the lath art owl will be thrilled. This project was designed, crafted and painted by Jerry and Becky Lipchik. It represents the first of several lath art gift projects in this book that you may want to consider crafting. They're great fun to make and to paint. As you may know, lath art has become extremely popular in recent years. Once you figure out how to make this type of art, you can begin the fun process of designing your own. The lath that is used is 1½″ wide, ⅜″ thick, and is generally available at local lumberyards. Normally, it's available in 36″ lengths and is relatively inexpensive. You will find that latex stains and/or paints work best for finishing the lath.

Front View Side View

Sawtooth Hanger

Top Lath

11½"

1½"

Eyeball

10"

Bcak

8¾"

11¾"

Side Lath

Bottom Lath

Wing   Feet   Wing

Illus. 150 (above). Lath art owl. Illus. 151 (right). Drawing of lath art owl. Illus. 152 (below). Drawings of lath art owl parts.

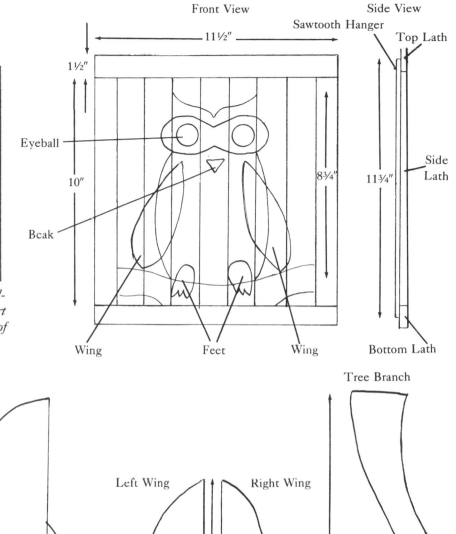

Tree Branch

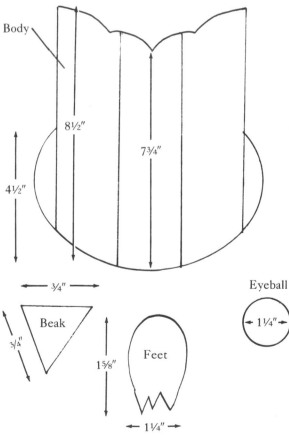

Body

8½"

7¾"

4½"

¾"

Beak

¾"

Feet

1⅝"

1¼"

Eyeball

1¼"

Left Wing   Right Wing

1½"

4"

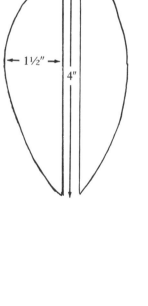

8½"

1¼"

MATERIAL:

- 1½" x ⅜" lath
- ⅝" No. 19 brads
- Construction paper
- Wood glue
- Sawtooth hanger
- Latex stains (brown, sky-blue, and white)
- Latex paints

TOOLS:

- Radial arm or table saw
- Scroll, sabre, or coping saw
- Try or steel square

DIRECTIONS:

1. Review Illus. 150–152. In addition to the frame and backing laths, each part of the owl must be separately made. Using construction paper, make full-size patterns of each body piece of the owl. Save the patterns because you may decide to make another one of these projects in the future.

2. Measure and cut laths for the frame. You will need two pieces for the top and bottom that are 11½" long. The two side pieces are 10" long. Unlike other projects, you should stain the parts as they are cut.

3. Stain the four frame pieces with a brown latex stain.

4. Measure and cut seven pieces of lath that are 11¾" long. These laths are for the background of the picture. They will be attached to the back of the frame.

5. Stain the seven background pieces with a sky-blue latex stain.

6. When the sky-blue stain is dry, brush on white stain or latex paint very lightly on the front surfaces of the background laths.

7. Allow the paint to dry.

8. Place the frame pieces together, front surfaces down. The back pieces, as indicated in the side view drawing in Illus. 151, extend to the middle of the top, bottom, and side pieces. Spread a bead of wood glue on the bottom half of the top piece and the top half of the bottom piece. Spread a bead of glue on the inside half of both side pieces. Place the seven back pieces, white-painted surfaces facing the front of the frame, on the glued surfaces, one next to the other. Nail them in place using ⅝" long brads. Allow the glue to dry.

9. Using the patterns prepared for the various body parts, trace and cut out the pieces using a scroll, sabre, or coping saw.

10. Paint the pieces as follows:

Body: Stain the body pieces brown and then sponge-streak them with an off-white stain or latex paint. By the way, you only have to finish one side of the pieces. On every area except the ears, stencil-brush on an off-white stain or paint and then a light brown. This will give the body a feathery appearance.

Wings: Stain or paint the two wings an off-white and then sponge-streak them with a dark-brown stain.

Beak: Paint the beak a school-bus yellow. Use a latex paint.

Feet: Paint the feet black, with school-bus yellow claws. Again, use latex paint.

Eyes: Paint the large circles white. Paint dry, black streaks all around the large circles. Paint the small circles black.

Tree Branch: Stain the branch a dark-brown and then sponge-streak it with black.

11. Using wood glue and ⅝" long brads, assemble the owl parts onto the sky-blue background pieces. Refer to Illus. 150 and 151 to note the placement of the various parts. When all the parts are in place, allow the glue to dry.

12. Nail a sawtooth hanger to the middle of the back of the top piece.

55: *Flower Pot Shelf* (Illus. 153 and 154)

Designed to hang and display small flowers or plants in pots, the shelf can also be used to showcase other pieces. To prevent any of the displayed pieces from falling off the shelf, a dowel runs the entire length of the project. This is a gift for someone who needs a specific kind of shelf for a certain location. As always, you may want to redesign the shelf to fit a particular location. It

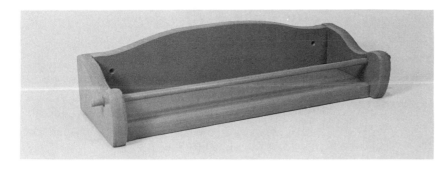

Illus. 153. Flower pot shelf.

Front View

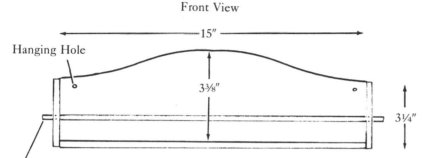

Hanging Hole

15″

3⅜″

3¼″

⅜″ Diameter Dowel: 18″ Long

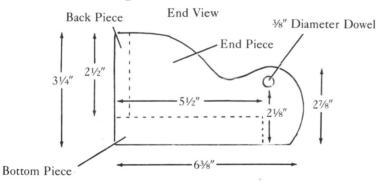

Back Piece

End View

⅜″ Diameter Dowel

End Piece

3¼″

2½″

5½″

2⅛″

2⅞″

6⅜″

Bottom Piece

Illus. 154. Drawings of flower pot shelf.

can also be enlarged to hold larger items. The project shelf has been painted, but you may want to consider a clear lacquer finish. Decorative touches on the back piece would be covered up by whatever is displayed on the shelf; thus, they should be omitted.

MATERIAL:
- 1″ x 4″ pine
- 1″ x 6″ pine
- ⅜″ diameter dowel
- Construction paper
- Wood glue
- Finishing nails
- Paint

TOOLS:
- Radial arm or table saw
- Scroll or sabre saw
- Electric drill, screw-sink, and ⅜″ bit
- Table-mounted router with roundover bit
- Finishing sander

DIRECTIONS:
1. Review Illus. 154. Make a pattern of the end pieces to actual size.
2. Measure and cut the back piece from a 1″ x 4″ pine board. The piece should be 15″ long.
3. Mark the top center of the back piece. Both ends of the top piece should be 2½″ high. Make a pattern or draw, freehand, curved lines from

the center point of the back piece to its ends. The curved lines should end at the 2½″ mark on the ends of the piece. Using a scroll or sabre saw, cut along the curved lines on the back piece.

4. Measure, mark and drill a hanging hole at both ends of the back piece. Note the placement of the holes in Illus. 154.

5. Measure and cut the bottom piece from a 1″ x 6″ pine board. As indicated in Illus. 154, the piece should be 5½″ wide, the exact width of a 1″ x 6″ board.

6. Using the end-piece pattern, trace two ends onto a piece of 1″ x 4″ pine. Cut the ends using a scroll or sabre saw.

7. Measure and mark the location of the dowel holes on both end pieces. Note the placement dimensions in Illus. 154.

8. Drill a ⅜″ diameter hole, where marked, through both end pieces.

9. Rout the top edges of the back piece and the front edges of the bottom piece with a roundover bit. The outside edges of the side pieces and a portion of the inside edges should also be routed. Don't rout edges that will be joined to other parts.

10. Prepare all surfaces for finishing using fine and extra-fine abrasive paper and a finishing sander.

11. Glue and nail the back piece to the top of the back of the bottom piece. Note its placement in Illus. 154.

12. Glue and nail the end pieces onto the back of the bottom of the assembly. Allow the glue to dry.

13. Measure and cut a ⅜″ diameter dowel to a length of 18″. Lightly round the edge on the ends of the dowel.

14. Place a dab of wood glue in the ⅜″ diameter holes in the end pieces and force the dowel through the holes. The dowel should extend equally on both ends. Wipe off any glue that gets on the dowel.

15. Wipe off any dust from the shelf. Paint the shelf or, if you prefer, finish it with a clear lacquer.

56: *Letter Opener* (Illus. 155 and 156)

This gift consists of a plain, brass letter opener dressed up with an attractive handle and decorative plugs. Placed on a desk, it quickly becomes a conversation piece. Also, the recipient of the gift will be inclined to expend nervous energy by playing with the opener. It's one of those things that's hard not to pick up and play with. Best of all, the wood used can be any piece of hardwood scrap you may have lying around. While the letter opener shown in Illus. 155 has a hard maple handle, you may have some red oak or walnut that you would rather use. By the way, brass letter openers can be purchased through mail-order suppliers or, in some instances, from a discount store or stationery supplier.

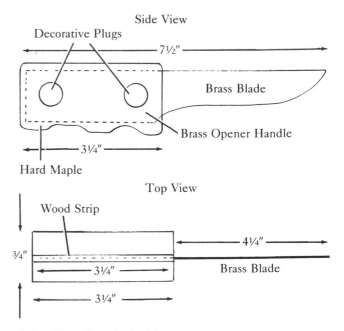

Illus. 155. Letter opener.

Illus. 156. Drawings of letter opener.

MATERIAL:
- ¾″ thick hardwood scrap
- Brass letter opener
- Epoxy glue
- Wood glue
- Lacquer

TOOLS:
- Band saw
- Electric grinder, rotary tool, or flex-shaft tool
- Carbide burrs
- Sanding sleeves
- Drill press and ½″ plug cutter
- Electric drill and ½″ wood bit
- Finishing sander

DIRECTIONS:
1. Measure and cut a piece of ¾″ thick hardwood to a length of 3¼″. As indicated, the handle for the letter opener shown in Illus. 155 is made from hard maple. You may prefer a different wood or have some other hardwood scrap available.

2. Measure the thickness and width of the letter-opener handle.

3. On the top edge of the hardwood handle, measure and make two lines reflecting the thickness of the letter-opener handle. On one end of the hardwood handle, make a mark indicating the width of the letter opener handle plus ⅛″. In other words, the top edge of the letter opener handle should be ⅛″ below the top edge of the wood handle. Note Illus. 156. This is the area where you will place a decorative strip.

4. Using a band saw and fence, with the hardwood handle standing on its unmarked end, align the fence and blade with one of the lines on the top edge of the handle. Saw through the handle at the line, stopping at the mark on the handle end.

5. Realign the band-saw fence and cut through the other line, again stopping at the mark on the handle end.

6. While holding the handle, carefully saw out the piece of wood that remains in the sawed area. Clean up the inside bottom of the cut with the band-saw blade. Take your time with this procedure and, as always, be careful.

7. Place the letter opener handle in the cut groove and check its fit. The top of the letter opener handle should be recessed at least ⅛″ below the top edge of the wooden handle. Remove any dust from the sawed area.

8. Measure and cut a strip of contrasting hardwood that will fit over the letter opener handle in the sawed groove. It should be the length of the handle, the thickness of the groove, and at least ¼″ wide. It should extend above the groove. It will be grounded down later. The letter opener handle in Illus. 155 has a black maple strip that contrasts nicely with the hard maple handle. If you have it, use padauk or some other scrap of exotic wood.

9. Mix two-part epoxy. Make sure you read the precautions before using the epoxy. The letter opener handle has to be glued into the wooden handle. You need enough epoxy to secure the letter opener handle in the sawed groove. Epoxy also needs to be placed above the letter opener handle and on the walls of the groove. Place the letter opener handle in the wooden handle and tap the decorative strip into the groove. Carefully wipe off any excess epoxy that squeezes out. Handle this glue with care. Allow the epoxy ample time to dry.

10. Measure and mark the location of ½″ diameter decorative plugs on each side of the handle. Drill plug holes to a depth of at least ⅜″.

11. Using a ½″ diameter plug cutter secured in a drill press, make enough decorative plugs for the letter opener handle.

12. Place a dab of glue in the drilled holes and tap a decorative plug in place. Allow the glue to dry.

13. Secure a carbide burr in an electric grinder, rotary tool, or flex-shaft tool, and begin the shaping process. Note in Illus. 155 and 156 how finger indentations are made in the bottom edge of the handle. Shape the handle until it feels comfortable in your hand. Grind the strip on the top of the handle and also the decorative plugs flush with the surface. Use sanding sleeves to shape the handle, but also to begin preparing its surface for finishing. Be careful when shaping that you don't hit the brass blade with the burrs or sand-

ing sleeves. Note from Illus. 155 and 156 how the back of the letter-opener handle shows at the back of the wooden handle. Be sure the two are flush. The brass should show. This assures the user that the brass does extend through the entire handle and that he or she has a well-made opener.

14. When the handle is shaped to your satisfaction, go over it with a finishing sander and fine and extra-fine abrasive papers. Prepare the surface for finishing. Wipe off the finishing dust.

15. Apply several coats of clear lacquer to the handle, rubbing the surface, between coats, with steel wool (0000).

57: *Bear Lamp* (Illus. 157 and 158)

The bear lamp will make a fine addition to a child's room. Lamps are easy to make, especially given the availability of electric components. You can either buy the lamp parts separately or, if you prefer, purchase lamp kits with everything in them, including a cord and plug. Wiring a lamp is easy and the kits usually include step-by-step directions for you to follow. The bear lamp shown in Illus. 157 is made from a 2″ x 10″ fir plank and is supported on a 9″ diameter round piece of pine. The round piece gives the lamp more stability, but also makes the entire project more attractive. Blue marbles are used for eyes on the project. The base is painted green, and the actual bear is light blue. You may want to paint detail on your bear lamp. Use your imagination when finishing the project. By the way, if you want, why not make a cat lamp instead of a bear lamp?

MATERIAL:
- 2″ x 10″ fir
- 1″ x 10″ pine
- Marbles
- Construction paper
- Lamp kit or components
- Wood screws
- Wood glue
- Electrical insulated staples
- Paint

Illus. 157. Bear lamp.

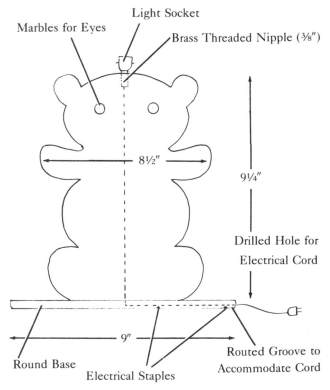

Front View

Light Socket

Marbles for Eyes

Brass Threaded Nipple (³⁄₈″)

8½″

9¼″

Drilled Hole for Electrical Cord

Round Base

Electrical Staples

Routed Groove to Accommodate Cord

9″

Illus. 158. Drawing of bear lamp.

TOOLS:

- Radial arm or table saw
- Band saw
- Scroll saw
- Table-mounted router and roundover and ⅜″ straight bits
- Drill press and ⅜″ bit
- 12″ lamp or airplane bit
- Electric drill and screw set
- School compass
- Finishing sander

DIRECTIONS:

1. Review Illus. 157 and 158, noting the design and dimensions of the project. Using construction paper, make a full-size pattern of the bear.
2. Measure and cut a piece of 2″ x 10″ plank. Trace the bear pattern on the surface of the piece. Cut out the bear using either a band or scroll saw.
3. Measure and cut a 10″ long piece of a 1″ x 10″ board. Using a school compass, make a 9″ diameter circle on the piece. Cut the round piece out using a scroll or band saw.
4. Rout the edges of the bear and also the round piece with a roundover bit.
5. Measure and mark the middle of the top of the bear. Assuming the brass nipple that will hold the light socket is ⅜″ in diameter, drill a ⅜″ diameter hole at the mark. If you have a long lamp bit that will drill through the entire length of the bear, drill the hole with it. If you have a shorter bit, drill as far as you can, again from the top. Measure and mark the middle location on the bottom edge of the bear. Drill upwards through the bear until you reach the hole extending from the top. You need a hole for the electrical cord that runs through the bear.
6. Where the school-compass point made its indentation, drill a hole through the round base.
7. With a ⅜″ straight bit in the router, rout, with the grain, a groove in the bottom surface of the round piece. The groove should run from the drilled hole to the edge of the piece. The groove should be deep enough to accommodate the electrical cord. Take your time with this procedure. You may have to make several passes with the router in order to achieve the needed depth.

8. Measure and mark the location of the eyes. Using a ⅜″ drill bit, make indentations at the marks that will accommodate the marbles. After finishing the bear, you will glue the marbles into these indentations.
9. Glue and screw the round base piece to the bottom of the bear. The drilled holes have to be in alignment. The screws should penetrate from the bottom of the round piece and into the bear.
10. Thread the electrical cord through the hole in the round base and up through the bear. Slip the cord through the ⅜″ brass nipple and tap it into the drilled hole at the top of the bear. Be careful that you don't damage the cord.
11. Strip the cord wires and attach them to the light socket as per the directions that accompany the lamp kit. Follow the instructions carefully, so no shocks result from a faulty wiring job.
12. Using electrical insulated staples, staple the cord inside the routed groove on the bottom of the round base. Be careful not to staple through the cord.
13. Secure a light bulb in the lamp and test your wiring.
14. Prepare all surfaces for finishing. Wipe off the sanding dust that results from using abrasive paper.
15. Paint the base and the bear. If you prefer, do some detail work on the bear. For example, you may want to paint on a nose, mouth, and other details.
16. When the paint is dry, dab some white glue in the eye indentations. With the bear lying on its back, place the marbles into the indentations and allow the glue to dry.
17. Buy a lampshade that is the appropriate size and appearance for the lamp. If using a large lampshade, you may want to add a lamp harp to the light socket.

58: Birdhouse with Tin Roof (Illus. 159 and 160)

Everybody enjoys sleeping under a tin roof when there is a rainstorm. Why not the birds? This

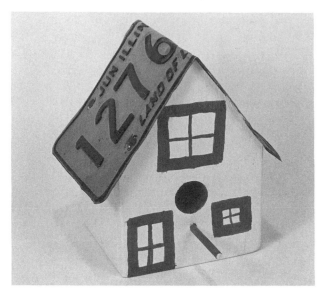

Illus. 159. Birdhouse with tin roof.

Front View

License Plate Roof

8"

4⅜"

1¼" Entry Hole

Perch ¼"
Diameter Dowel

← 5½" →

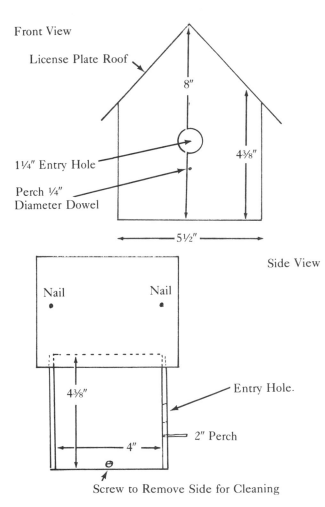

Side View

Nail   Nail

4⅜"

Entry Hole.

4"   2" Perch

Screw to Remove Side for Cleaning

Illus. 160. Drawings of birdhouse with tin roof.

house, using an old license plate for a roof, will be a gift enjoyed by both the recipient and the birds that get to live in it. It is designed for one of the smaller birds, but can be made larger, if you prefer. Oddly enough, many people seem to be collecting and displaying birdhouses in their own homes these days. If you like, paint some windows and a door on the house. If it will be used for birds, use screws to hold the bottom piece in place; this way, you can remove the bottom piece to clean the house. Even birds need their houses cleaned.

MATERIAL:

- ½" thick pine
- License plate
- ¼" diameter dowel
- Wood screws
- Shingle nails
- Finishing nails
- Waterproof wood glue
- Paint

TOOLS:

- Radial arm or table saw
- Band saw
- Drill press and Forstner or 1¼" multi-spur bit
- Electric drill and ¼" bit
- Finishing sander

DIRECTIONS:

1. Review Illus. 160. As indicated, you will need ½" thick pine for crafting the birdhouse. It should be 6" wide and ½" thick.
2. Measure, lay out and cut the front and back pieces of the birdhouse. As you might guess, the two pieces need to be exactly the same.
3. Measure and mark the locations of the entry hole and the perch on the front piece. Drill a 1¼" diameter entry hole where marked, and a ¼" diameter hole for the dowel perch.
4. Measure and cut two side pieces to the dimensions given in Illus. 160.
5. Using waterproof wood glue and finishing nails, assemble the front, back, and side pieces.
6. Measure the opening in the bottom of the house and cut a piece that will fit inside it.

7. Secure the bottom piece in place with a wood screw. The screw should penetrate each side piece and extend into the bottom piece. The screw can be removed, thus allowing the bottom piece to be removed when the birdhouse has to be cleaned.

8. Measure and cut a piece of ¼″ diameter dowel and glue it into the drilled hole. The perch should be about 2″ long.

9. Prepare the surfaces for finishing using abrasive paper and a finishing sander. Wipe off all the finishing dust.

10. Paint and decorate the birdhouse. If it's going to be hung outside, use outside paint on it. Have fun painting it. Make it look like a house.

11. The license plate has to be bent in the middle. Mark the middle and bend it over a straight edge of some kind. Bend it to the angle needed to fit onto the birdhouse. Place the license plate roof on the house and nail it down with finishing nails.

59: *Windowsill Flower Box* (Illus. 161 and 162)

This project is designed to sit, inside, on a windowsill and be filled with pots of flowers. Its sides are cut at an angle so it looks more attractive. It's the kind of gift for someone who enjoys house plants and wants them displayed around the house. Plants are often set on a windowsill, but this box gives the user the opportunity to place them there in a more organized fashion. It is also a more attractive way to display plants, because the pots are not visible. The sill box can be made to fit any windowsill. It's a good project to paint and add some stencils to.

MATERIAL:
- ½″ thick pine
- Construction paper
- Wood glue
- Wood filler
- Finishing nails
- Paint

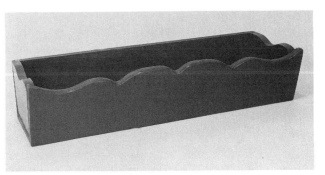

Illus. 161. Windowsill flower box.

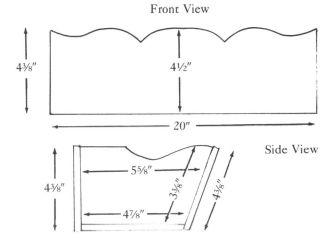

Illus. 162. Drawings of windowsill flower box.

TOOLS:
- Radial arm or table saw
- Band saw
- Scroll or sabre saw
- Table-mounted router
- Nail set
- Finishing sander

DIRECTIONS:
1. As indicated, you need ½″ thick pine for the project. If you can plane an 8′ long, 1″ x 6″ pine board to a ½″ thickness, you should have adequate wood for the project. If you have to, resaw a pine board on the band saw using a ½″ wide blade. In a pinch, you can always make the box from standard-thickness pine.

2. Prepare a pattern of the scrolls for the front piece. Also, prepare a pattern for the side pieces.

3. Measure and cut the front piece to length.

Trace the scroll pattern onto the top area of the board. Cut out the scroll area using either a scroll or sabre saw.

4. Measure and cut the back piece. As indicated in Illus. 162, the back piece is 20″ long and 4⅜″ wide or high.

5. Trace the side-piece pattern on ½″ stock and make two side pieces. Cut them out using a scroll or sabre saw. Make sure the top and bottom lengths are different and reflect the project dimensions. This is what will give the front piece its angled appearance.

6. Measure and cut the bottom piece to a length of 20″. The width of the piece should be 4⅞″, but its front edge should be cut at an angle. The angle on the side pieces should be continued down onto the ends of the bottom piece. This can be drawn freehand. Cut the front edge of the bottom piece at the drawn angle using a band saw. Adjust the band saw to cut the required angle.

7. Rout the top scroll edges of the front piece with a roundover bit. You do not have to rout any other edges on this project.

8. Using wood glue and finishing nails, attach the back piece to the bottom piece. Note in Illus. 162 how they should be assembled.

9. Glue and nail the end pieces to the back and bottom pieces.

10. Glue and nail the front piece to the assembly. Drive all the nail heads under the wood's surface using a nail set. Fill the holes with wood filler.

11. Prepare the surfaces and edges for finishing using a finishing sander and fine and extra-fine abrasive paper. Sand over the wood-filled areas. Wipe off all the sanding dust.

12. Paint the sill box and decorate the front piece with stencils or some other design. The box shown in Illus. 161 was painted dark green.

60: *Bird Tree* (Illus. 163 and 164)

This project will prove a joy to bird carvers, and a delight to the person receiving it as a gift. As Illus. 163 indicates, it's a branch filled with 12

Illus. 163. Bird tree.

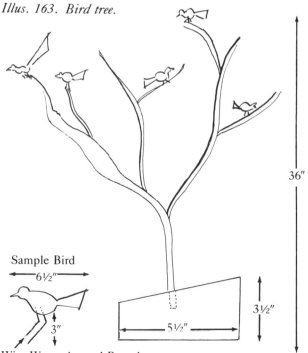

36″

Sample Bird

6½″

3″

5½″

3½″

Wire Wraps Around Branches

Illus. 164. Drawing of bird tree.

birds that are all painted different colors and have different designs. Each bird has two wire legs that wrap around a branch and hold it in place. The tree or branch is secured to a log slice that is heavy and large enough to support everything. While you may strive for ornithological accuracy, I choose instead to have a good time making a collection of wild-looking birds. They are painted and decorated unlike any birds you have ever seen. The birds are cut from a standard pine board, and the tree is a branch from my backyard. The log slice is from my backyard wood pile.

MATERIAL:
- 1″ x 6″ pine
- Tree branch
- Construction paper
- 1/32″ thick wire
- White glue
- Log slice
- Paint

TOOLS:
- Band saw
- Scroll or sabre saw
- Electric grinder, rotary tool, or flex-shaft tool
- Carbide burrs and sanding sleeves
- Carving tools
- Electric drill and 1/32″ and 1/2″ bits
- Long-nose pliers
- Finishing sander

DIRECTIONS:
1. While you may want to draw some or all of the birds freehand onto the wood's surface, patterns also should be made. When you make patterns, you're forced to spend more time drawing the object the way you want it to appear. The project birds vary in size from a 3″ long wren-like creature to one that is 8″ long. Use your own judgement as to the desired lengths and overall shapes of the birds. If necessary, look in a bird book for some ideas. You may want to check the profiles of various birds. Make as many different patterns and birds as you want in your tree.

2. Trace the patterns, with the wood grain, onto the surface of a 1″ x 6″ pine board. Maximize the area on the board by filling it with traced and freehand-drawn birds. Again, make as many birds as you think you will need in the bird tree.

3. Cut out the traced and drawn birds using a scroll saw, sabre saw, or a band saw and a 1/4″ wide blade.

4. Use a band saw for some initial wood removal and shaping of the birds. It's easier to saw off some of the excess wood than it is to grind or carve it off. Be careful with this procedure.

5. Shape the birds with a tool of choice. The electric grinder and a carbide burr is a great way to shape the birds. The same results can be accomplished using a rotary or a flex-shaft tool and smaller carbide burrs. It may take a bit longer, but you can also do detail work with these smaller tools and burrs. If you prefer, using carving knives and tools.

6. Sanding sleeves can be used to shape and also prepare the surface for finishing. A finishing sander can also be used to prepare the surfaces for painting. If you want, sanders with a coarse-grit abrasive also work well for shaping the birds.

7. When you have finished shaping and carving the birds, drill two 1/32″ diameter holes into the bottom of each bird. The holes should be at least 3/8″ deep.

8. Cut two 1/32″ diameter wires 3″ long for each bird. Place a dab of white glue on the end of each wire and insert the wire into the drilled holes in the birds. Allow the glue to dry.

9. Paint and decorate all the birds. Be creative.

10. While the paint is drying on the birds, find a tree branch with lots of smaller branches on it. The branch should be approximately 36″ long.

11. Using a band saw, cut a slice of log that has an approximate diameter of 5½″. The log should be at least 3½″ thick.

12. Drill a 1/2″ diameter hole into the middle of the log slice. Whittle the end of the branch so that it will fit tightly into the drilled hole.

13. Place the birds in the tree by wiring them to a branch. You may want to refer to Illus. 163.

61: Flower Pot Holder (Illus. 165 and 166)

This is a gift for the person who likes to hang plants in his house. It is designed so that a 4″ flower pot can be placed in the large hole in the front piece of the holder. This is shown in Illus. 166. The back piece of the holder has sufficient surface for either a wood-burned or a stencilled decoration. The holder shown in Illus. 165 has cattails wood-burned into the back piece surface.

MATERIAL:
- 1″ x 8″ pine
- Construction paper
- Wood glue
- Finishing nails
- Lacquer

TOOLS:
- Radial arm or table saw
- Band saw
- Scroll or sabre saw
- Table-mounted router and roundover bit
- Drill press, circle cutter, screw-sink
- Clamp
- School compass
- Wood-burning set
- Finishing sander

DIRECTIONS:
1. Review Illus. 166. You may want to make a pattern for the side pieces and the front piece. Also, make a pattern of the back piece and its scroll.
2. Measure and cut the back piece from a 1″ x 8″ pine board. Trace the scroll pattern on the top portion of the piece and cut it out using a scroll or sabre saw.
3. Trace two side pieces, using a pattern, onto the surface of a pine board. Align the pattern so that the backs of the side pieces will be the edges of the board. Make sure that the bottom of each side piece and the front edge that will join the front piece all have a straight edge. Refer to Il-

Illus. 165. Hanging flower pot holder.

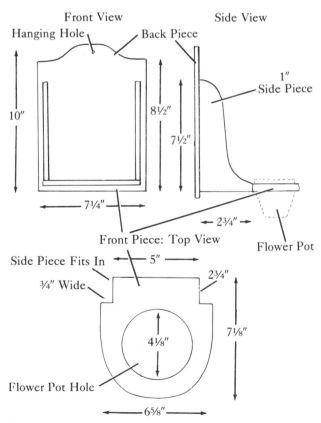

Illus. 166. Drawings of hanging flower pot holder.

lus. 166 and note how the side piece fits into the other pieces.

4. If a pattern was made for the front piece, trace it, with the wood's grain, onto the surface of a 1″ x 8″ board. Cut out the two areas where the side pieces will fit with a band saw.

5. Using a school compass, draw a 4⅛″ diameter circle on the surface of the front piece. Secure the circle cutter in the drill press and set it to cut a 4⅛″ diameter circle. Clamp the front piece to the drill-press table. The center indentation made by the school compass point should be under the circle cutter's drill bit. Cut out the circle. If you do not have a drill press, drill a hole through the circle in the front piece and cut out the area using a sabre saw.

6. Rout all the edges, including those on the pot hole in the front piece, using a roundover bit. Don't rout any of the edges that will be joined to another piece. For example, don't rout the back edges of the two side pieces.

7. Measure and drill a hanging hole in the top of the middle of the back piece.

8. Using wood glue and finishing nails, attach the two side pieces to the front piece.

9. Spread glue on the backs of the side pieces and the back edge of the front piece. Place the assembly on the back piece and nail it. Finishing nails should be driven from the back of the back piece and into the side pieces. Make sure the assembly is centered on the back piece. There should be about a ⅜″ overlap on each side of the back piece.

10. Draw a design on the front of the back piece and wood-burn it.

11. Using a finishing sander, along with fine and extra-fine abrasive paper, prepare all the surfaces and edges for finishing. Sand over the wood-burned design to clean it up. Remove all the dust.

12. Finish the holder with a clear lacquer. Use several coats, and rub each coat with steel wool (0000). Remove the wool hairs before applying an additional coat.

62: *Playing Card Holder*
(Illus. 167 and 168)

Here is a handy device that will appeal to anyone who plays cards. It provides a place on which to place cards. This will prove especially helpful to children who like to play different card games but whose hands are too small to hold the cards. The holder shown in Illus. 167 is made from a piece of wild cherry. You may prefer some other hardwood or, if necessary, a piece of pine can be used. You may want to make several of these holders for gifts. As always, feel free to change the dimensions of the project. Maybe someone needs an especially long holder for a particular card game.

Illus. 167. *Playing card holder.*

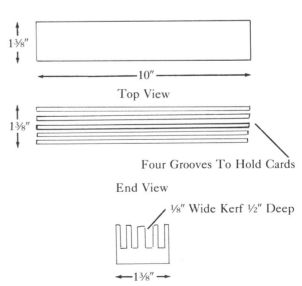

Illus. 168. *Drawings of playing card holder.*

109

MATERIAL:
- 1½" (6/4's) thick piece of hardwood
- Lacquer

TOOLS:
- Table saw
- Belt or finishing sander

DIRECTIONS:
1. Measure and cut a piece of 1⅜" (approximate) thick hardwood to a length of 10". The holder shown in Illus. 167 is made from wild cherry, but you may prefer some other hardwood. If you want, the project can also be made from a piece of 2" thick pine or fir.
2. Cut the slots that hold the cards using a table saw and fence. Use a push stick for making the cuts. Cut four slots, ½" deep, the full length of the holder. The kerf cut by the table-saw blade is approximately ⅛" wide.
3. Measure and mark the location of the card slots on one end of the holder. Place the holder on the table saw and adjust the fence so that the blade aligns with the first mark. Set the blade to cut to a depth of ½". Make the first slot by pushing the holder, held tightly against the fence, over the blade with a push stick. Repeat the aligning and sawing process until the four slots have been cut.
4. Prepare the surfaces of the holder for finishing with fine and extra-fine abrasive papers and a finishing or belt sander.
5. Apply several coats of lacquer to the holder.

63: *Fish on a Stick II* (Illus. 169 and 170)

A colorful and fun project to make, fish on a stick are always a welcomed gift. Fish decoys and wooden plugs have become popular collectibles in recent years. The two fish shown in Illus. 169 will make some collector friend very happy. The fish are shaped from standard pine, but their fins are pieces of aluminum. You can also use tin from a can or any other kind of sheet metal you

Illus. 169. Fish on a stick II.

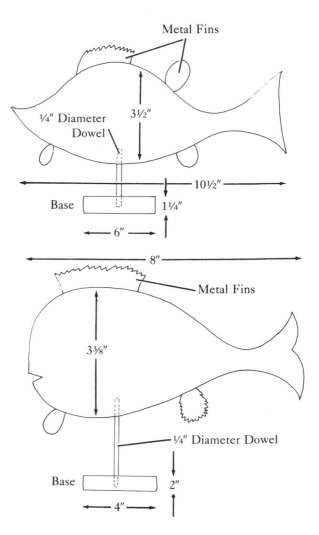

Illus. 170. Drawings of fish on a stick II.

can find. The real fun, in addition to making the fish, is in the painting and decorating. The fish shown in Illus. 169 are painted green, yellow, black and white. Fish this colorful dwell only in the depths of the sea.

MATERIAL:
- 1″ x 6″ pine
- Construction paper
- Aluminum or tin
- ¼″ dowels
- Log slices
- White glue
- Paint

TOOLS:
- Scroll or sabre saw
- Band saw
- Hobby knife
- Tin snips or scissors
- Electric drill and ¼″ bit
- Electric grinder, rotary tool, or flex-shaft tool
- Carbide burrs and sanding sleeves
- Carving tools
- Finishing sander

DIRECTIONS:
1. Whether you plan to make fish similar to the ones shown in Illus. 169 or totally different ones, you should make patterns from construction paper. Make the patterns to the actual size of the fish body. Do not include the fins on the patterns. They will be designed and cut separately.
2. Trace the fish patterns onto the surface of the 1″ x 6″ pine. Cut out the fish using either a scroll or sabre saw.
3. Shape the fish using an electric grinder, rotary tool, or flex-shaft tool, or a combination of these tools. My own preference is to use an electric grinder with a carbide burr. The fish should be thick in the middle and become thin near the top and bottom edges. Add as much detail as you want with the various tools. Sanding sleeves and a finishing sander with a coarse-abrasive paper both work well for shaping.
4. Prepare the surfaces for finishing using fine and extra-fine abrasive paper and a finishing sander.

5. Drill a ¼″ diameter hole in the bottom center of each fish. The hole should be at least ⅜″ deep.
6. Using a band saw, measure and cut log slices to be used as bases for the fish. Drill ¼″ diameter holes into the middle of each base. The holes should be at least ⅜″ deep.
7. On pieces of aluminum or tin, draw fins for the fish. Refer to Illus. 169 to note some of the fins used. An alcohol pen works well for drawing on the metal. You may want to serrate the top edge of the larger fins. Be creative. Don't hesitate to make the fins large. You must have a straight edge on the bottom of each fin.
8. Cut the fins from the metal using either tin snips or a pair of scissors.
9. Cut slots into the top and bottom edges of each fish. The various fins will be glued into these slots. To cut the slots, use a hobby knife with a pointed blade. Take your time with this procedure and be very careful. You don't want the knife to slip. Cut one slot at a time and then check the fit of the fin. The slots should be deep enough to hold the fins in place. Glue will be used to secure the fins in the slots.
10. Spread some white glue in a slot and slide a fin in place. Repeat the process until all the fins are in the slots. Allow the glue to dry.
11. Paint the fish and the fins. If you need some help getting started, take a look at the fish shown in Illus. 169. Remember that these fish are products of my imagination.

64: *Loon Plant Holder* (Illus. 171 and 172)

For those who enjoy the loons who haunt the Northern lakes, this is an ideal gift. If the person also enjoys plants, this will be especially appreciated. A rather sizeable planter affords the user the option of planting directly into the box area or placing flower pots into the area. Either way, the holder can accommodate many plants. The loons shown in Illus. 171 are painted black and white, the natural colors of loons. Exterior-grade paint is used in anticipation of placing dirt in the planter area. Waterproof wood glue should also be used for the project.

Illus. 171. Loon plant holder.

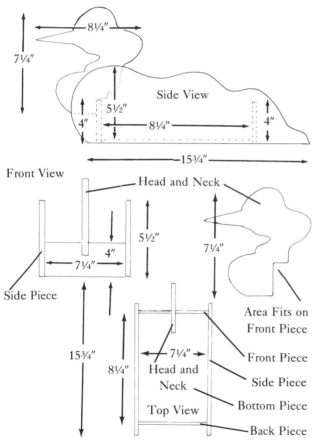

Illus. 172. Drawings of loon plant holder.

MATERIAL:

- 1″ x 8″ pine
- Construction paper
- Waterproof wood glue
- Wood filler
- Finishing nails
- Exterior-grade paint

TOOLS:

- Radial arm or table saw
- Scroll or sabre saw
- Nail set
- Finishing sander

DIRECTIONS:

1. Review Illus. 172. You will have to make a pattern of the head and neck area and a pattern of the side area of the holder. Make the sides look like a loon. Give them some nice rolls and taper them off at their back ends.

2. Measure and cut two pieces of 1″ x 8″ pine to length for use as the side pieces. Trace the side-piece pattern on both pieces of wood and cut it out. Use a scroll or sabre saw to cut out the side pieces.

3. Measure and cut the front and back pieces to a width of 7¼″ (the actual width of a 1″ x 8″ board) and a length of 4″.

4. Cut a piece of 1″ x 8″ pine to a length of 8¼″ for the bottom piece.

5. Trace the head and neck pattern onto a piece of 1″ x 8″ pine. Cut out this piece using a scroll or sabre saw. Make sure that the two surfaces that will fit over the front piece are straight.

6. Using waterproof wood glue and finishing nails, assemble the front and back pieces to the bottom piece.

7. Center the assembly on one side piece and, with glue and nails, secure the side piece to the assembly. Illus. 172 shows how the parts are to be assembled.

8. Glue and nail the other side piece to the assembly.

9. Drive all nail heads under the surface using a nail set. Rub wood filler into the holes.

10. Glue and nail the head and neck piece to the top center edge of the front piece. Nail into the neck from the back of the front piece.

11. Allow the glue to dry. Prepare the surfaces and edges for finishing using abrasive paper and a finishing sander. Wipe off all the dust when done.

12. Paint the loons black and white. You may want to refer to Illus. 171 or a picture of a loon.

65: *Toothpick Holders* (Illus. 173 and 174)

This is a wood-turning project that is fun and easy to make. Best of all, it results in some attractive and useful gifts. Small, turned containers are ideally suited for use as toothpick holders. As a matter of fact, these small containers have many uses. They can also be displayed as attractive turned pieces. The holders shown in Illus. 173 are turned from scraps of black walnut and wild cherry. You may have some pieces of hardwood lying around that would be ideal for making small, turned containers. The holders are faceplate-turned using either a chuck or glue block. Finish the holders with a clear lacquer finish and rub and polish them with paste wax.

MATERIAL:
- 2¼″ (9/4's) thick hardwood
- 1″ x 4″ pine
- White glue
- Lacquer

TOOLS:
- Band saw
- Wood lathe
- Turning tools
- Faceplate
- School compass
- Clamp
- Electric drill and screw set
- Belt sander

DIRECTIONS:
1. Using a school compass, make 3½″ diameter glue blocks on a 1″ x 4″ pine board. Cut the round blocks using a band saw.

2. With a school compass, make several 3″ diameter circles on pieces of hardwood. Use wood that is at least 2″ (8/4's) to 2¼″ (9/4's) thick. Cut out the hardwood circles using a band saw.

3. Spread white glue on the surface of a pine block and place, in its middle, a hardwood block. Clamp the assembly until the glue is dry. Prepare several turning blocks this way.

4. Attach a 3″ diameter faceplate to the glue block and secure the assembly on the lathe.

Illus. 173. Toothpick holders.

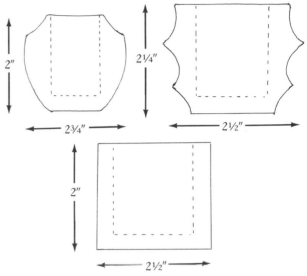

Illus. 174. Drawings of toothpick holders.

5. With a revolving center in the tailstock, bring it forward into the front surface of the turning block. This will provide both stability and safety during the turning process.

6. Align the tool rest and, using either scrapers or gouges, turn the block to its desired shape. Its surfaces should be prepared for finishing.

7. Move the tailstock out of the way and align the tool rest in front of the turned piece. Using a ½″ or 1″ flat-nose scraper, make a storage hole in the piece. Make the hole large enough to accommodate many toothpicks. If you prefer, secure a multi-spur bit in the tailstock and drill out the holes.

8. Using a parting tool, cutting slightly into the bottom of the turned piece, separate the turning from the glue block. If you prefer, separate the turning and the glue block using the band saw. Leave the faceplate attached, because it gives you something to hold on to while sawing.

9. Prepare the bottom for finishing using a belt sander and a fine-grit abrasive belt.

10. Apply several coats of lacquer. Rub the surface with steel wool (0000) between coats. Wipe off any steel hairs that remain before applying another coat. When the lacquer is dry, apply paste wax and polish the surface.

11. Turn additional holders using the above methods, and finish them.

66: *Hanging Memo Pad*
(Illus. 175 and 176)

The hanging memo pad is a functional gift that can be hung on a wall or set on the counter. It uses standard 2¼″ adding machine rolls for memos. There's a drilled hole in the memo pad dowel to hang a pencil on with a piece of string, to ensure that one is always available. The pad is designed to provide a writing surface that is over 8″ long. This makes it ideal for a grocery list. The memo pad shown in Illus. 175 is made from ½″ thick pine and is painted. You may want to use a clear lacquer finish or stain the pad.

MATERIAL:
- ½″ thick pine
- ½″ diameter dowel
- ¼″ thick batting
- 2¼″ x 2¾″ adding machine rolls
- Finishing nails
- Wire brads
- Wood glue
- Paint

TOOLS:
- Radial arm or table saw
- Band saw
- Scroll or sabre saw
- Electric drill, screw-sink, and ¹⁄₁₆″ and ½″ bits
- Finishing sander

DIRECTIONS:
1. Review Illus. 176. As indicated, you need ½″ thick pine for the project. You may want to plane

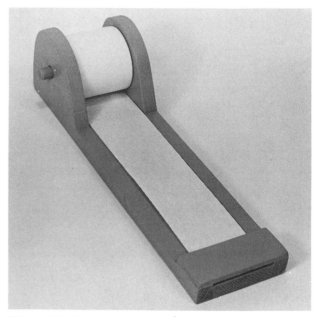
Illus. 175. Hanging memo pad.

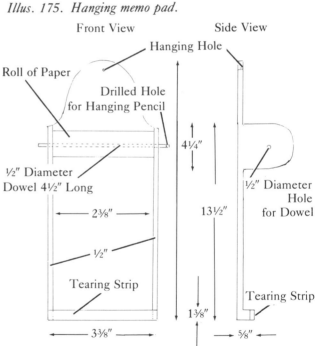
Illus. 176. Drawings of hanging memo pad.

a 1″ x 4″ pine board to ½″ thickness for the project. If necessary, resaw standard-thickness pine to ½″ using a band saw and ½″ wide blade.

2. Measure and cut the back piece. Note the scroll top as shown in Illus. 175 and 176. The piece should be 14½″ long and 2⅜″ wide. Use a scroll or sabre saw to cut the scroll.

3. Make a hanging hole in the middle of the top of the back piece using a screw-sink and an electric drill.

4. Lay out one side piece on a board. Draw the rounded area, making it 3½″ wide and 4¼″ long. Note in Illus. 176 how the bottom end of the side piece is wider where the tearing strip is placed. The bottom 1⅜″ should be ⅝″ wide, while the remainder of the side, except the round area, should be ½″. Mark this area on the surface of the wood, so you remember to cut it correctly. Cut the rounded area with a scroll or sabre saw, but cut the rest of the side piece using a band saw. A good, straight cut the length of the side piece should be made.

5. Using the first finished side piece as a pattern, trace the second side piece on a board. Cut it out using a scroll or sabre saw and a band saw. Again, remember the wider area at the bottom of the piece.

6. Determine the location of the dowel for the roll of paper. Place the roll of paper to be used on the side of the round area and mark the location of the dowel hole. Stick a pencil through the roll and mark the wood's surface. Place the roll as near to the top of the round area as possible. There should be plenty of room between the roll and the surface of the back piece.

7. While holding both side pieces tightly together, drill a ½″ diameter hole at the location marked and through both pieces.

8. Cut a ½″ diameter dowel 4½″ long. Near one end of the dowel, drill a ¹⁄₁₆″ diameter hole through the dowel. Attach a string through the hole to attach a pen or pencil to.

9. Using wood glue and finishing nails, attach both side pieces to the back piece. The side pieces should be flush with the bottom end of the back piece.

10. Measure and cut a ¼″ thick piece of batting to a length of 3⅜″ and a width of 1⅜″. If you don't have batting, resaw a piece of pine on the band saw to the required dimensions.

11. Secure the tearing strip to the elevated ends of the side pieces using wood glue and wire brads. Allow the glue to dry.

12. Place a roll of paper, on the dowel, between the side pieces. Pull the paper down and under the tearing strip. Pull out a length of paper and tear it off using the tearing strip. Remove the paper roll for the project.

13. Prepare all surfaces for finishing using fine and extra-fine abrasive paper. Wipe off all the dust.

14. Paint the project. When the paint is dry, place a roll of paper on the dowel and tie a piece of string through the dowel hole. Tie a pencil or pen to the string. Make sure that the string is long enough so that the pencil can be used to write on the full length of the pad.

67: *Musical Pig Bank on Wheels* (Illus. 177 and 178)

This attractive project has two features that will encourage children to save their money. First, when a coin passes through the slot a tune plays. Second, the child can see the coins accumulating inside the bank. This bank will not only hold money, it can also be used as a pull toy. The bank itself is crafted from a 2″ x 10″ fir plank, and the wagon from 1″ x 6″ pine board. The musical movement, the clear-plastic sides, and the wheels and axles are all items that you can find either locally or through mail-order suppliers. You will also have lots of fun painting and decorating the bank. By the way, the pig on the project shown in Illus. 177 is painted blue, the wagon is red, and the wheels green with yellow streaks.

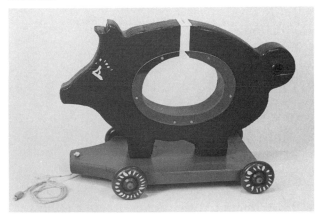

Illus. 177. Musical pig bank on wheels.

115

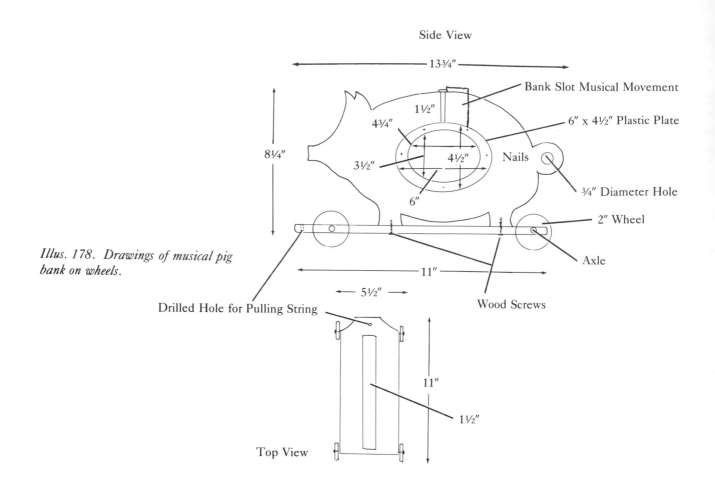

Side View

13¾″

1½″

Bank Slot Musical Movement

4¾″

8¼″

6″ x 4½″ Plastic Plate

3½″

4½″

Nails

¾″ Diameter Hole

6″

2″ Wheel

Axle

Illus. 178. Drawings of musical pig bank on wheels.

11″

5½″

Drilled Hole for Pulling String

Wood Screws

11″

1½″

Top View

MATERIAL:
- 2″ x 10″ fir plank
- 1″ x 6″ pine
- Construction paper
- Four 2″ diameter wheels and axles
- Two 4½″ x 6″ clear-plastic side plates
- Bank slot musical movement
- Nails
- Wood glue
- Wood screws
- String
- Paint

TOOLS:
- Radial arm or table saw
- Band saw
- Scroll saw
- Electric drill, screw set, and ¼″ and ¾″ bits
- Table-mounted router and roundover bit
- Finishing sander

DIRECTIONS:
1. Review Illus. 178 and the material list. Obtain all the material prior to beginning the project.

2. Using construction paper, make a full-size pattern of the pig. Do not include the middler cutout areas on the pattern.

3. Trace the pig pattern onto the surface of a 2″ x 10″ fir plank. Cut the traced piece from the plank using a table or radial arm saw. With a scroll saw or a band saw with a ¼″ wide blade, cut out the traced pig.

4. Measure and mark the location of the bank slot musical movement on the top edge and one side of the pig. Cut out this marked area using a band saw. Saw on the inside of the lines, so that the movement will fit snugly in the slot.

5. Lay the pig on its side. Slide the slot movement in the cut slot. Place one of the clear-plastic plates on the side of the pig so that it touches the

116

bottom edge of the slot movement. You may want to refer to Illus. 178 to note how the plate and slot relate to one another. While holding the plate in place, using a pencil, trace its outline onto the side of the pig. Remove the plate and the slot movement.

6. With a pencil, freehand, draw an oval inside the traced plate oval. There should be a ⅝″ wide area between the two ovals. The second oval is the area that is cut out. The clear plate will later be nailed to the ⅝″ space.

7. Thread the blade of either a scroll or band saw down through the bank slot area and cut out the second oval. Take your time with the cut, so you leave a neat, clean oval.

8. Drill a ¾″ diameter hole through the tail area of the pig.

9. Rout the outside edges of the pig using a roundover bit. Do not rout the oval money area.

10. Measure and cut the wagon base from a piece of 1″ x 6″ pine. The base should be 11″ long and 5½″ wide, the exact width of a 1″ x 6″.

11. Draw the curved areas on the front of the wagon and cut them out using a scroll saw.

12. Measure and mark the location of the four wheel axles. Drill ¼″ diameter holes for the axles where marked. Make sure the holes are drilled deep enough. While you're drilling, drill a ¼″ hole for the pull string in the middle of the front portion of the wagon.

13. Rout the edges of the wagon with a round-over bit, but do not rout the edges by the drilled axle holes.

14. Glue and screw the pig to the top of the wagon. The screws should penetrate from the bottom surface of the wagon and into the pig's feet. Secure the pig to the middle of the wagon using screws and wood glue.

15. Place the axles through the wheels and glue the axles in the ¼″ holes. Allow ample clearance between the back surface of the wheels and the sides of the wagon. The wheels should roll freely. Allow the glue to dry.

16. Prepare all the surfaces and edges for finishing using fine and extra-fine abrasive paper. Wipe off the dust when done.

17. Now comes the fun part. Paint and decorate everything: the pig, the wagon, the wheels and the axles. Let your imagination run wild! Maybe the child who will be the proud owner of the pig bank can help, if not with the actual painting, then with the color selection.

18. When the paint is dry, slide the bank slot musical movement in place. If it's too loose, place a very small drop of white glue on one side of it and slide the musical movement in place. Allow the glue to dry.

19. Using small brads with heads, nail the clear-plastic plates on each side of the pig. Don't drive the nails in too far or hit the plastic's surface or it will shatter.

20. Secure a pulling string in the wagon hole and tie it to a small piece of wood at the other end. Maybe you should test out the bank with a few quarters.

68: *Desk Thermometer* (Illus. 179 and 180)

A quality thermometer housed in a black walnut case makes a fine gift for someone special. While this gift looks nice on a desk, it also looks great on a shelf or a mantel. You may want to use red oak, wild cherry, or some other wood for the project. The actual thermometer can be ordered from any number of mail-order suppliers. Some local stores may also stock these instruments. The thermometer does require a 2⅜″ diameter hole that is at least 1″ deep. You may have to buy a Forstner or multi-spur bit of this size for the project. If you do, the bit can also be used for making clocks and other projects. The project is finished with a clear lacquer and rubbed with paste wax. Adhesive felt is attached to the bottom surface, to prevent scratching.

MATERIAL:
- 2″ (8/4's) thick black walnut
- 1″ (4/4's) thick black walnut
- Construction paper
- Thermometer
- Wood glue
- Adhesive felt
- Lacquer

Illus. 179. Desk thermometer.

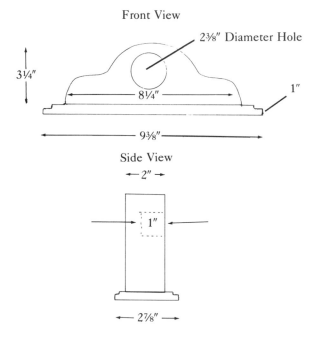

Illus. 180. Drawings of desk thermometer.

TOOLS:

- Radial arm or table saw
- Band saw
- Drill press and 2⅜" Forstner bit
- Table-mounted router and roundover bit
- Clamp
- Belt and finishing sander

DIRECTIONS:

1. Using construction paper, make a full-size pattern of the top portion of the project. The top should be round, the sides should slope and match one another.

2. Measure and cut a piece of 2" (8/4's) thick hardwood to a length of at least 8½" and a width of 3½". Trace the pattern onto the surface of the piece.

3. Cut the traced piece using a band saw and a ¼" wide blade. If you prefer, use a scroll saw to cut out the piece.

4. Measure and cut a piece of 1" (4/4's) thick hardwood to a length of 9⅜" and a width of 2⅞". This should be the same kind of wood as used for the top of the project. Cut the piece slightly large, because the edges will have to be cleaned up on a belt sander.

5. Measure and mark the location on the front surface for the thermometer hole. Clamp the piece to the drill-press table while drilling the hole. Place a piece of scrap between the surface of the wood and the clamp. This is to prevent the surface from being damaged by the clamp. Using a 2⅜" diameter Forstner or multi-spur bit, drill a 1" deep hole where the mark is.

6. Using finishing and belt sanders, remove any saw marks from the surfaces of the thermometer piece.

7. Rout the top edges of the thermometer piece using a roundover bit. Don't rout the bottom edges.

8. Set the roundover bit to make a deeper cut on the top edges of the base piece. Make a more radical cut on these edges, leaving an elevated area on the surface.

9. Prepare all surfaces of both pieces for finishing using fine and extra-fine abrasive paper and a finishing sander. Wipe off all the dust.

10. Glue and clamp the two pieces together. Put a scrap of wood between the surfaces and the clamp. Make sure the top piece is aligned perfectly on the bottom piece. Allow the glue to dry.

11. Finish the project with several coats of lacquer. Rub the surface, between coats, with steel wool (0000). Wipe off any remaining steel hairs before applying another coat. When the lacquer is dry, rub the project with paste wax and polish it.

12. Place the thermometer into the drilled hole. Cut and attach adhesive felt to the bottom surface of the project.

69: *Spalted Clock* (Illus. 181 and 182)

Wood decays as a result of moisture and fungi. As the fungi break down the wood structure, they change the color of the wood and also create what are called "black zone lines." This results in very attractive wood, called spalted wood. When the wood is dried, the fungi are killed and the decay process is stopped. Spalted wood can be found in the backyard wood pile, in the woods, and sometimes at the local hardwood dealer. When a quartz clock movement is inserted into a block of spalted wood, the result is a great gift. The clock movement can usually be purchased locally but, if not, can be obtained from mail-order suppliers. You will need a 2⅜" diameter Forstner or multi-spur bit for this project. The clock shown in Illus. 181 is finished with a clear lacquer.

MATERIAL:
- 3" (12/4's) thick spalted wood
- Clock movement
- Adhesive felt
- Lacquer

Illus. 181. Spalted clock.

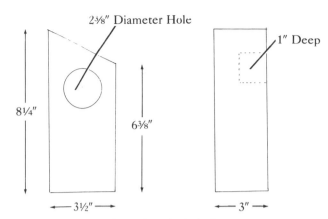

Illus. 182. Drawings of spalted clock.

TOOLS:
- Band saw
- Radial arm or table saw
- Drill press and either 2⅜" Forstner or 2⅜" multi-spur bit
- Clamp
- Belt and finishing sanders

DIRECTIONS:
1. If spalted wood is not available, use a similar size piece of some other hardwood. You could even use a thinner piece of wood.
2. Measure and cut the block to length using a radial arm or table saw.
3. Measure and mark the angle of the cut on the top of the block. Set the mitre gauge on the band saw and cut the angle as marked.
4. Mark the location of the clock movement on the front surface of the block. Clamp the block to the drill-press table. Place a piece of scrap between the block and the clamp. Align the location mark under the 2⅜" diameter bit and drill a 1" deep hole.
5. Remove all the saw marks from the various surfaces using a belt sander and a fine-grit abrasive belt.
6. Prepare all surfaces for finishing using fine and extra-fine abrasive paper and a finishing or belt sander. Wipe off all the dust.
7. Finish the project with lacquer. You will have to apply many coats of lacquer, because spalted

wood tends to absorb it. Keep applying coats until they start to build up. Rub the surface with steel wool (0000) between coats. Wipe off the steel hairs before applying more lacquer. A final coat of paste wax makes for a fine finish. Polish the wood after applying the wax.

8. Measure and cut a piece of adhesive felt and attach it to the bottom surface.

9. Set the time and place the clock in the drilled hole.

70: *Tiered Plant Stands*

(Illus. 183 and 184)

This project is the ideal gift for the plant lover. It's well-suited for displaying and growing African violets, Christmas cacti, or other plants. Each stand is a different height so the project better displays the plants. The hole in the top of the stands is designed to hold a 4″ flower pot. The bottom portion of the pot drops into the hole, while its top edge rests on the surface of the stand. If you want, the hole can be enlarged to hold a larger flower pot. The stands in Illus. 183 are finished with lacquer, but you may prefer painting them.

MATERIAL:
- 1″ x 8″ pine
- Finishing nails
- Wood glue and wood filler
- Lacquer

Illus. 183. Tiered plant stands.

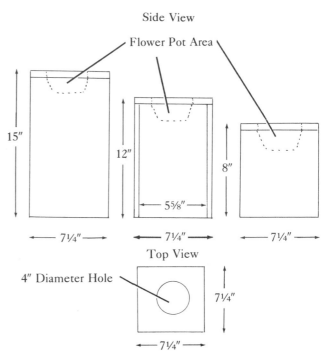

Illus. 184. Drawings of tiered plant stands.

TOOLS:
- Radial arm or table saw
- Band saw
- Sabre saw
- Table-mounted router and roundover bit
- Drill press and circle cutter or ⅜″ bit
- Clamp
- Finishing sander
- Nail set

DIRECTIONS:
1. Measure and cut the side pieces and the top piece for the *tallest* stand from 1″ x 8″ pine. Two of the four side pieces should be 15″ long and 7¼″ wide. As you know, 7¼″ is the standard width of a 1″ x 8″ pine board. The other two side pieces should also be 15″ long, but they should be ripped to a width of 5⅝″. Use a band or table saw to rip them to width. Measure and cut the top piece to a length of 7¼″ and a width of 7¼″.

2. The second tallest stand requires two sides that are 12″ long and 7¼″ wide. The other two sides are 12″ long, but 5⅝″ wide. The top piece should be cut to a length of 7¼″, and a width of 7¼″, which is standard on a 1″ x 8″ board.

3. For the shortest stand, measure and cut two side pieces to a length of 8″ and a width of 7¼″. The other two side pieces should be cut to a length of 8″, but a width of 5⅝″. The top piece is 7¼″ x 7¼″.

4. Measure and mark the middle point on the surface of each top piece.

5. If a drill press is to be used, secure a circle cutter in the chuck. Set the cutter to make holes that are 4″ in diameter. Clamp each top piece to the drill-press table, align the cutter drill over the marked hole location, and cut.

6. If you don't have a drill press, draw 4″ diameter circles on the surfaces of the top pieces using a school compass. Drill a ⅜″ diameter hole through the circle. Thread the blade of a sabre saw through the drilled hole and cut along the line.

7. Rout the outside edges of the 7¼″ wide side boards. Do not rout the ends or the back edges. Also, do not rout the edges of the 5⅝″ wide boards.

8. Rout the top edges and ends on each of the top pieces. Do not rout the bottom edges or ends. Also, do not rout the flower pot hole.

9. Using wood glue and finishing nails, assemble each of the stands. Remember, the 5⅝″ wide pieces go between the 7¼″ pieces. Glue and nail the top piece to each stand.

10. Drive in the heads of the finishing nails using a nail set. Wipe some wood filler into each hole.

11. Prepare the outside surfaces for finishing using fine and extra-fine abrasive paper and a finishing sander. Remove any excess wood filler with the sander. Wipe off the finishing dust.

12. Finish the stands with several coats of lacquer.

71: *Snake Family* (Illus. 185 and 186)

For the child or adult who enjoys snakes, this is a perfect gift. You don't have to be a herpetologist to be fascinated by snakes or to make wooden ones. If you like to carve or shape wood, this is a

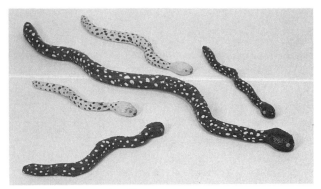

Illus. 185. Snake family.

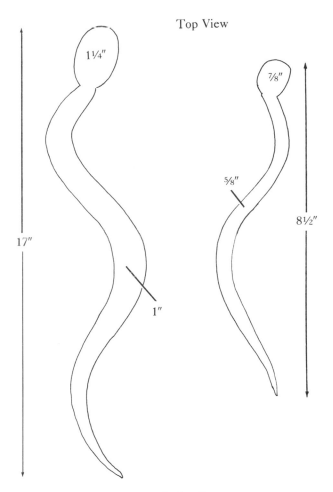

Illus. 186. Drawings of snake family.

project that you will enjoy doing. The snakes are rough-cut from a pine board and then shaped as you see fit. You will especially enjoy painting them. Lots of colors and imagination can be used. By the way, these are nonvenomous snakes.

MATERIAL:
- 1″ x 4″ pine
- Paint

TOOLS:
- Scroll or sabre saw
- Electric grinder, rotary tool, or flex-shaft tool
- Carbide burrs
- Sanding sleeves
- Carving tools
- Finishing sander

DIRECTIONS:

1. Measure and cut a piece of 1″ x 4″ pine board to a length that will permit you to cut out the snake family.

2. Draw the snakes, freehand, full-size on the surface of the board. Make their heads wider than their bodies. Refer to Illus. 185 and 186.

3. Using either a scroll or sabre saw, cut out the snakes.

4. Shape the snakes using either electric grinders, burrs, and sanding sleeves or, if you prefer, carving tools. Make them as realistic as possible. Make the heads stand out. Make their bodies round and their bottoms flat.

5. Go over the snakes with fine and extra-fine abrasive paper and a finishing sander. Prepare the surfaces for finishing. Wipe off the dust.

6. Paint and decorate the snakes. Use some bright colors. The snake family shown in Illus. 185 is painted yellow, blue, and green. If a child is around, have him or her help with the painting. Children always have good ideas on how things should appear.

72: Cutting Board with Bowl (Illus. 187 and 188)

Unlike most cutting boards, this one is designed so a bowl can be slid under it. The user can cut the items that need cutting and then scrape them into a bowl placed under the rounded area of the board. The project was designed by Andy Ma-

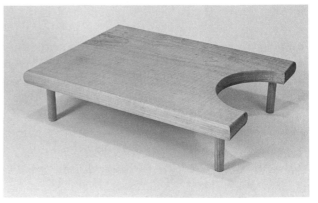

Illus. 187. Cutting board with bowl.

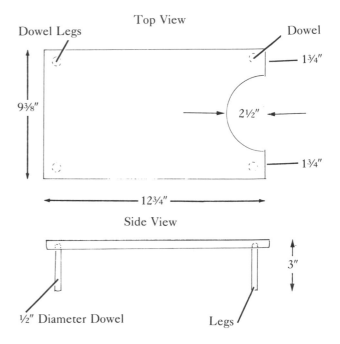

Illus. 188. Drawings of cutting board with bowl.

toesian for use in preparing Armenian cuisine in his kitchen. The cutting board should be made from a piece of hard maple and elevated on four ½″ diameter dowels. The board should be finished with mineral oil.

MATERIAL
- 1″ (4/4's) thick hard maple
- ½″ diameter dowel
- Waterproof wood glue
- Mineral oil

TOOLS:

- Radial arm or table saw
- Band, scroll, or sabre saw
- Electric drill and ½" bit
- Table-mounted router and roundover bit
- Finishing sander

DIRECTIONS:

1. Measure and cut a 1" (4/4's) thick piece of hard maple to a length of 12¾".

2. On one end, using a coffee can or another round object, trace the round area on the surface of the wood. Allow 1¾" on each side of the rounded area.

3. Cut out the traced area using a band, scroll, or sabre saw.

4. Measure and mark the location of the ½" diameter dowels on the bottom surface of the board. Pick the best-looking surface for the top.

5. Drill the ½" diameter dowel holes as marked to a depth of at least ½". All the holes should be drilled to the same depth.

6. Rout the edges of the cutting board using a roundover bit.

7. Prepare the surfaces and edges for finishing using fine and extra-fine abrasive paper and a finishing sander. Wipe off all the finishing dust.

8. Measure and cut four ½" diameter dowels to their proper lengths. The design for the cutting board shown in Illus. 188 requires dowels 3" long. The length of the dowels you use will be determined by the size bowl you plan on sliding under the board.

9. Place a dab of waterproof wood glue in the dowel holes and tap the dowels in place. Use waterproof glue because the cutting board will be washed. Regular wood glue breaks down in water.

10. Apply mineral oil to the board and legs and allow it to soak in. If the board is warm, the oil will soak in faster and deeper. Apply several coats. Occasionally apply a coat when you start using the cutting board.

73: *Shorebird II* (Illus. 189 and 190)

Assign your own special name to describe this shorebird. You may decide on something very technical like shorus birdus or something simpler. Whatever you call the bird, the person who will receive it will be delighted. These kinds of gifts are very popular; people like to have them sitting around the house. You will have lots of fun painting this project. Note the detail given to the wing of the bird shown in Illus. 189.

Illus. 189. Shorebird II.

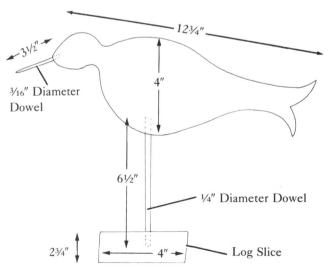

Illus. 190. Drawing of shorebird II.

123

MATERIAL:

- 1" x 6" pine
- ³⁄₁₆" diameter dowel
- ¼" diameter dowel
- Wood glue
- Construction paper
- Log slice
- Paint

TOOLS:

- Radial arm or table saw
- Scroll or sabre saw
- Electric drill and ³⁄₁₆" and ¼" bits
- Finishing sander

DIRECTIONS:

1. Note the dimensions of the bird in Illus. 190. Using construction paper, make a full-size pattern of the bird.

2. Trace the bird pattern onto a piece of 1" x 6" pine. Cut it out using either a scroll or sabre saw.

3. Measure and cut a slice of log that is at least 4" long, 2¾" high, and 3" wide. A bird this size needs a large block, for stability.

4. Cut a 3½" long piece of ³⁄₁₆" diameter dowel for the beak.

5. Measure and cut a 6½" long piece of ¼" diameter dowel for the stand.

6. Drill a ³⁄₁₆" diameter hole into the nose of the bird. The hole should be at least ³⁄₈" deep.

7. In the middle of the bottom of the bird drill a ¼" diameter hole to a depth of at least ½". Drill a ¼" diameter hole into the middle of the log slice.

8. Using a sander, taper the beak to a dull point.

9. Place a dab of glue in the nose hole and force the beak dowel into the hole.

10. Place the stand dowel into the hole in the bottom of the bird and into the base.

11. Sand the surfaces and edges in preparation for painting. Wipe off the dust before painting.

12. Paint and give the bird some detail. Make it look like a shorebird even though it's an unknown species. Don't forget to paint the beak.

74: Hand Mirrors (Illus. 191 and 192)

Illus. 191. Hand mirrors.

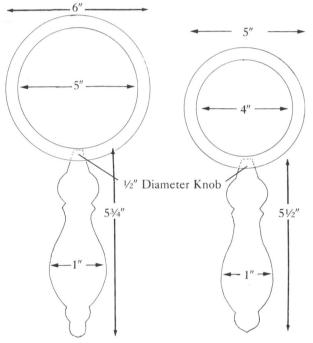

½" Diameter Knob

Illus. 192. Drawings of hand mirrors.

These handsome mirrors make a fine gift. The frame and handle are turned from black walnut—though you may prefer another hardwood—and the mirror is a high-quality bevelled mirror. Andy Matoesian, a master turner, spindle-turned the handles using gouges. I turned the mirror frame using scrapers. You may prefer other tools for turning the project, and perhaps even different mirror designs. Bevelled mirrors are available from a number of mail-order suppliers and in a variety of sizes. You may even be able to find them locally at a mirror store.

MATERIAL:
- 1″ (4/4's) thick black walnut
- 1½″ (6/4's) thick black walnut
- 5″ bevelled mirror
- 4″ bevelled mirror
- Epoxy
- White glue
- Lacquer

TOOLS:
- Radial arm or table saw
- Band saw
- School compass
- Wood lathe
- Turning tools
- Vernier caliper
- Clamp
- Drill press and ½″ wood bit
- Drill press vise
- Belt sander

DIRECTIONS:
1. Review Illus. 192, noting the dimensions of the project. The handles are turned with a ½″ diameter tenon that fits into a ½″ diameter hole in the mirror frame.

2. Measure and cut spindles for turning the handles. The spindles should be at least 6½″ long and 1½″ square. This should provide ample wood for turning the handles.

3. Secure a spindle between centers on the lathe, and turn it. You may want to use Illus. 191 as a guide. Remember to turn a ½″ diameter tenon that is at least ½″ long on the handle end that penetrates into the mirror frame. Turn both handles.

4. Using a school compass, make one 6″ diameter circle and one 5″ diameter circle on a piece of 1″ thick hardwood. Cut out the circles using a band saw.

5. Make two 3½″ diameter glue blocks from pine scraps. Make the circles with a school compass and cut them using a band saw.

6. Spread white glue on one surface of the pine glue blocks and place them in the middle of the hardwood circles. Clamp the pieces until the glue is dry.

7. Attach a faceplate to one of the glue blocks and secure it to the headstock of the lathe. Turn the piece round and shape its edge. Align the tool rest in front of the piece and, using a 1″ square-nose scraper, turn the area for the mirror. Set a vernier caliper to the exact diameter of the mirror. For example, the two project mirrors are 4″ and 5″ in diameter. Check the diameter of the turned area frequently. The mirror area should be recessed to a depth of at least ⅜″. Make certain that its bottom is flat. When the turning is complete, carefully place the mirror into the turned area to check its fit. Don't drop the mirror.

8. Realign the tool rest to the side of the frame and, using a parting tool, separate the frame from the glue block. Make sure you catch the frame as the two separate. If you feel this procedure will pose a problem, separate the pieces using a band saw. Leave the faceplate attached, to give you something to hang onto when sawing.

9. Turn the second mirror frame.

10. Mark the location of the ½″ diameter tenon hole on the mirror frame. The wood grain of the handle should be running up and down when the handle is in place. Secure the frame in a drill-press vise, being careful not to damage the wood. The tenon location mark should be aligned under a ½″ diameter wood bit. Drill the tenon hole to a depth of ½″. Don't let the bit break through the inside edge of the mirror area. If it does, patch it with wood filler or sawdust mixed with white glue. Drill the tenon hole on both frames.

11. Using a belt or finishing sander, prepare the back surface of the mirror frames for finishing. It is assumed that the other surfaces were prepared while they were being turned.

12. Dab epoxy on a scrap of wood. You will need enough epoxy to attach both handles to both mirror frames. Spread epoxy inside the ½″ diameter holes in the mirror frames. Insert the handle tenons, forcing them in place, and allow the epoxy to dry. Wipe off any excess epoxy. Make sure you read the directions before you start working with epoxy.

13. Finish the frames and handles with lacquer. You do not need to finish the inside area of the frame, because the mirror will be glued to that surface. Rub the surfaces down with steel wool (0000) between coats of lacquer. Spend some time on the projects so that you get a nice finish. Add paste wax to the surfaces and polish them. This will enhance the finish.

14. Spread white glue on the inside surfaces of the frames. Set the mirrors in place and press them down into the glue. Allow the glue to dry. Clean the mirrors.

75: *Christmas Tree* (Illus. 193 and 194)

This small, decorative seasonal gift may be just the item for someone special. This Christmas tree can be assembled for the holiday season and taken down when it's over. The design of the tree allows you to make it as large or small as you want or need. You can also cut the boughs so that small ornaments can be hung on them. The tree shown in Illus. 193 is made from ¼" thick construction plywood and is painted green. As Illus. 194 indicates, you make two identical trees, cut slots in the trees, and slide them together. This is explained in the Directions section.

Illus. 193. Christmas tree.

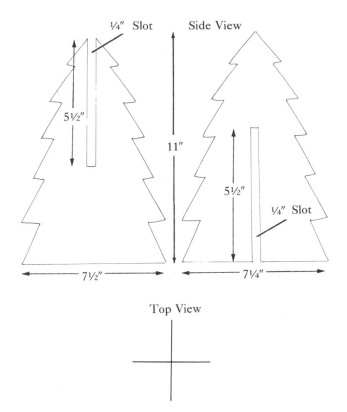

Illus. 194. Drawings of Christmas tree.

MATERIAL:

- ¼" thick plywood
- Construction paper
- Green paint

TOOLS:

- Radial arm or table saw
- Band saw
- Scroll or sabre saw
- Finishing sander

DIRECTIONS:

1. Decide how large a Christmas tree you want to make. The tree shown in Illus. 193 is rather small, but is adequate to serve as part of a Christmas display on a mantel or table. Make a full-size pattern of the tree you would like to make. You may want to use thicker plywood for the project.

2. Measure and cut two pieces of plywood to the desired length.

3. Trace the tree pattern onto the surfaces of both pieces of plywood. Cut out the trees using a band, scroll, or sabre saw. Use whatever is available and easiest for you.

4. Cut the assembling slots into the trees. These slots must be exactly one-half the height or length of the trees. Refer to Illus. 193 to note how this is done. The width of the slots is determined by the thickness of the plywood used. For example, if ¼" thick plywood is used the slots should be ¼" wide. The slot on one tree is cut from the top downwards; the slot on the other tree is cut from the bottom upwards. Measure and cut the slots. Make sure you make straight cuts for the slots.

5. Slide one slotted tree over the other slotted tree and check the assembly for fit. If the fit is too tight, you may have to widen the slots a bit. If one tree doesn't slide all the way to the surface, you may have to cut the slots longer. Hopefully, you will have a good initial fit. Take the tree apart.

6. Prepare the surfaces for finishing using fine-grit abrasive paper and a finishing sander. Wipe off all the dust when done.

7. Paint the trees a Christmas-tree green and, if you want, paint on some decorations.

76: *Fish Plaque* (Illus. 195 and 196)

This gift project is a trophy for a dry fly fisherman. The plaque displays a brown trout with a fly still hooked to its upper lip. You may want the plaque to display a smallmouth bass or some other fish. Make a fish of your choice or one that the recipient of the gift will especially enjoy. This is a fun project to make and paint. Some of the details on the fish shown in Illus. 195 were done with a wood-burning set.

MATERIAL:
- 1" x 8" pine
- Construction paper
- Wood glue
- Wood screw
- Hanger
- Lacquer
- Paints

Illus. 195. Fish plaque.

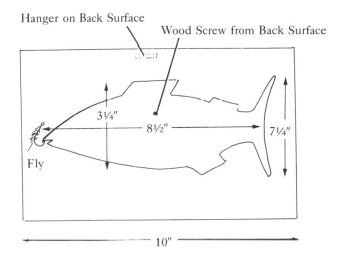

Illus. 196. Drawing of fish plaque.

TOOLS:
- Radial arm or table saw
- Band saw
- Scroll or sabre saw
- Table-mounted router and roundover bit
- Electric grinder, rotary tool, or flex-shaft tool
- Sanding sleeves and carbide burrs
- Carving tools
- Wood-burning set
- Finishing sander

DIRECTIONS:
1. Note the dimensions of the project as indicated in Illus. 196. Decide on the type of fish you want on the plaque. You may want to check in a

fish book for some ideas or details. Using construction paper, make a full-size pattern of the fish you want to make.

2. Measure and cut a piece of 1″ x 8″ pine and trace the fish pattern onto its surface. Cut out the fish using either a scroll or sabre saw.

3. If you have a band saw, begin shaping the fish and remove some of the excess wood.

4. Using an electric grinder, rotary tool, flex-shaft tool, or a combination of these tools, shape and carve the fish. The fish should taper at both the bottom and top. Give special attention to shaping the various fins and the tail. While the fish has to be shaped on both sides, you do not have to do detail work on the side that will be attached to the board.

5. Prepare the surfaces for finishing using a finishing sander and fine and extra-fine abrasive papers.

6. Wood-burn some details into the fish. You may want to review Illus. 195 to note some of the burned-in details. Clean up the wood-burned areas with a fine-grit abrasive paper.

7. Measure and cut the back piece of the plaque from a 1″ x 8″ board. The piece should be at least 10″ long if the fish was cut to a length of 8½″.

8. Rout the edges of the back piece using a round-over bit.

9. Paint and add detail to the fish. Also, lacquer the back piece. Make your fish look like a real one.

10. Using wood glue and a wood screw, secure the fish to the back piece. The screw should enter from the back of the back piece and into the side of the fish. Align the fish in the middle of the back piece.

11. Nail a hanger in the middle of the top of the back surface of the back piece.

12. If your project plaque displays a trout, secure a dry fly to its upper lip.

77: *Reaction Toy* (Illus. 197 and 198)

The reaction toy is the ultimate executive gift. It's a superb instrument for measuring reaction time. It's my understanding that numerous ex-

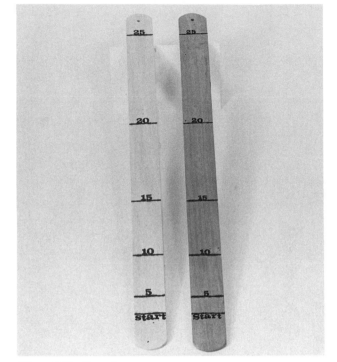

Illus. 197. Reaction toy.

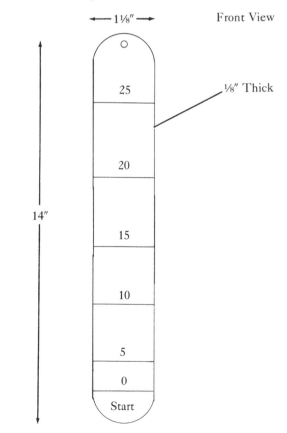

Illus. 198. Drawing of reaction toy.

128

ecutives who have the slowest reaction time now head major corporations and governmental agencies. To measure a person's reaction time, hold the instrument at its top hole while the testee places his or her thumb and index finger within ½" of the point marked "start." Be certain that their fingers are not touching the surface of the instrument. When you, the tester, say go, release the instrument. The testee should try to catch it between his/her two fingers. There is a scale on the toy with different numerical values that become greater the further they are from the starting position. The higher the number, the slower the person's reaction time. By the way, the toy was designed by Mike O'Meara, an individual with a keen interest in physics. It should be made from an ⅛" thick strip of hardwood. The lines can be wood-burned, but you may want to stencil on the numbers.

MATERIAL:
- ⅛" thick piece of hardwood
- Stencil numbers and paint
- Lacquer

TOOLS:
- Band saw
- Scroll or sabre saw
- Electric drill and ⅛" bit
- Finishing sander
- Wood-burning set

DIRECTIONS:
1. Measure and cut a ⅛" thick strip of hardwood to a length of 14" and a width of 1⅛". As you might guess, these dimensions are all approximate. Work with whatever wood you may have in the shop. If necessary, resaw a piece on the band saw to an approximate thickness.
2. Cut both ends round using a scroll or sabre saw. Note Illus. 197.
3. Drill a ⅛" diameter hole in the middle of the top of the strip.
4. Using a finishing sander, prepare the surfaces and edges for finishing. Wipe off the dust.
5. Set up some kind of scale with lines and numbers. Wood-burn the lines into the strip. Sand

over the burned area with extra-fine abrasive paper.
6. Finish the toy with lacquer. When the lacquer is dry, numbers can be stencilled onto the surface. If the numbers are painted on first, the lacquer could ruin the paint. Assign any numbers to the lines that you want. Below the bottom line you should stencil in the word "start."

78: *Lath Art Lighthouse*
(Illus. 199–201)

Designed, crafted, and painted by Jerry and Becky Lipchik, the lath art lighthouse is a gift project that will require more time and effort on your part, but is well worth it. As indicated in the earlier lath art owl project (project 54), the lath used is approximately 1½" wide, ⅜" thick, and 36" and 48" long. It's available at most local lumber dealers and is relatively inexpensive. While specific directions for making the project are presented, it is left to you to draw patterns of the various parts of the design. Make a full-size pattern for each piece of the picture. You may find it helpful to review project 54. Drawings and specific dimensions are presented for the frame, the inside area, and the back support piece. For those who enjoy making puzzles, lath art is especially fun and challenging.

Illus. 199. Lath art lighthouse.

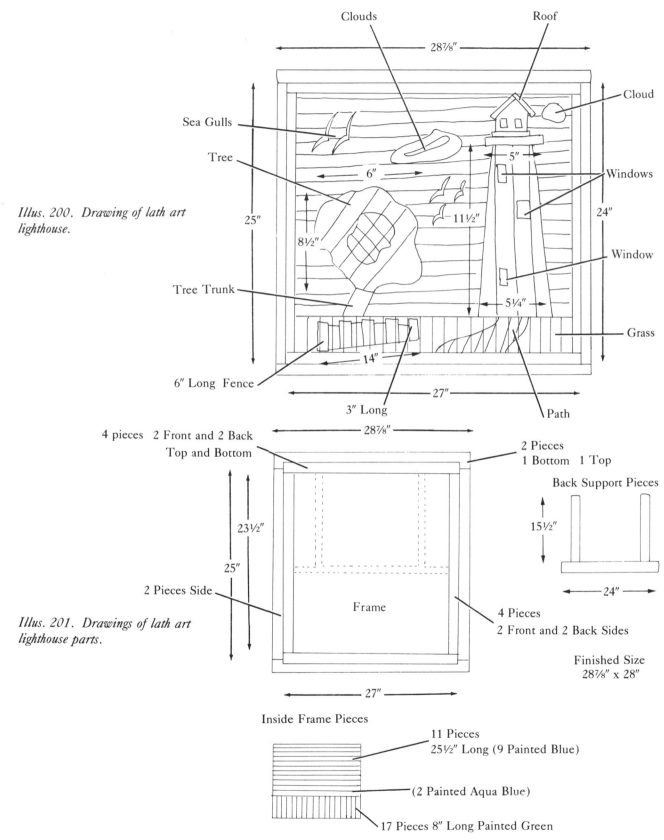

Clouds   Roof

Cloud

Sea Gulls

Tree

Windows

Window

Tree Trunk

Grass

6" Long Fence

3" Long

Path

28⅞"

6"

5"

25"

11½"

8½"

24"

5¼"

14"

27"

Illus. 200. Drawing of lath art lighthouse.

4 pieces 2 Front and 2 Back
Top and Bottom

2 Pieces
1 Bottom 1 Top

Back Support Pieces

28⅞"

23½"

25"

15½"

2 Pieces Side

Frame

4 Pieces
2 Front and 2 Back Sides

24"

Illus. 201. Drawings of lath art lighthouse parts.

Finished Size
28⅞" x 28"

27"

Inside Frame Pieces

11 Pieces
25½" Long (9 Painted Blue)

(2 Painted Aqua Blue)

17 Pieces 8" Long Painted Green

130

MATERIAL:

- Wood lath 1½″ x ⅜″
- ⅝″ No. 19 nails
- Wood glue
- Construction paper
- Eye screws
- Picture-hanging wire
- Latex stains: redwood, sky-blue, grass-green, and white
- Stiff bristle brush
- Liner brush
- Craft sponge
- Stencil brush
- Rags for wiping
- Craft paint in different colors

TOOLS:

- Scroll or coping saw
- Try or steel square

DIRECTIONS:

1. Measure and cut the following: 4 pieces 27″ long; 4 pieces 23½″ long; 2 pieces 25½″ long; 2 pieces 28⅞″ long; 2 pieces 15½″ long; and 1 piece 24″ long.

2. Brush redwood latex stain on the above pieces. Wipe off the excess stain with a rag.

3. Measure and cut eleven, 25½″ long wood lath pieces for the sky-and-sea background area.

4. Brush blue latex stain on the 11 pieces and wipe off any excess.

5. Paint over 2 of the blue-stained pieces with aqua paint. When they are dry, paint on white, using a small amount at a time and blending it in.

6. Measure and cut seventeen, 8″ long lath pieces for the grass background. Brush on green stain and wipe off the excess.

7. To assemble the frame, you may want to work on the floor where you will have ample room. Refer to the Illus. 199–201 to assist you in assembling. Begin the process by organizing the inside frame pieces and then securing, on both the front and the back, the actual frame pieces. Secure the pieces together using wood glue and ⅝″ No. 19 nails. As suggested earlier, this is a project for those who enjoy putting together puzzles.

8. Using the patterns prepared earlier, trace and cut, using either a scroll or coping saw, the various parts of the picture. Take your time with this task and keep the parts separated. It sometimes helps to place the cut pieces in their proper places on the assembled frame after they've been cut.

9. Paint the cut parts as follows:

House: *Bottom part*, white
Top part, bright red
Trim, black
Top windows, pale yellow sponged with white
Bottom windows, medium grey
Door, black

Path: pale gold, sponge-streaked with light brown

Tree: *Large bottom leaf section*, dark green sponged-streaked with light brown
small top-leaf section, bright green, sponge-streaked with light brown
trunk dark brown, sponge-streaked with black

Fence: medium rust brown, sponge-streaked with ivory

Clouds: light blue, sponge-streaked with white. Let it dry and then sponge-streak it with more white.

Gulls: white

10. Measure and cut a fence-support piece to a length of 13″. Brush on redwood stain. Note where the fence is placed in Illus. 199 and 200. Glue and nail the fence-support piece, at an angle, in place. The fence pieces are later secured to it.

11. Glue and nail the picture pieces in place.

12. Thread eye screws into edges on the back portion of the frame and attach hanging wire to them. Allow ample slack in the wire for hanging the picture.

79: *Desk Pencil Holder* (Illus. 202 and 203)

Everyone needs a place to put pens and pencils. This gift project is a functional piece for use ei-

Illus. 202. Desk pencil holder.

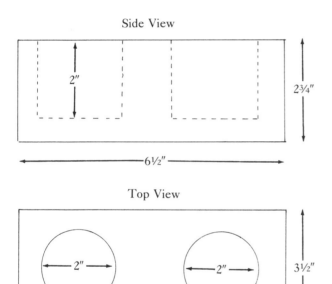

Illus. 203. Drawings of desk pencil holder.

ther on a desk at the office or at home. The pencil holder shown in Illus. 202 is made from spalted sycamore. You may want to review project 69 for a brief description of spalted wood. You can, of course, make it from a hardwood you prefer. If you're so inclined, cut a piece of hardwood in two and glue a piece of veneer between

the pieces. You can also decorate a large block of hardwood with wood plugs of a contrasting wood.

MATERIAL:
- 2¾" (11/4's) thick hardwood
- Adhesive felt
- Lacquer

TOOLS:
- Radial arm, table, or band saw
- Table-mounted router and roundover bit
- Drill press and 2" multi-spur or 2" Forstner bit
- Drill press vise or clamp
- Finishing or belt sander

DIRECTIONS:
1. Use any type of 2¾" (11/4's) or larger hardwood for the project. If you have a dry piece of oak from the wood pile, cut it on the band saw to a useable block for a pencil holder. If you can, find a piece of spalted wood for the project.

2. Measure and cut the holder to a length of 6½" and a width of 3½".

3. Mark the location for the two drilled holes. The holes should be at least 2" in diameter. The larger the holes, the more pencils and other desktop items can be stuck into them.

4. Clamp the block in a drill press vise or secure it to the drill-press table with a clamp. Place a piece of scrap on the block to protect it from the metal clamp. Align the marked holes under a Forstner or multi-spur bit and drill the holes. The holes should be at least 2" deep.

5. Using a table-mounted router and roundover bit, rout the edges of the holder and the edges of the drilled holes.

6. Prepare the surfaces for finishing using either a finishing or belt sander and fine and extra-fine abrasive grits. Wipe off the sanding dust. Remember to wipe it from the drilled holes.

7. Finish the holder with lacquer. If spalted wood is used, apply many coats of lacquer because the wood is very porous.

8. Apply a piece of adhesive felt to the bottom surface, to prevent the holder from scratching the desktop or other surfaces.

80: *Recipe Holder* (Illus. 204 and 205)

A recipe holder made from a block of walnut or some other hardwood is a high-quality gift. This recipe holder can be designed in any shape. The only stipulation is that you cut an area in the top surface where a recipe card can be placed. The holder shown in Illus. 204 is made from walnut, has an angled cut for holding a recipe card, and has three ½" diameter Indian padauk plugs overlaying one another as a decorative touch. You may want to use some veneer for a decorative inlay. By the way, the holder is small enough that you should be able to use a piece of scrap hardwood. Certainly the decorative plugs can be cut from scraps.

Illus. 204. Recipe holder.

MATERIAL:
- 1¾" (⅞'s) thick black walnut
- Indian padauk
- Wood glue
- Lacquer

TOOLS:
- Radial arm or table saw
- Band saw
- Table mounted router and roundover bit
- Drill press, ½" plug cutter, and ½" wood bit
- Finishing sander

DIRECTIONS:
1. Decide on the kind of hardwood you want to use. The dimensions of the holder can vary in relation to how much wood you have available. You should also decide on whether you want to use plugs or veneer for decoration.

2. Measure and cut a block of hardwood to the desired dimensions and shape. You may want to refer to Illus. 204 and 205 to note the design and dimensions of the holder.

3. On the top surface of the block, make a cut with a band saw that is ⅝" deep and at an angle. Review Illus. 205. This, of course, is the cut that will hold the recipe card. It should be at an angle so the card, when in place, can be more easily read.

4. Rout the edges of the holder using a roundover bit.

5. Using a ½" diameter plug cutter in a drill press, cut three plugs from Indian padauk or some other attractive wood that will contrast well with the holder.

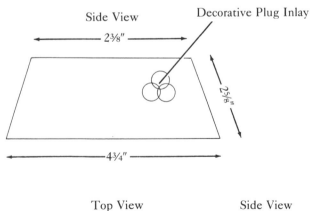

Side View

2⅜"

2⅝"

Decorative Plug Inlay

4¾"

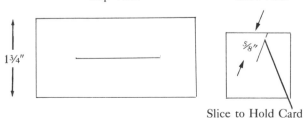

Top View

1¾"

Side View

⅝"

Slice to Hold Card

Illus. 205. Drawings of recipe holder.

6. Drill a ½″ diameter hole into the side of the holder where you want the decorative inlay to be placed. The depth of the hole should be the length of the wood plug. Place a dab of glue into the drilled hole and tap a plug in place. Allow the glue to dry. It's important that the glue dry before you drill the next hole.

7. Drill a second ½″ diameter plug hole. The drilled hole should overlap, by about ¼″, the first plug. Place glue in the hole and tap the second plug in place. Allow the glue to dry.

8. Drill the final ½″ diameter plug hole so that it overlaps a portion of the previous two plugs. Place some wood glue into the hole and tap the final plug in place. Allow the glue to dry.

9. Prepare the surfaces for finishing using a finishing sander and fine and extra-fine abrasive paper. Make sure the plugs are sanded flush with the surface of the holder. Wipe off the dust.

10. Finish the recipe holder with lacquer. Rub the surfaces between coats with steel wool (0000) and wipe off the wool hairs and dust before applying the next coat. A final coat of paste wax will give the holder a strong finish.

81: *Wooden Spoon Caddy* (Illus. 206 and 207)

This project will make a useful gift for someone who needs a place to hold all those wooden spoons, forks, and other wooden kitchen utensils. While the caddy shown in Illus. 206 is designed to hold eight items, you can make your gift as large and as tall as needed. Measure the handles of the spoons and other items before deciding on the height of the caddy. A clear lacquer finish makes the caddy blend in with the wooden ware.

MATERIAL:
- 1″ x 8″ pine
- 1″ diameter dowel
- Wood screws
- Wood glue
- Lacquer

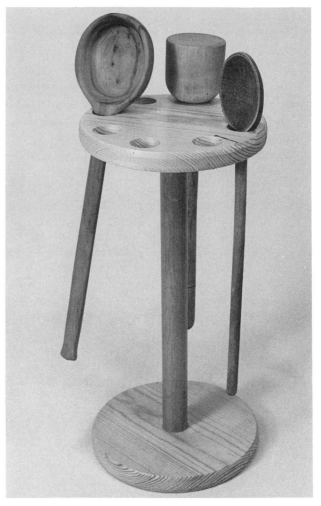

Illus. 206. Wooden spoon caddy.

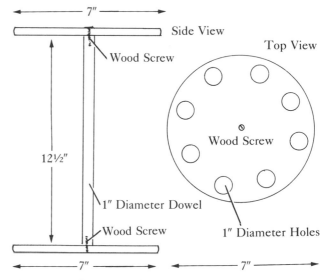

Illus. 207. Drawings of wooden spoon caddy.

134

TOOLS:

- Radial arm or table saw
- Band or sabre saw
- Table-mounted router and roundover bit
- Electric drill, screw set, 1" wood bit, and 1/32" bit
- School compass
- Finishing sander

DIRECTIONS:

1. Measure and cut two pieces of 1" x 8" pine to a length of at least 8".

2. With a school compass, draw a 7" diameter circle on each piece of pine.

3. Cut out the traced circles using either a band or sabre saw. Take your time with the sawing. The circles should be as close to perfect as you can get.

4. On one circle, measure and mark the location of eight drilled 1" diameter holes. The wooden utensils will hang through these holes, handles pointing downwards. Drill the holes using a 1" diameter wood bit.

5. Rout the edges of both round pieces with a roundover bit.

6. Measure and cut a 1" diameter dowel to a length of at least 12½".

7. Prepare all surfaces for finishing.

8. Using the compass point indentations as the center point of each round piece, drill a 1/32" pilot hole through the pieces. Start wood screws through both round pieces, one from the top and the other from the bottom. The screw points should penetrate through the pieces.

9. Place the approximate middle of each end of the dowel on the point of a screw. Press on the point to indent the surfaces of the dowel. Drill a 1/32" pilot hole into the dowels at these indentation points.

10. Spread glue on the dowel ends. Then place screws on the dowels and thread the screws in place. There should be a tight fit between the dowel ends and the surfaces of the round pieces. Make sure each screw head is slightly recessed into the wood's surface. Wipe off any glue that squeezes out.

11. Wipe off all the finishing dust and finish the caddy with a clear lacquer finish.

82: Shorebird III (Illus. 208 and 209)

As you probably can guess, I not only like to give shorebirds as gifts but I also enjoy making them. Actually, it's fun to design different shapes and then, using black and white paint, give them a bird-like appearance. My birds tend to be a generic-type species.

MATERIAL:

- 1" x 5" pine
- ¼" diameter dowel
- Construction paper
- Log slice
- Black and white paint

TOOLS:

- Radial arm or table saw
- Band saw
- Scroll or sabre saw
- Electric drill and ¼" bit
- Finishing sander

DIRECTIONS:

1. As always when it comes to making shore-

Illus. 208. Shorebird III.

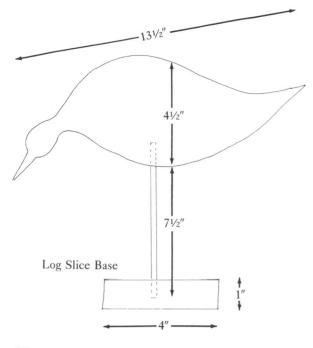

Illus. 209. Drawing of shorebird III.

birds, design and cut a full-size pattern of the bird. Construction paper works well for making patterns. You may want to review Illus. 206 and 207 to note the design and dimensions.

2. Measure and cut a piece of 1″ x 5″ pine to the appropriate length. You may want to make several of these birds while you're at it. Trace the bird pattern onto the wood.

3. Cut out the bird using either a scroll or sabre saw.

4. Measure and cut a ¼″ diameter dowel to a length of approximately 7½″.

5. Slice a piece of log to a length of at least 4″ and about 1″ or more high. It should be wide enough so that the bird won't tip over.

6. Drill a ¼″ diameter hole in the middle of the bottom of the bird and in the middle of the top of the log slice. The holes should be about ½″ deep.

7. Insert the dowel into the hole in the bird and then into the log to check for stability.

8. Prepare the surfaces of the bird for finishing using fine and extra-fine abrasive paper and a finishing sander. Wipe off the dust.

9. Paint the bird. Don't paint the dowel or the log slice. What does a shorebird look like? It looks like the bird you just finished painting.

83: *Apple Cutting Board*
(Illus. 210 and 211)

Cutting boards of all sizes and shapes make excellent gifts. The apple board is another example of what's possible when it comes to cutting board shapes. It is designed for cutting cheese or for doing small food preparation tasks. For example,

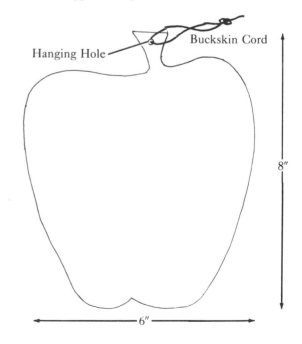

Illus. 210. Apple cutting board.

Illus. 211. Drawing of apple cutting board.

it's ideal for slicing black olives, onions, or other items where little board space is required. Design the project to meet the needs of the gift recipient. Make the cutting board from hard maple. A piece of buckskin for hanging the apple is always a useful touch.

MATERIAL:

- 1″ (4/4's) thick hard maple
- Construction paper
- Buckskin
- Mineral oil

TOOLS:

- Radial arm or table saw
- Scroll, sabre, or band saw
- Table-mounted router and roundover bit
- Electric drill and ¼″ bit
- Finishing or belt sander

DIRECTIONS:

1. Decide on the size of the apple cutting board. Make a pattern of the apple using construction paper.
2. Measure and cut a piece of 1″ (4/4's) thick hard maple to length.
3. Trace the pattern onto the hard maple and cut it out using a scroll, sabre, or band saw. Hard maple requires a sharp blade, no matter which saw you plan on using.
4. Rout the edges of the board using a roundover bit. As with saw blades, a sharp router bit is required when routing hard maple. Dull bits tend to burn the edges as they're being routed.
5. Drill a ¼″ diameter hole in the stem. A piece of buckskin can be later threaded through the hole for hanging. If you prefer, omit the hole.
6. Prepare the surfaces and edges for finishing using fine and extra-fine abrasive paper. Wipe off the dust.
7. Apply several coats of mineral oil to the board. If the board is warm, the oil will be absorbed more quickly. Occasionally reoil the board.
8. Cut a piece of buckskin to length, thread it through the hole, and tie it in a knot.

84: *Small Open Shelf* (Illus. 212 and 213)

This gift is for someone who needs a small hanging shelf to display collectibles or other items. The shelf is small enough to be used on a small wall or in an area where space is at a minimum. You may want to make several shelves, so that the user can stagger them on the same wall. The shelf is made from pine, which makes it light enough so it's not difficult to hang. Some hardwood shelves are so heavy that it's a major task just getting them to stay on the wall. The project can be painted, if you prefer, but it looks very nice with a clear lacquer finish. Secure a sawtooth hanger or similar hanger on the upper back of the shelf.

MATERIAL:

- 1″ x 4″ pine
- ½″ thick pine
- ¼″ thick pine
- Finishing nails and wire brads
- Wood filler
- Wood glue
- Sawtooth hanger
- Lacquer

TOOLS:

- Radial arm or table saw
- Band saw
- Table-mounted router and rabbeting and roundover bits
- Nail set
- Finishing sander

DIRECTIONS:

1. Review Illus. 212 and 213, noting the design and dimensions of the shelf. As you will note, the top, bottom, and side pieces are made from 1″ (4/4″) thick pine. The two shelves are ½″ thick pine and the back slats are ¼″ thick pine. In that you only need a few pieces of these thicknesses, you can easily resaw standard-thickness pine on a band saw.
2. Measure and cut two side pieces from 1″ x 4″

Illus. 212. Small open shelf.

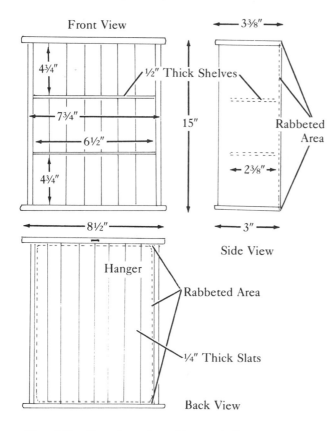

Illus. 213. Drawings of small open shelf.

pine to a length of 15″. Using either a table or band saw, cut them to a width of 3″.

3. Measure and cut the top and bottom pieces from 1″ x 4″ pine. Each piece should be 8½″ long. With a band or table saw, cut the pieces to a width of 3⅜″. If you prefer that the top and bottom pieces be slightly wider, use their full width, which, for a 1″ x 4″ piece of pine, is 3½″ wide.

4. Secure a rabbeting bit in a table-mounted router. Review the back view of the project shown in Illus. 213 and note how the inside edges of the top, bottom, and side pieces are rabbeted. The rabbeted area is ¼″ deep, in order to accommodate ¼″ wide back slats. While the rabbets of the two side pieces are cut the entire length of the pieces, the top and bottom piece rabbets should stop approximately ¼″ from the ends of each piece. This is done to prevent the rabbets from being seen. Rout the rabbeted areas. You may want to make several passes to achieve the ¼″ depth. Trying to rout too deeply in one pass can be dangerous.

5. While you're using the router, secure a round-over bit in it. Rout all the edges, except the rabbeted ones, on the top, bottom, and side pieces.

6. Measure and cut two shelf pieces from ½″ thick pine to a length of 6½″ and a width of 2⅜″. As suggested, if necessary, resaw a piece of 1″ x 4″ pine using a band saw and ½″ wide blade to get the ½″ thick shelf pieces. Cut them slightly oversize and sand off their saw marks on a belt sander.

7. Rout the front edges of the two shelves using a roundover bit. Reduce the depth of cut of the bit when routing thin material.

8. Prepare all surfaces for finishing using fine and extra-fine abrasive paper and a finishing sander. Wipe off the dust.

9. Using wood glue and finishing nails, assemble the top, bottom, and side pieces. Place the shelves inside the side pieces when assembling, so they will fit properly when secured in place.

10. Measure and mark the location of the two shelf pieces. Glue and nail them in place. The nails should penetrate from the outside surface of the side pieces and into the ends of the shelves.

If you miss a shelf end with a nail, pull it out and try again.

11. Using a nail set, drive all nail heads under the surface of the wood. Fill each hole with a touch of wood filler. When the filler is dry, sand over the areas.

12. Measure the length from the rabbeted area on the top area to the rabbeted piece on the bottom area. Also, measure the width of the area from the rabbeted area in one side piece to the rabbeted area in the other side piece. Measure and cut slats that are ¼" thick to fit into this area. Use 1" x 4" pine and a band saw with a ½" blade to resaw slats to a thickness of ¼". You can leave the surfaces of the slats rough, even the ones facing into the shelf. The saw marks do not distract from the overall appearance of the shelf.

13. Using wire brads, nail the slats into the rabbeted areas.

14. Finish the project with lacquer. Secure a sawtooth hanger or similar hanger to the back of the top piece.

85: *Toy Car* (Illus. 214 and 215)

The design for this toy car is based on old roadsters. With long engines requiring an extended front end, these cars often had oversize tires on their rear. Maybe this is a gift you should make for yourself. The car itself is made from a piece of 2" x 4" pine, and the wheels from ¾" thick construction-grade plywood. As you will note from looking at Illus. 214, the details have been wood-burned into the wood.

Illus. 214. Toy car.

Side View

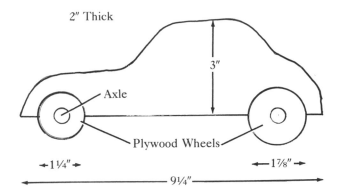

Illus. 215. Drawing of toy car.

MATERIAL:

- 2" x 4" pine
- ¾" thick plywood
- ³⁄₁₆" diameter axles
- Construction paper
- Wood glue
- Lacquer

TOOLS:

- Radial arm or table saw
- Scroll, sabre, or band saw
- Electric drill and ³⁄₁₆" bit
- School compass
- Wood-burning set
- Finishing sander

DIRECTIONS:

1. Design the car of your dreams and then make a full-size pattern from construction paper.

2. Measure and cut a piece of 2" x 4" pine to the appropriate length.

3. Trace the pattern onto the piece of 2" x 4" material. Maybe you should make more than one.

4. Using a scroll, sabre, or band saw, cut out the car.

5. With a school compass, trace the wheels onto a piece of ¾" plywood. You may want to use the

139

diameters suggested in Illus. 215. Cut out the wheels with a scroll, sabre, or band saw, or drill press and circle cutter if you have them.

6. Drill ³⁄₁₆″ diameter holes through the middle of each wheel for the axles.

7. Measure and mark the location of the axles and wheels on the body of the car. Drill ³⁄₁₆″ diameter holes into the car, where marked. The holes should be deep enough to accommodate the axles after they have penetrated the wheels.

8. Prepare the car and wheels for finishing using fine and extra-fine abrasive paper and a finishing sander. Wipe away all the dust and blow it out of the drilled holes.

9. Thread the axles through each wheel, place a dab of wood glue into the axle holes in the car body, and insert the axles into the body. Make sure that there's enough room between the wheels and the car body so the wheels will roll freely. Allow the glue to dry.

10. Pencil in the details you want on the surface of the car and wheels. Using a wood-burning set, burn in the pencilled areas. Give your car some realistic detail. Sand over the wood-burned areas when done.

11. Wipe off all the dust and finish the car with a clear lacquer.

86: The What-Kind-of-a-Bird-Is-It Bird (Illus. 216 and 217)

This is the perfect gift for someone who enjoys birds and has a sense of humor. The bird, part stork and part crane, is definitely different. You should have fun with this gift project, especially when it comes to painting it.

MATERIAL:
- 1″ x 4″ pine
- 1″ x 6″ pine
- ³⁄₈″ diameter dowels
- Construction paper
- Wood screws and wood glue
- Paints

Illus. 216. The what-kind-of-a-bird-is-it bird.

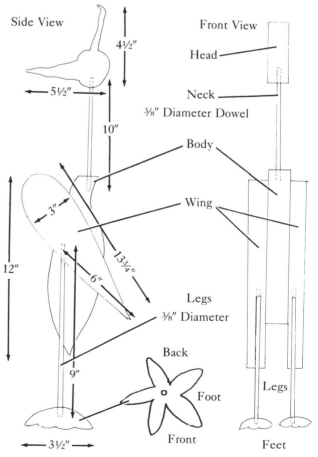

Illus. 217. Drawings of what-kind-of-a-bird-is-it bird.

140

TOOLS:

- Radial arm or table saw
- Scroll or sabre saw
- Electric drill, screw set, and ⅜" bit
- Table-mounted router and roundover bit
- Finishing sander

DIRECTIONS:

1. Review both Illus. 216 and 217. While you may want to design your own bird, the project dimensions should provide some guidance. Make patterns for the head, body, wings, and feet, unless you prefer doing them freehand.

2. Measure and cut two 14" long pieces of 1" x 4" pine for the wings. Trace the wing pattern onto each piece and cut it out using a scroll or sabre saw.

3. Measure and cut one 12" long piece of 1" x 4" pine for the body. Trace the body pattern onto the piece and cut it out.

4. For the two feet, measure and cut two pieces that are 3½" square. As you may recall, a 1" x 4" pine board is 3½" wide. Trace the patterns onto the pieces and cut the feet.

5. Cut a 6" long piece of 1" x 6" pine for the head piece. Trace the pattern onto the wood and cut it out.

6. Measure and cut two 9" long pieces of ⅜" diameter dowels for the legs.

7. Measure and cut one 10" long piece of ⅜" diameter dowel for the neck.

8. Using an electric drill or drill press, drill a ⅜" diameter hole into the middle of the top of both feet. The hole should be at least ½" deep.

9. Drill a ⅜" diameter hole into the top of the end of the body piece. Make the hole at least ½" deep.

10. Drill a ⅜" diameter hole into the bottom of the edge of each wing. The holes should be 6" from the pointed ends of the wings. Drill the holes correctly, to ensure that the bird is able to stand without tipping over.

11. In the bottom of the head, drill a ⅜" diameter hole ½" deep. Note the location of the hole in Illus. 216 or 217.

12. With the exception of the feet, rout the edges of all the parts using a roundover bit.

13. Using a finishing sander and coarse-grit abrasive paper, sand over the ends of the toes on the feet. Make them look like bird toes.

14. Prepare all the surfaces for finishing using fine and extra-fine abrasive paper and a finishing sander. Remove all the dust from the holes and surfaces.

15. Using wood glue and wood screws, secure the two wings to the body. Note Illus. 216 for their placement.

16. Glue the 9" long dowels into each foot and then into the holes in the wings. Allow the glue to dry.

17. Glue the 10" long dowel into the head and top of the body. Allow the glue to dry.

18. Now comes the challenging part. With lots of different colors, paint the bird. Don't forget a dab of paint on the legs indicating knees and also on the end of the toes suggesting nails.

87: *Cat Birdhouse* (Illus. 218 and 219)

This gift is for the person who happens to enjoy both cats and birds. Given that cats and birds are natural enemies, it's a rather clever design that will have birds flying into the mouth of a cat. This is another project that some may prefer displaying in the house rather than hanging outside. The house does have a tin roof nailed to a wooden one. If you prefer, you can omit the tin one. It's a fun project to both make and paint. The entry hole should be of a size specific to a given bird's preference.

MATERIAL:

- 1" x 8" pine
- ½" pine
- ¼" diameter dowels
- Construction paper
- Tin
- Wood glue
- Wood filler
- Wood screws
- Eye screws and wire
- Finishing and flathead nails
- Paints

Illus. 218. Cat birdhouse.

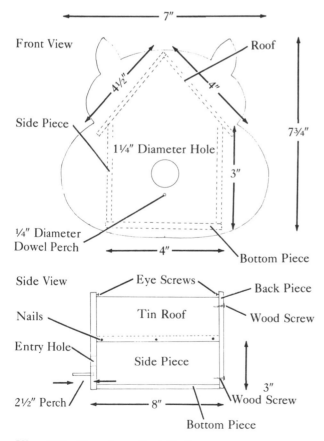

Illus. 219. Drawings of cat birdhouse.

TOOLS:

- Radial arm or table saw
- Band saw
- Scroll or sabre saw
- Table-mounted router and roundover bit
- Drill press and 1¼" Forstner or multi-spur bit
- Electric drill, screw set, and ¼" bit
- Nail set
- Tin snips
- Finishing sander

DIRECTIONS:

1. After reviewing Illus. 218 and 219, make a pattern, from construction paper, of the cat head. Use ½" thick pine for the roof, the sides, and the bottom piece. If necessary, resaw standard-thickness pine using a band saw and a ½" wide blade.

2. Measure and cut two pieces of 1" x 8" pine to a length of 8". Trace onto the pieces the cat head pattern. Using a scroll or sabre saw, cut out the front and back of the house.

3. From a piece of ½" thick pine, cut the bottom piece to a length of 8" and a width of 4".

4. Cut two side pieces that are 8" long and 3" high. Both should be cut from ½" thick pine.

5. Measure and cut roof pieces from ½" thick pine. One side should be 4½" wide and 8" long. The other side should be 4" wide and 8" long.

6. Locate the bird-entry hole on the front piece of the house. Drill a 1¼" diameter hole or one that is more appropriate for the size of the planned guests.

7. Drill a ¼" diameter hole just below the entry hole for placement of the perch. The hole should be at least ½" deep.

8. Rout the edges of the front and back pieces using a roundover bit and table-mounted router.

9. Glue and nail the two side pieces to the top surface of the bottom piece.

10. Glue and nail the 4" rooftop piece to the 4½" wide roof piece. Illus. 219 shows the placement of the narrower piece.

11. With an equal overlap on both sides, nail the assembled roof to the side pieces/bottom assembly.

12. If you would like to also have a tin roof,

measure and cut a piece of tin that will fit over the roof. You can use a large coffee can or something similar for the tin, and cut it to size using tin snips. Bend the tin in the middle, lay it on the wooden room, and nail it in place with flat-head nails.

13. Spread glue on the edges of the assembly and nail the front piece to it using finishing nails. Secure the back piece to the roof assembly with wood screws. This will allow the owner to remove the back piece and clean the house.

14. Using a nail set, drive the nail heads under the surface and fill the holes with wood filler.

15. Measure and cut a ¼″ diameter dowel to a length of at least 2½″ and glue it into the drilled perch hole.

16. Attach eye screws to the top of the back surfaces of both the front and back pieces. A wire can be strung between them for hanging the birdhouse from a tree.

17. Prepare the surfaces for finishing using abrasive papers and a finishing sander. Wipe off all the dust.

18. Paint the house as desired and then paint a cat's face on the front piece.

88: *Plant Stand* (Illus. 220 and 221)

This is a very popular and useful gift. You may want to plan on building several of these stands. The stand can be designed to meet specific needs. Its post can easily be made higher. If necessary, the top and bottom pieces can also be enlarged. In that the project is made from pine, it can be painted, stained, or lacquered. The stand shown in Illus. 220 is finished with a clear lacquer.

MATERIAL:
- 1″ x 10″ pine
- 1″ x 8″ pine
- 1″ x 4″ pine
- Wood glue and wood filler
- Wood screws
- Lacquer

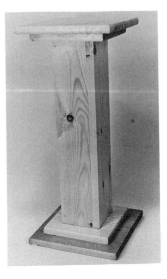

Illus. 220. Plant stand.

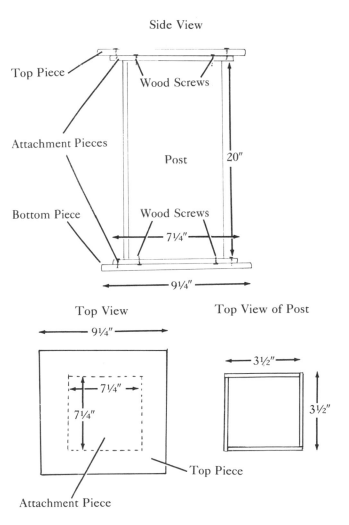

Illus. 221. Drawings of plant stand.

TOOLS:

- Radial arm or table saw
- Table-mounted router and roundover bit
- Electric drill and screw set
- Nail set
- Finishing sander

DIRECTIONS

1. Measure and cut the top and bottom pieces from 1″ x 10″ pine. The pieces should be 9¼″ square.

2. Cut the two attachment pieces from 1″ x 8″ pine. The pieces should be 7¼″ square.

3. Measure and cut four 20″ long post pieces from 1″ x 4″ pine. The pieces should be 3½″ wide, the standard width of a 1″ x 4″ pine board.

4. Rout, using a roundover bit, all edges on the top and bottom pieces. Rout the edges on only one surface of the attachment pieces. Do not rout the post pieces.

5. Prepare all surfaces for finishing using fine and extra-fine abrasive paper and a finishing sander.

6. Using wood glue and finishing nails, assemble the four post pieces. Refer to Illus. 221 to note how the pieces should be assembled.

7. Drive the nail heads under the surface using a nail set. Fill the holes with wood filler. When the filler is dry, sand over the areas, removing any excess.

8. Center the post on the top and bottom attachment pieces and secure it with wood screws and wood glue. Use an electric drill and screw set to drive in the screws. The routed edges on both pieces should face the post.

9. Center the top attachment piece and post assembly onto the bottom of the top piece. Make sure it's centered. Secure them together using wood glue and wood screws. The screws should penetrate through the attachment piece and into the bottom of the top piece.

10. Center the bottom piece on the bottom attachment piece. Secure them together with wood glue and wood screws. The screws should penetrate from the bottom surface of the bottom piece and into the attachment piece. Bury the screw heads into the surface of the bottom piece.

11. Wipe away or sand off any excess wood glue.

Be certain all the surfaces and edges are prepared for finishing. Wipe off all the dust.

12. Finish the plant stand with several coats of clear lacquer. Rub on several coats of paste wax and polish to make the finish more durable.

89: Calculator Stand (Illus. 222 and 223)

While this stand will accommodate most small, hand-held calculators/computers, it was designed and developed by Mike O'Meara for use with his Hewlett-Packard calculator. The stand places the calculator at both an angle and a height that make it easier to use and read. A support piece that fits into grooves controls both the height and the angle of the stand. The stand shown in Illus. 222 is made from black walnut. This is one of those unique gifts that both novice and professional users of these kinds of instruments will find useful.

MATERIAL:

- ¾″ (3/4's) thick black walnut
- Wood glue
- Lacquer

TOOLS:

- Radial arm or table saw
- Band saw
- Table-mounted router and roundover bit
- Clamps
- Finishing sander

Illus. 222. Calculator stand.

144

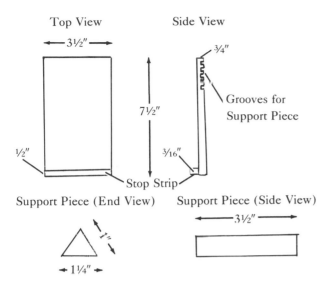

Top View   Side View

3½"

7½"

¾"

Grooves for
Support Piece

3/16"

½"

Stop Strip

Support Piece (End View)   Support Piece (Side View)

3½"

1"

1¼"

Illus. 223. Drawings of calculator stand.

DIRECTIONS:

1. Measure and cut the base from ¾" (3/4's) thick walnut or another hardwood. If you prefer, use pine. The base should be 7½" long and 3½" wide.

2. Measure and cut a stop strip to a length of 3½". The strip should be 3/16" square.

3. Cut the support piece to a length of 3½". Using a band saw, cut the piece to the needed angles so it forms a triangle. Two sides should be 1" wide, and the third 1¼" wide. Refer to Illus. 223 to note how the support piece should look. Make two support pieces, just in case the user loses one.

4. Using a table saw and fence or, if you prefer, a radial arm saw, cut grooves into the bottom surface of the base piece. The kerfs should be 3/16" deep and placed approximately ¼" apart. Cut at least five kerfs. These grooves will hold the edge of the support piece and allow the user to raise or lower the height of the unit.

5. Rout the top and side edges on the top surface of the base. Do not rout the edges where the stop strip will be placed, or the bottom surface edges.

6. Glue and clamp the stop strip onto the bottom edge of the top surface of the base. Allow the glue to dry.

7. Prepare all surfaces and edges for finishing using fine and extra-fine abrasive paper and a finishing sander. Wipe off all the dust before finishing.

8. Finish the stand and support pieces with several coats of lacquer. Rub the finish with steel wool (0000) between coats. Be sure to wipe off the dust and steel hair left by the wool.

90: *Magazine Holder* (Illus. 224 and 225)

Magazine holders are always a practical and much enjoyed gift. What household doesn't need several holders to accommodate the many magazines in the home? This holder is sufficiently large that it will hold and organize a sizeable number of magazines. Made from pine, it can be stained and lacquered or, if you prefer, painted some appropriate color. A clear lacquer finish also looks good. The ends of the holder have a heart cut into them to add to the overall attractiveness of the unit.

MATERIAL
- 1" x 6" pine
- Construction paper
- Wood glue
- Finishing nails
- Wood stain
- Lacquer

TOOLS:
- Radial arm or table saw
- Band saw
- Scroll or sabre saw
- Electric drill and 3/8" bit
- Table-mounted router and roundover bit
- Finishing sander

DIRECTIONS:

1. Measure and cut the two side pieces from 1" x 6" pine. The pieces should be 12" long and 5½" wide. Their width, of course, is the standard thickness of 1" x 6" pine.

Illus. 224. Magazine holder.

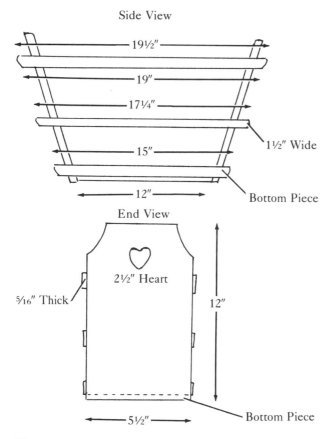

Side View

19½"

19"

17¼"

15"

1½" Wide

12"

Bottom Piece

End View

2½" Heart

5/16" Thick

12"

5½"

Bottom Piece

Illus. 225. Drawings of magazine holder.

2. Make a pattern for the two curved, cutout areas on the top edges of the two end pieces. Trace and cut out the areas using a scroll or sabre saw.

3. Make a 2½" long heart pattern from construction paper. Trace the pattern on the top area of the side pieces. Refer to Illus. 225 for placement of the heart. Drill a ⅜" diameter hole through the traced pattern. Insert the blade of a sabre saw through the hole and cut out the heart on both side pieces.

4. Measure and cut the bottom piece of the holder from 1" x 6" pine. The ends need to be cut at an angle. To make cutting the angle easier, the top of the board should be 12½" long and the bottom of the board should be 12" long. Lay out the dimensions and cut the board accordingly.

5. The six side strips are 1½" wide and 5/16" thick. Cut the six strips to length from 1" to 6" pine. Two strips should be 19½" long, two strips 17¼" long, and two strips 15" long. Using a band saw and a ½" wide blade, resaw the strips to a thickness of 5/16". You want one planed surface on each strip, so resaw the strips accordingly.

6. Cut the ends of the strips at an angle. The top edge of each strip should be ½" longer than the bottom edge. For example, the top strips should be 19½" long on their top edge and 19" long on their bottom edge. This will provide an angle that will match the side pieces when they are assembled.

7. Rout the top edges, the heart cutouts, and the outside edges on the side pieces using a round-over bit. Also, rout the outside edges of all the strips.

8. Prepare all surfaces for finishing using fine and extra-fine abrasive paper and a finishing sander. Wipe off the dust.

9. Using wood glue and finishing nails, attach the side pieces to the ends of the bottom piece. Make sure the routed edges are facing out.

10. Secure the side strips, according to their length, on the edges of the side pieces. Use glue and finishing nails to attach them. Place them an equal distance apart, from top to bottom.

11. Finish the holder using stain and lacquer.

91: Spice Rack (Illus. 226 and 227)

Designed to hold and display 12 standard jars of spices, this makes a welcomed housewarming

Illus. 226. Spice rack.

Front View

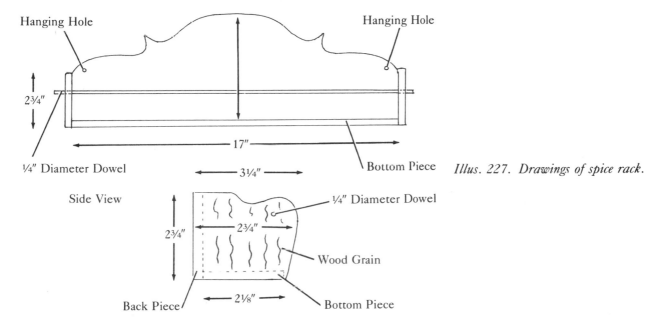

Hanging Hole

Hanging Hole

2¾"

17"

¼" Diameter Dowel

3¼"

Bottom Piece

Illus. 227. Drawings of spice rack.

Side View

¼" Diameter Dowel

2¾"

2¾"

Wood Grain

Back Piece

2⅛"

Bottom Piece

gift. The size of the rack permits it to be hung over most cooking ranges or under one of the counters. The rack can be redesigned to accommodate small cans or even small jars of spices. It can also be enlarged to hold standard-size jars of spices. The project is made from pine and looks good with a clear lacquer finish. Note the two hanging holes in the back piece of the rack.

MATERIAL:

- 1" x 5" pine
- Construction paper
- ¼" diameter dowel
- Wood glue
- Finishing nails
- Wood filler
- Lacquer

TOOLS:

- Radial arm or table saw
- Band saw
- Scroll or sabre saw
- Electric drill, screw-sink, and ¼" bit
- Table-mounted router and roundover bit
- Nail set
- Wood-burning set
- Finishing sander

DIRECTIONS:

1. Review Illus. 227 and its suggested dimensions. Decide what size rack you want to make. Using construction paper, make patterns for the back piece and ends. You may prefer a different design for the top area of the back piece.

2. Measure and cut a piece of 1" x 6" pine to a length of 17".

3. Trace the back piece pattern onto the 17" long piece of pine and cut it out, using either a scroll or sabre saw.

4. Measure and cut the bottom piece to a length of 17" and a width of 2⅛". You may want to rip the bottom piece to its proper width using either a band saw and fence or a table saw and fence.

5. Cut two pieces that are approximately 3½" wide and 2¾" long for the end pieces. Trace the end piece pattern onto the pieces and cut it out, using a scroll or sabre saw.

6. Measure and mark a dowel hole on each side piece. The hole should be at least 2¾" from the back edge and about ½" from the top edge of the end piece. Drill holes where marked in both pieces.

7. Rout all edges, except those that will be joined to another part, with a roundover bit.

8. Measure and mark a hanging hole on the top of the front of the back piece. Drill the holes with a screw-sink.

9. Prepare all surfaces for finishing using fine and extra-fine abrasive paper and a finishing sander. Wipe off the dust.

10. If you plan on wood-burning a design onto the back piece, do it before the pieces are assembled. It will be somewhat easier. Sand over the wood-burned design to clean it up.

11. Using wood glue and finishing nails, secure the end pieces to the back piece. Note in Illus. 235 how it is to be assembled.

12. Nail and glue the bottom piece in place. Nail it from both the end pieces and the back piece.

13. Using a nail set, drive all the nail heads under the surface. Fill the holes with wood filler. When the filler is dry, sand off any excess.

14. Cut and measure a ¼" diameter dowel to a length of 19¼". Glue it into the drilled holes in the side pieces.

15. Finish the rack with a clear lacquer finish.

92: *Lath Art Bear* (Illus. 228 and 229)

This is another special gift project designed, crafted, and painted by Jerry and Becky Lipchik.

Illus. 228. Lath art bear.

Front View

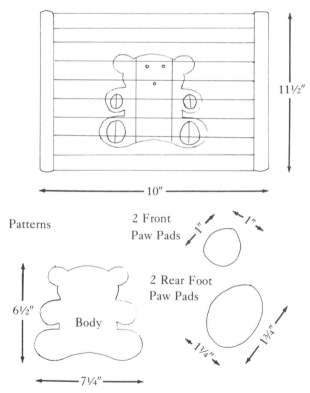

Illus. 229. Drawings of lath art bear.

It is ideal for a child's room or for that adult who truly enjoys touches of Americana around the house. This is also one of those projects that you can use to launch your craft show career. Made from standard lath, which is available at most local lumberyards, this project requires a minimum of tools. You may want to consider making several of these lath art bears. These are fun projects for the whole family to design, craft, and paint.

MATERIAL:

- 1½" x ⅜" wood lath
- ½" roundhead plugs
- ⅝" x No. 19 wire nails
- Construction paper
- Sawtooth hanger
- Wood glue
- Brown, blue, and white latex stains
- Craft paints

TOOLS:

- Scroll, sabre, or coping saw
- Try or steel square

DIRECTIONS:

1. For the frame, measure and cut two pieces of lath to a length of 11½", and two pieces to a length of 10".
2. Stain the four frame pieces with brown stain. Wipe off the excess stain.
3. Measure and cut, for the frame background, seven pieces of lath to a length of 11¾".
4. Stain the seven background pieces with blue stain. Wipe off any excess stain.
5. Brush white stain or paint lightly on top of the blue-stained background pieces.
6. Lay the seven background pieces down with their edges touching. Note by referring to Illus. 237 how they are placed. Squeeze a bead of glue on all the pieces, ¼" from their edges.
7. Place the brown border pieces across the edges of the blue background pieces, on the glue, half on and half off. Nail the border pieces in place with the ⅝" x No. 19 wire nails. Refer to Illus. 228 or 229 to note how the frame pieces are placed.
8. Using construction paper, make patterns of the bear, the two front paw pads, and the two rear paw pads. Note the dimensions for the parts in Illus. 229.
9. Trace the patterns onto the lath and cut them

out, using a scroll, sabre, or coping saw. Keep the pieces together, so none are lost.
10. The bear pieces should be painted as follows:
Body: dark brown
Paw Pads: rust-brown
Ears: sponge rust-brown paint in a circle inside the ears
Eyes: black
11. Refer to Illus. 228 and 229 and note the placement of the various body parts on the background. Glue and nail the parts in place using wood glue and ⅝" x No. 19 wire nails. Allow the glue to dry.
12. On the top of the back center of the frame, nail the sawtooth hanger.

93: *Spool Tree* (Illus. 230 and 231)

This unusual gift is perfect for the serious sewer. It is very useful because it not only displays the available threads, but also gives immediate access to them. The dowels are removable, to allow the user to place extra-large spools on the tree. Additional removable dowels are placed around the base for placement of some larger spools. If the user wants, a pin cushion can be hung from the dowel that protrudes from the top of the tree. You can modify the tree to meet the specific needs of the gift recipient. It's an easy and fun project to make. Finish it with a clear lacquer.

MATERIAL:

- 1" x 8" pine
- 1⅜" diameter dowel
- ¼" diameter dowels
- Wood screw
- Wood glue
- Lacquer

TOOLS:

- Sabre or band saw
- Electric drill, screw-sink, 1/32" and ¼" bits
- School compass
- Table-mounted router and roundover bit
- Finishing sander

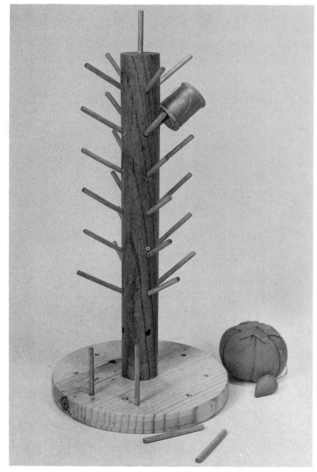

Illus. 230. Spool tree.

DIRECTIONS:

1. Using a school compass, draw a 7″ diameter circle on a piece of 1″ x 8″ pine. Cut out the round base using a band or sabre saw.

2. Rout the top and bottom edges of the base with a roundover bit.

3. Measure and cut a 1⅜″ diameter dowel to a length of 12″. Any dowel that is at least 1″ or more in diameter will work fine.

4. Measure and mark the location of the ¼″ diameter dowels on the large dowel and the ¼″ diameter dowels on the base. Make four rows of dowels on the larger dowel to hold the spools. Starting from the bottom edge of the larger dowel, place the dowels at least 1½″ apart. The rows should have at least 1″ between them. Try to place at least eight dowels in the base.

5. Drill the dowel holes to a uniform depth of ⅜″. If you don't have a drill bit stop, wrap a piece of duct or masking tape around a ¼″ drill bit, ⅜″ up from the point. This will serve as a stop guide when you are drilling the holes.

6. Drill the holes in the large dowel where marked. The holes should be drilled at an angle. Hold the electric drill at approximately the same angle for each hole. Take your time with the procedure.

7. Drill the holes, where marked, in the base.

8. Measure and cut enough ¼″ diameter dowels for each of the drilled holes. The dowels should be at least 2″ long. Sand the sharp edges off the ends of the dowels.

9. Drill a ¹⁄₃₂″ diameter pilot hole through the base at the middle indentation made by the school compass.

10. Mark the middle on the bottom end of the large dowel and drill a ¹⁄₃₂″ pilot hole.

11. Thread a wood screw through the base pilot hole, from the bottom surface, until its point penetrates above the top surface.

12. Spread wood glue around the screw point and on the bottom end of the large dowel. Place the dowel on the screw point and thread the wood screw into the dowel. Wipe away the excess glue.

13. Sand the base in preparation for finishing. Wipe off all dust.

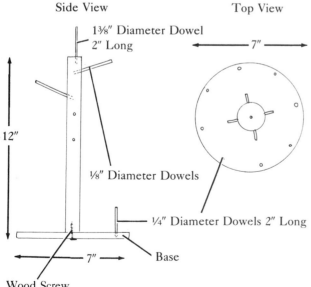

Side View   Top View

1⅜″ Diameter Dowel
2″ Long

7″

12″

⅛″ Diameter Dowels

¼″ Diameter Dowels 2″ Long

7″

Base

Wood Screw

Illus. 231. Drawings of spool tree.

14. Don't glue the small dowels in their holes. You want to be able to remove them for use with larger spools.

15. Using a clear lacquer, finish the tree and the dowels.

94: Cat Bank (Illus. 232 and 233)

Though designed for children, this musical bank, which features a mischievous-looking cat, will also appeal to adults. As indicated earlier with the previous bank projects, these kinds of gifts are fun to design, make, and paint.

MATERIAL:
- 2″ x 10″ fir plank
- 4″ x 5″ clear-plastic ovals
- Nails
- White glue
- Construction paper
- Musical bank slot
- Paints

TOOLS:
- Radial arm or table saw
- Band, scroll, or sabre saw
- Finishing sander

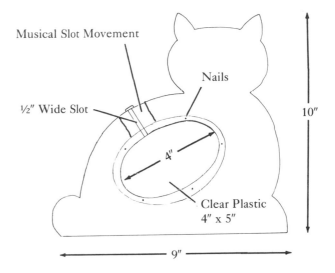

Illus. 233. Drawing of cat bank.

DIRECTIONS:

1. Review Illus. 232 and 233 and note the design and dimensions of the project. Using a large piece of construction paper, make a pattern of the project cat or one of your own design.

2. Measure and cut an 11″ long piece of 2″ x 10″ fir plank. You will find that pine is not available in these larger dimensions.

3. Trace the cat pattern onto the surface of the 10″ piece. Cut out the cat using a scroll, band, or sabre saw.

4. Measure the length and width of the musical bank slot and transfer these dimensions onto the slot's location on the cat.

5. Note the placement of the plastic oval on the side of the cat in Illus. 232. Place a plastic oval on one side of the cat and trace its outline onto the surface. The edge of the oval should touch the bottom of the musical bank slot.

6. Make another oval ½″ inside the first oval. This second oval is the one that must be cut out for the money storage area. The ½″ area is the surface needed for nailing the plastic oval to the side of the cat.

7. Using a band, scroll, or sabre saw, cut down both sides of the bank slot on the marked lines.

Illus. 232. Cat bank.

Cut on the inside of the lines, so that the musical movement will fit snugly into the slot. Continue the cut down to the second and smaller oval and cut it out. Take your time with the cut, so you have a perfectly shaped oval.

8. Prepare all surfaces for finishing using fine and extra-fine abrasive paper and a finishing sander. Wipe away the dust.

9. Paint and decorate the cat to suit your fancy or that of the gift recipient. Allow the paint to dry.

10. Secure the musical movement into the slot. You may have to use a touch of white glue on it. Allow the glue to dry.

11. Nail the plastic ovals in place. Be careful not to hit the plastic with a hammer or a nail head, because it will shatter.

12. Drop a coin in the slot and enjoy your bank!

95: *Shorebird IV* (Illus. 234 and 235)

If you've made all three of the previous shore-birds, the recipient of these gifts should now have a covey, but will no doubt still want more. Now that you know how to design and craft them, come up with some new shapes. The one shown in Illus. 234 is made from 1" x 6" pine and uses a log slice for a base. Unlike the other birds, the eyes on this one are a 1/8" diameter piece of dowel that penetrates through the bird. The beak is also a dowel.

MATERIAL:
- 1" x 6" pine
- 1/8" diameter dowel
- 1/4" diameter dowel
- Construction paper
- Log slice
- Wood glue
- Paint

TOOLS:
- Radial arm or table saw
- Scroll or sable saw 1/8" and 1/4"
- Electric drill and bits
- Finishing sander

Illus. 234. Shorebird IV.

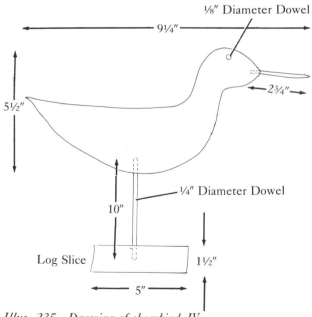

Illus. 235. Drawing of shorebird IV.

DIRECTIONS:

1. Note the design and dimensions for the project as shown in Illus. 234 and 235. Make a

152

full-size pattern of the bird from construction paper.

2. Measure and cut a piece of 1″ x 6″ pine to a length of 10″.

3. Trace the shorebird onto the surface of the piece of pine. Cut out the bird using a scroll or sabre saw.

4. Measure and cut a log slice for a base that is at least 1½″ high, 5″ long, and 2½″ wide.

5. Measure and cut a piece of ¼″ diameter dowel to a length of 10″.

6. Cut two pieces of ⅛″ diameter dowel. One piece should be 2¾″ long, and the other 1″ long. The shorter piece will penetrate the head and serve as the bird's eyes.

7. Drill a ¼″ diameter hole into the middle of the bottom of the bird and into the middle of the top of the log slice. The holes should be at least ½″ deep.

8. Drill a ⅛″ diameter hole through the head at the area where the eyes will appear. Also, drill a ⅛″ diameter hole in the front of the head for the beak. The hole should be at least ½″ deep.

9. Using a finishing sander, taper one end of the beak dowel to a point.

10. Glue the beak into the drilled head hole, and glue the eye dowel into its hole.

11. Prepare the bird for finishing using abrasive paper and a finishing sander. Wipe off the dust.

12. Place the ¼″ diameter support dowel into the hole in the bird and into the base hole.

13. Decide on how you want to paint and decorate the shorebird and then do it. By the way, a black eye is a nice touch.

96:
Pencil/Note/Paper-Clip Holder (Illus. 236 and 237)

This desktop gift is turned from red oak and is designed to be featured on a large rolltop or standard oak desk. The holder shown in Illus. 236 was designed and turned by Andy Matoesian for

Illus. 236. Pencil/note/paper-clip holder.

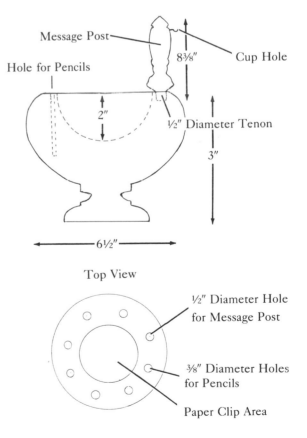

Illus. 237. Drawings of pencil/note/paper-clip holder.

use on his oak desk. It has eight holes for placement of pens or pencils, and a small brass cup hook on its message post that can be used to hang important notes or messages. The paper-clip hole in the middle is deep enough to accommodate a variety of different size clips. To prevent the holder from scratching, adhesive felt is attached to its bottom surface. This project presents you with the opportunity to do both faceplate and spindle turning. The holder shown in Illus. 236 is finished with a clear lacquer.

MATERIAL:
- 3″ (12/4's) thick red oak
- 1″ (4/4's) thick red oak
- Cup hook
- Pine scraps
- White glue
- Wood glue
- Adhesive felt
- Lacquer

TOOLS:
- Radial arm or table saw
- Wood lathe
- Turning tools
- Band saw
- School compass
- Scissors
- Clamps and vernier caliper
- Drill press or electric drill and ⅜″ and ½″ bits
- Belt or finishing sander

DIRECTIONS:
1. Review the project design and dimensions as shown in Illus. 236 and 237. While the holder shown in Illus. 236 is turned from red oak, you may prefer a different kind of hardwood. You may also want to make the project smaller.
2. Measure and cut a 3″ (12/4's) thick block of red oak that is approximately 7″ square.
3. Using a school compass, make the largest circle possible on the block. You want to leave as much extra wood as possible on the block. Cut out the traced round block on a band saw.
4. With a school compass and scrap pine, make a 3½″ diameter glue block. If you have an appro-

priate chuck, use it rather than the glue block.
5. Spread white glue on the pine glue block, place the block on the center of the bottom of the turning block, and clamp it. Allow the glue to dry. Use the least-attractive surface or portion of the block for the bottom.
6. Secure a faceplate to the glue-block assembly and secure it to the lathe. Place a revolving center in the tailstock and force it into the turning block. This will provide both stability and security during the turning process.
7. Align your tool rest and, using turning tools, turn the holder to shape. Realign the tool rest with the front of the holder and turn the clip area. Prepare the surfaces for finishing. You may want to refer to Illus. 236 for ideas on shaping the holder.
8. Using a parting tool, separate the turned holder from the glue block. Make sure you catch the holder when it separates. If you prefer, use a band saw to cut the glue block from the bottom surface of the turned holder. Use a belt or finishing sander to clean up the bottom. You will have adhesive felt covering it, so it need not be perfect.
9. Measure and cut a 1″ (4/4's) thick piece of red oak to a length of at least 9″. The piece should be square.
10. Secure the spindle block between centers. If you prefer, use a chuck. Turn a tenon that is at least ½″ long and ½″ in diameter. Use a vernier caliper to check on the diameter of the tenon. Glue the tenon into a ½″ diameter hole in the top surface of the holder. Spindle-turn the block to the shape desired for the message post. You may want to refer to Illus. 236 and 237 to determine how Matoesian turned the project post. If you're a good cutter, no abrasive paper should be needed on the post.
11. Measure and mark the locations for at least eight ⅜″ diameter holes on the top surface of the holder. Also, mark the location for the ½″ diameter tenon hole for the message post.
12. With a drill press or electric drill, drill the ⅜″ diameter holes to a depth of at least 1½″. Drill the ½″ diameter message post hole to a depth of at least ½″.
13. With a small wire brad, make a pilot hole in

the upper area of the message post for the cup hook. Thread the cup hook in place.

14. Place wood glue in the message post tenon hole and set the post into the hole. Align the post so that the cup hook points away from the holder.

15. Finish the holder and post with several coats of lacquer. Rub the surface with steel wool (0000) between coats. Wipe off the dust and wool hairs before applying the next coat. When the lacquer is dry, rub on a coat of paste wax and polish the surface.

16. Using a school compass and a pair of scissors, cut a piece of adhesive felt for the bottom surface of the holder. Attach it.

97: *Shaker Pegboard* (Illus. 238 and 239)

These kinds of projects are always a popular and very useful gift. The Shaker pegboard can be used for hanging coats, cups, or almost anything else the user wants to hang. The pegboard can be placed in almost any room. Shaker pegboards are always popular in bedrooms, near the back

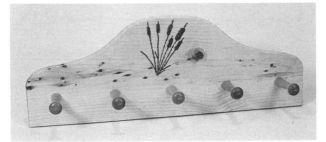

Illus. 238. Shaker pegboard.

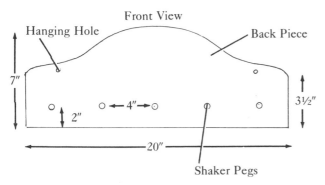

Illus. 239. Drawing of Shaker pegboard.

door, or in a stairwell. You may want to increase the size of the project so that more pegs can be used. Space the pegs according to the type of items that can be hung on them. A wood-burned design or a stencil looks nice on the upper back surface. Two holes for hanging the holder are usually adequate.

MATERIAL:
- 1″ x 8″ pine
- Shaker pegs
- Construction paper
- Wood glue
- Lacquer

TOOLS:
- Radial arm or table saw
- Scroll or sabre saw
- Table-mounted router and roundover bit
- Electric drill or drill press, screw-sink, and ½″ bit
- Wood-burning set
- Finishing sander

DIRECTIONS:
1. Make a pattern from construction paper for the top curved area of the board.

2. Measure and cut a piece of 1″ x 8″ pine to a length of 20″.

3. Trace the pattern onto the pine board and cut it out using a scroll or sabre saw.

4. Measure and mark the locations of the Shaker peg holes. Note the suggested dimensions in Illus. 239.

5. Mark the location of the two hanging holes.

6. Using a ½″ diameter bit, drill the Shaker peg holes. Also, with a screw-sink, drill the two hanging holes.

7. Rout, using a roundover bit, the front and back edges of the board.

8. If you want to have a wood-burned design on the board, draw it on in pencil and then burn it in.

9. Prepare the board for finishing using fine and extra-fine abrasive paper and a finishing sander. Wipe off the dust and blow it out of the drilled peg holes.

10. Place wood glue in the holes and tap the Shaker pegs in place. Wipe off any glue that squeezes out. Allow the glue to dry.

11. Finish the board and pegs with several coats of clear lacquer. Rub and polish the board and pegs with paste wax.

98: *Spalted Spoon/Scoop*
(Illus. 240 and 241)

Traditional wooden ware is very much a part of Americana, and is something that many people like to collect. This project is crafted from a chunk of spalted wood. As you may recall, spalting is the result of fungal infestation of the wood. The unpredictable black lines are made by the fungi and are called, appropriately, black zone lines. Their work in the decay process results in extremely attractive wood for us to use. When the wood is dried, the decay process and the fungal activity stops. Spalted wood can be found in the backyard wood pile, in the woods, or sometimes at the local hardwood dealer. If necessary, carve or shape the project from a chunk of basswood, or pine, or some piece of wood from your backyard.

MATERIAL:
- 2″ (8/4's) thick spalted wood
- Lacquer

TOOLS:
- Band saw
- Carving tools
- Electric grinder, rotary tool, or flex-shaft tool
- Carbide burr and sanding sleeves
- Finishing sander

DIRECTIONS:
1. Measure and cut a chunk of spalted wood or some other wood to a length of at least 7½″. The wood should be at least 2″ (8/4's) thick and 3″ wide, to make a good-sized spoon/scoop.

2. Draw the shape of the spoon/scoop onto the surfaces of the block. Draw both the handle and the scoop on the wood's surface.

Illus. 240. Spalted spoon/scoop.

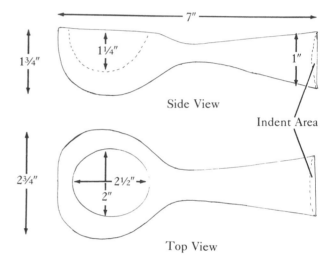

Illus. 241. Drawings of spalted spoon/scoop.

3. Cut out the spoon/scoop using a band saw and a ¼″ wide blade. Use a band saw to shape the project and remove as much wood as possible.

4. Shape or carve the project using an electric grinder, rotary tool, or flex-shaft tool. I prefer using an electric grinder with a carbide burr and sanding sleeves. The tough part of the job is cutting out the inside area of the spoon/scoop. If you want, drill some of the wood out of the area. Make the handle and the spoon/scoop end round and smooth. Indent the end of the handle area slightly. Sanding sleeves and a finishing sander with coarse-abrasive paper work well for giving the project its final shape and finish. You have to finish the inside of the spoon/scoop area by hand, using abrasive paper.

5. When the project is shaped to your satisfaction, prepare the surfaces for finishing using fine and extra-fine abrasive paper. Much of this work needs to be done by hand. Wipe off all the dust.
6. Finish the project using a clear lacquer. Spalted wood is very porous, so you will have to apply many coats to build up a finish. When the finish begins to build up, rub it with steel wool (0000) between coats. Wipe off the dust and hairs from the wool. Finish the project by rubbing paste wax on it and polishing it.

99: *Turned Letter Opener* (Illus. 242 and 243)

For those who enjoy turning their gift projects, this letter opener will be fun and challenging. Use hard maple for this project. It makes turning easier, but it also makes for a more durable and functional letter opener. This project was designed by Michael Field. Finish it with either lacquer or Danish oil.

MATERIAL:
- 1½″ (6/4's) thick hard maple
- Lacquer

TOOLS:
- Wood lathe
- Turning tools
- Band saw
- Wood rasp

DIRECTIONS:
1. Measure and cut a piece of 1½″ (6/4's) thick hard maple to a length of 11″. The piece should be cut square.
2. Mount the turning block between centers. Use a drive center in the headstock and a revolving center in the tailstock.
3. Bring the handle portion of the spindle to roundness. Do *not* round the blade portion of the holder. Then turn the handle portion of the letter opener. The handle should be turned on the headstock end of the spindle. Refer to Illus. 242 if you need some ideas for turning the handle.

Illus. 242. Turned letter opener.

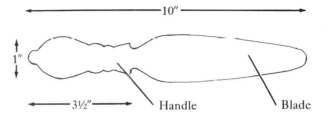

Illus. 243. Drawing of turned letter opener.

4. While holding the spindle against the drive center, remove the revolving center from the spindle and move it about ½″ to one side. Tighten the revolving center against the spindle. You will now be turning off-center.
5. Turn the concave area between the handle and the blade, and then turn the blade itself. While turning the blade, note how it is being shaped. Taper the blade towards its point as you shape it.
6. Shut the lathe off and give the blade its final shape using a wood rasp or file. You may also want to use coarse abrasive paper for shaping.
7. When the blade is done, prepare it for finishing using fine and extra-fine abrasive paper. Leave the letter opener between centers as you sand its surfaces. After sanding its surfaces, carefully remove the letter opener from the lathe.
8. Separate the letter opener from the scrap ends of the spindle using a band saw. Clean the top of the handle and the point of the blade with abrasive paper. The blade end should be rounded and somewhat sharp. Don't put a point on it.
9. Finish the letter opener with either Danish oil or lacquer. Rub a paste wax on it and polish it, to give the project a nice feel and appearance.

100. Coffee Can Birdhouse (Illus. 244 and 245)

Why not make a birdhouse from a coffee can and save some wood? This project uses a painted, 26-ounce coffee can. You may want to use a can that is covered with a paper label and then paint it yourself. How about some reflective green, or-ange, or some other weird color? A wooden insert is prepared that fits into one end of the can. It is screwed in place so that it can be removed for cleaning the house. Some holes should be drilled in the back (bottom) of the house to permit air to move through the house. Screws on the top of the can allow the user to attach wire for hanging the house in a tree.

Illus. 244. Coffee can birdhouse.

MATERIAL:

- 1″ x 6″ pine
- 26-ounce coffee can
- ¼″ diameter dowel
- Wood screws
- Hanging wire
- Wood glue
- Paint

TOOLS:

- Band or sabre saw
- Drill press, multi-spur or Forstner wood bit, and ¼″ and 1¼″ bits
- Nail
- School compass

DIRECTIONS:

1. Measure the inside diameter of the coffee can to be used.
2. Set a school compass to the required diam-eter, trace a circle onto a piece of 1″ x 6″ pine, and cut the circle out. Use a band or sabre saw to make the cut. Take your time with the sawing, so that you have a neat, round insert that will fit snugly into the can.
3. Refer to Illus. 245 and note that the center of the wooden insert has an indentation from the school compass. Drill a 1¼″ diameter entry hole at this point.
4. Approximately ½″ below the entry hole, drill a ¼″ diameter hole for the perch.
5. Cut a piece of ¼″ diameter dowel to a length of 2½″ for a perch.
6. Place the wooden insert inside the can open-ing. With a nail, punch a hole through the sur-face of the can and slightly into the edge of the insert. Place a small wood screw into the hole and thread it into the wooden insert. The screw

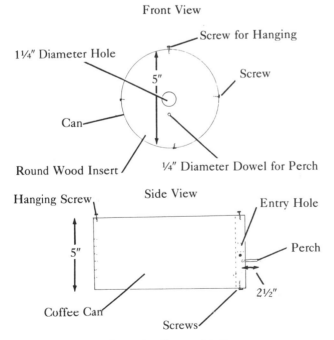

Illus. 245. Drawings of coffee can birdhouse.

should enter into the middle of the edge of the insert. Repeat this procedure until the insert is securely in place.

7. Glue the ¼" diameter perch into the drilled hole.

8. Using an old drill bit, drill air holes into the back of the can.

9. Thread a screw, partially, into the top front and the top back of the can. This will be used to attach the hanging wire.

10. Paint and decorate the front of the wooden insert and the perch. The insert for the birdhouse shown in Illus. 244 is painted red with white polka dots. The birds will love it, and so will the gift recipient.

11. Attach a piece of hanging wire to the protruding screws on the top of the can.

101: Veneer Bookmarks (Illus. 246 and 247)

What could be a nicer gift for someone who enjoys reading than a collection of custom-made bookmarks? Made from strips of veneer, these bookmarks can be cut to various sizes and shapes. They can also be wood-burned or, if you prefer, stencilled with some design. This project was designed by Carol Banghart, an avid reader. While the bookmarks shown in Illus. 246 are made of ash veneer, you can use any of the thicker cut veneers. Many of the dyed veneers make attractive and unusual looking bookmarks.

MATERIAL:
- Wood veneer
- Lacquer

TOOLS:
- Hobby knife
- Cutting board
- Wood-burning set
- Finishing sander

DIRECTIONS:

1. Cut a series of bookmarks to different lengths, widths, and shapes. Use a hobby knife and cut

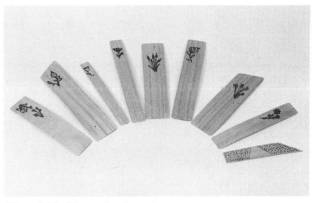

Illus. 246. Veneer bookmarks.

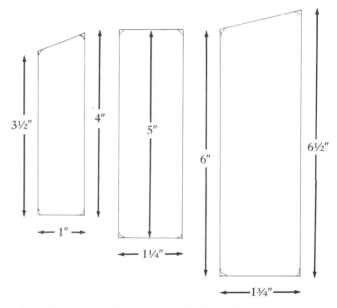

Illus. 247. Drawings of veneer bookmarks.

on either an old cutting board or a piece of scrap pine.

2. If you want to round the corners of some designs, use a finishing sander and a fine abrasive paper.

3. You may want to punch a hole in the top of the middle of some bookmarks and attach an attractive string or ribbon.

4. Wood-burn designs into some of the bookmarks. Sand over the burned area with extra-fine abrasive paper. Wipe off the dust and finish the bookmark with several coats of lacquer.

5. You may want to paint some of the bookmarks and, as a final decorative touch, paint a small stencil on them.

Index

Metric Conversion Chart

⅛ inch = 3.18 millimetres
¼ inch = 6.35 millimetres
⅜ inch = 9.53 millimetres
½ inch = 12.70 millimetres

⅝ inch = 15.88 millimetres
¾ inch = 19.05 millimetres
⅞ inch = 22.23 millimetres
1 inch = 25.40 millimetres
10 millimetres = 1 centimetre

1½ inch = 38.10 millimetres
2 inches = 50.80 millimetres
1 foot = 30.48 centimetres
1 yard = 0.9144 metre